# DATE DUE

BRODART, CO.                    Cat. No. 23-221

# ETHICS
## FOR
# CRIMINAL
# JUSTICE
# PROFESSIONALS

## CLIFF ROBERSON
## SCOTT MIRE

CRC Press
Taylor & Francis Group
Boca Raton London New York

CRC Press is an imprint of the
Taylor & Francis Group, an **informa** business

CRC Press
Taylor & Francis Group
6000 Broken Sound Parkway NW, Suite 300
Boca Raton, FL 33487-2742

© 2010 by Taylor and Francis Group, LLC
CRC Press is an imprint of Taylor & Francis Group, an Informa business

No claim to original U.S. Government works

Printed in the United States of America on acid-free paper
10 9 8 7 6 5 4 3 2 1

International Standard Book Number: 978-1-4200-8670-6 (Paperback)

---
### Library of Congress Cataloging-in-Publication Data
---
Roberson, Cliff, 1937-
    Ethics for criminal justice professionals / Cliff Roberson and Scott Mire.
      p. cm.
    Includes bibliographical references and index.
    ISBN 978-1-4200-8670-6 (alk. paper)
    1. Criminal justice, Administration of--Moral and ethical aspects--United States. 2. Legal ethics--United States. 3. Police ethics--United States. I. Mire, Scott. II. Title.

HV9950.R627 2010
174'.9364--dc22                                                               2009025349
---

Visit the Taylor & Francis Web site at
http://www.taylorandfrancis.com

and the CRC Press Web site at

# Table of Contents

# Preface

The text *Ethics for Criminal Justice Professionals* is designed for ethics-related classes in criminal justice and for the professional in the field who desires to increase his or her knowledge in this critical area. The text is intended to be a reader-friendly introduction to the practical study of ethics. It is also designed to provide students with a vehicle to promote critical thinking and engaging discourse on ethics.

Ethics in criminal justice is a subject that has gained prominence in the past two decades with the increasing concerns about the accountability of criminal justice professionals, from the police chief to the officer on the beat, from the warden to the correction officer on the ward, and from the judge to the court clerks. Each of these professionals is currently under examination by the public.

The approach is to examine each aspect and each element within the criminal justice system with the goal of encouraging critical examinations of the various decisions that criminal justice professionals are required to make and stand accountable for in the performance of their public duties.

In the study of ethics, we are reminded of an excerpt from Lewis Carroll's *Alice in Wonderland*:

"Where shall I begin, please your Majesty?"asked the White Rabbit.
"Begin at the beginning," the King said gravely, "and go on till you come to the end: then stop."

# Acknowledgments

**Cliff Roberson:** While the text lists Scott Mire and myself as the sole authors, this book would not have been possible without the assistance and help of many. First, I wish to acknowledge the support and assistance that our editor at Taylor & Francis, Carolyn Spence, provided. I also want to thank the project coordinator for this publication, Jill Jurgensen, who did a professional job and made us look good.

In the text, we reprinted some exceptional and practical journal articles. For permission to use these works, we gratefully thank Major H. Wayne Duff, Jr. and Captain Brandon Zuidema of the Lynchburg, Virginia, police department; former Chief of Police Bob Harrison of the Vacaville, California, police department; Chief Charlie Sewell of the McMinnville, Tennessee, police department; Editor John E. Ott, *FBI Law Enforcement Bulletin*; and Pamela W. Leupen, associate director for National Training and Resources, Office for Crime Victims, U.S. Department of Justice.

**Scott Mire:** I would like to thank my wife, Crystal, for all of the support she has provided throughout this journey. The constant pressure of having to write was much more tolerable as a result of your understanding and compassion. Thank you!

# About the Authors

**Cliff Roberson** is the academic chair of the Graduate School of Criminal Justice at Kaplan University and editor in chief of the journal *Professional Issues in Criminal Justice* (http://www.picj.org). He is also an emeritus professor of criminal justice at Washburn University and a retired professor of criminology at California State University, Fresno. His previous academic experience includes professor of criminology and director of the Justice Center, California State University, Fresno; professor of criminal justice and dean of arts and sciences at the University of Houston–Victoria; associate vice president for academic affairs, Arkansas Tech University; and director of programs for the National College of District Attorneys, University of Houston.

His nonacademic legal experience includes being the head of the Military Law Branch, U.S. Marine Corps; trial and legal services supervisor, Office of State Counsel for Offenders, Texas Board of Criminal Justice; private legal practice; judge pro tem in the California courts; and trial and defense counsel and military judge as a marine judge advocate. Cliff is admitted to practice before the U.S. Supreme Court, the federal courts in California and Texas, the Supreme Court of Texas, and the Supreme Court of California.

His educational background includes a PhD in human behavior from the U.S. International University; an LLM in criminal law, criminology, and psychiatry from George Washington University; a JD from American University; a BA in political science from the University of Missouri; and one year of postgraduate study at the University of Virginia School of Law.

Cliff has authored or coauthored numerous books and texts. His recent texts on criminal justice subjects include the following:

- *Constitutional Law and Criminal Justice* (Taylor & Francis, 2009)
- Roberson and Das, *An Introduction to Comparative Legal Models of Criminal Justice* (Taylor & Francis, 2008)
- *Identify Theft Investigations* (Kaplan, 2008)
- Birzer and Roberson, *Police Operations* (Pearson, 2008)
- Birzer and Roberson, *Policing Today and Tomorrow* (Prentice Hall, 2006)
- Wallace and Roberson, *Principles of Criminal Law*, 4th ed. (Allyn and Bacon, 2008)

- *Criminal Procedure Today: Issues and Cases*, 2nd ed. (Prentice Hall, 2000)
- Roberson, Wallace, and Stuckey, *Procedures in the Justice System*, 9th ed. (Prentice Hall, 2009)
- Roberson and Wallace, *Introduction to Criminology* (Copperhouse, 1998)
- *Introduction to Criminal Justice* (Copperhouse, 1994; 2nd ed. 1998; 3rd ed. 2000)
- Masters and Roberson, *Inside Criminology* (Prentice Hall, 1996)
- Birzer and Roberson, *Introduction to Private Security* (Pearson, 2008)

**Scott Mire** is an assistant professor of criminal justice at the University of Louisiana at Lafayette. Scott received his PhD in criminal justice at Sam Houston State University in August 2005. He is a former police officer, narcotics agent, and U.S. federal agent. Scott also served as training coordinator for the Texas Police Corps while completing his graduate studies. Scott has published numerous articles in various journals, including the *Journal of Offender Rehabilitation* and *Criminal Justice*.

# What Is Ethics?

1

## Working Definition of Ethics

No man is above the law and no man is below it, nor do we ask any man's permission when we require him to obey it. (Theodore Roosevelt, 1913)

Serving in law enforcement provides officers with many privileges not conferred upon most other professions. ... The law enforcement profession is highly revered by those employed within its ranks and by the public. Officers, regardless of rank or position, must be leaders in their departments and communities. Most criminal justice professionals, as well as citizens, will follow the example set by their respected leaders. When charged with enforcing the social contract society has with its citizens, officers must realize that their actions must represent, at a minimum, the same behaviors expected by society. Law enforcement officers who hold themselves to a higher ethical standard offer their communities the appropriate example to follow. (Boetig, 2007, pp. 12–13)

*Ethics* is a difficult term to define. Cyndi Banks (2004, p. 3) noted that ethics provides us with "a way to make moral choices when we are uncertain about what to do in a situation involving moral issues." Banks also noted that ethics involves making moral judgments about what is right or wrong, good or bad.

A few years ago, sociologist Raymond Baumhart asked businesspeople, "What does the term 'ethics' mean to you?" Among their replies were the following:

"Ethics has to do with what my feelings tell me is right or wrong."
"Ethics has to do with my religious beliefs."
"Being ethical is doing what the law requires."
"Ethics consists of the standards of behavior our society accepts."
"I don't know what the word means." (Velasquez et at. 1987, p.4)

### What Ethics Is Not

It may be helpful to identify what ethics is not. Manuel Velasquez, Claire Andre, Thomas Shanks, and Michael J. Meyer (1988) provided a list of what ethics is not. Their list includes the following:

- Ethics is not the same as feelings. According to Velasquez et al., feelings provide important information for our ethical choices. Some people have developed habits that make them feel bad when they do something wrong, but many people feel good even though they are doing something wrong. Many times, our feelings will tell us it is uncomfortable to do the right thing if it is hard.
- Ethics is not religion. Religions for the most part advocate high ethical standards. But what about those people who are not religious, ethics also apply to them.
- Ethics is not the same as following the law. While legal systems incorporate many ethical standards, law can become ethically corrupt, as some totalitarian regimes. Law can be a function of power alone and designed to serve the interests of narrow groups.
- Ethics is not following culturally accepted norms. Some cultures are quite ethical, but others become corrupt or blind to certain ethical concerns. As noted by Velasquez et al., "When in Rome, do as the Romans do" is not a satisfactory ethical standard.
- Ethics is not science. While social and natural science provide important information to help us make better ethical decisions, science alone does not tell us what we ought or ought not to do.

Ethics is not the same as values. Values are judgments of worth of attitudes, statements, and behaviors. Value judgments are subjective in nature and can be verified only through reason. Ethics may also be considered as moral philosophy because we are concerned with the study of questions of right and wrong. Often, individuals mistake morals for ethics. Morals constitute acceptable rules of behavior, whereas ethics is the study of morality, that is, an analysis of what constitutes good conduct. Ethics is central to criminal justice since morality is what distinguishes right from wrong. Only by being moral can we distinguish our conduct from the conduct of criminals that the system condemns (Albanese, 2008, p. 3).

For the purpose of our discussions on ethics, "ethics" will be used to refer to the study of the standards of behavior that tell us what choices we should make in the many situations in which we find ourselves as criminal justice professionals. In other words, ethics is the study of morality. This is by far not a perfect definition, but it provides us with a framework in which to discuss ethical issues.

## Role of Critical Thinking

We should be teaching students how to think. Instead, we are teaching them what to think. (Clement & Lochhead, 1980, p. 1)

Critical thinking means correct thinking in the pursuit of relevant and reliable knowledge about the world. Another way to describe it is reasonable, reflective, responsible, and skillful thinking that is focused on deciding what to believe or do. A person who thinks critically can ask appropriate questions, gather relevant information, efficiently and creatively sort through this information, reason logically from this information, and come to reliable and trustworthy conclusions about the world that enable one to live and act successfully in it. (Schafersman, 1991, p. 1)

Jay Albanese (2008) contended that critical thinking is fundamental to ethics. Critical thinking is the process of evaluating viewpoints, facts, and behaviors in an objective manner in order to access the presentation of information or methods of argumentation in order to ascertain the worth of an act or course of conduct. According to Albanese (2008), continued examination of one's beliefs or actions is the only way to know all aspects and implications of a belief or an action and whether that belief or action constitutes ethical conduct. Albanese also noted that education currently is largely based on the accumulation of facts, and critical thinking involves the development of abilities to intelligently sort through those facts, as well as half-truths, lies, and deceptive arguments.

The ethical problems encountered by police can generally be divided into two classes. The first class is concerned with integrity, for example, taking bribes, giving perjured testimony, or inflicting serious injury on suspects by the use of illegal force. This class of problems involves obvious cases of misconduct or corruption, and it does not take an understanding of ethical concepts to know that these actions are wrong. The second class involves those problems that require hard choices in law enforcement and moral judgments. An issue that would fit in the second class is whether or not it is acceptable to accept a free cup of coffee offered by a restaurant owner (Heffernan, 2001).

Heffernan (2001) contended that we should use two approaches in the ethical training of officers. According to him, our first approach should be to develop police integrity. Education involving this approach should only devote incidental time to the justification of moral values and be primarily concerned with developing both the capacity to recognize basic values and the strength of character to act on this recognition. Heffernan contended that effective law enforcement in a democratic society is possible only when the police honor basic standards of integrity. Police integrity can be applied in police academies by example and by direct instruction.

Heffernan's (2001) second approach concerns the making of hard moral choices. According to him, hard choices in policing usually arise within the confines of the law. The distinction between the first and second approaches is that the first approach always focuses on the illegality of the act or conduct whereas the second approach generally does not. Some of the choices involving the second approach include the use of deceit in undercover operations, the selection of targets in undercover operations, privacy issues in police supervision, the exercise of police discretion, and loyalty to one's peers. According to Heffernan, the best strategy for stimulating reflection on hard choices in professional life is to foster the development of an appropriate literature of applied ethics. In making the hard choices, we generally do not question one's disposition to do the right thing but seek to answer the question: what is the right thing to do?

## Teaching of Morality

Morality is concerned with what is "right" and what is "wrong." In Plato's dialogues, which are discussed in Chapter 2, Socrates is credited as the first philosopher to ask the question as to whether morality can be taught. This question is still relevant today in our world, which is filled with all sorts of confusions, misunderstandings, physical conflicts, and disasters after disasters. According to Delattre (1990, p. 1), "morality is the achievement of good character and of the aspiration to be the best person you can be. But what is good character and what kind of person should one aspire to become?" Delattre explained that since achieving integrity or character excellence is a matter of forming habits, and since both good and bad habits can be formed only by repeating actions over and over again, morality cannot be taught. But because people can become habituated by repeated behavior under responsible and loving training and supervision, the habits of morality can be learned.

Delattre (1990) noted that it is possible to train and habituate the young with respect, generosity of spirit, and intellectual honesty. Accordingly, he contended that it is possible to help the young learn habits of integrity without imposition, and it is possible to teach them and help them learn to think with real acumen and rigor. Delattre concluded his argument that morality can be taught with the following statement:

> If their teachers, who are supposed to care about them, and their parents, who are supposed to love them, do not take life that seriously, then the young will learn their habits from the streets, from demagogues, and from entertainment and commercial media that neither care about them nor love them. That is a consequence no adult of integrity can be willing to tolerate. (Delattre, 1990, pp. 11–12)

## Morality Theories

When discussing or formulating ethical opinions, individuals generally take certain viewpoints. Four of the most common viewpoints or theories are utilitarianism, deontological, virtue, and religious. In some cases, the study of ethics is approached from one or more than one of these viewpoints. We discuss these viewpoints in greater detail in Chapter 4 in our discussion of ethical schools.

Most of our concepts involving utilitarianism are based on John Stuart Mill's essay *Utilitarianism*. According to utilitarianism, the moral worth of an action is judged by its contribution to overall utility or its contribution to happiness or pleasure as summed among all persons. Under this concept, the moral worth of an action is determined by its outcome, or the ends justify the means. Utilitarianism can be contrasted with deontological ethics. When determining the moral worth of an act, deontological ethics disregards the consequences of performing the act (Capaldi, 2004, p. 31).

*Deontology* as a word is derived from the Greek words for duty (*deon*) and science (or study of; *logos*). Deontology is a normative theory that considers which choices are morally required, forbidden, or permitted. Deontology is one of the moral theories that guide and assess our choices of what we ought to do (deontic theories), in contrast to aretaic (virtue) theories that guide us and assess what kind of person (in terms of character traits) we are and should be (Gert, 1970).).

Immanuel Kant (1724–1804) emphasized the necessity of virtue or moral character. *Virtue* is a general term that was translated from the Greek word *arete*. *Arete* is also translated as excellence. Virtue refers to what guides us, and it assesses what kind of person we are in terms of character traits (Foot, 1985).

The religious viewpoint refers to the practice of making ethical determinations and choices based on one's religious viewpoint or using one's religious beliefs and doctrines as the foundation for making ethical decisions (Geach, 1969).

**Branches of Ethics**

Often, ethics is divided into three branches:

- Metaethics which is concerned with methods, language, logical structure, and the reasoning used in the interpretation of ethical terms; for example, what does "good" mean?
- Normative ethics which is concerned with ways of behaving and standards of conduct.
- Applied ethics, which is concerned with solving practical ethical issues as they arise. A good example of applied ethics is the case discussed later in this chapter regarding attorney Staples Hughes.

## Metaethics

Metaethics, also referred to as "analytic ethics," is the branch of ethics that seeks to understand the nature of ethical properties and ethical statements, attitudes, and judgments. Metaethics addresses the question "What is goodness?" It seeks to understand the nature of ethical properties and evaluations. Some of the issues examined under metaethics include the following (Ackerman, 1980):

- Is morality more a matter of taste than truth?
- Are moral standards culturally relative?
- Are there moral facts?
- If there are moral facts, what is their origin? How is it that they set an appropriate standard for our behavior?

Metaethics examines the issues and connection between values, reasons for action, and human motivation. It seeks to understand how it is that moral standards might provide us with reasons to do or refrain from doing as it demands (Ackerman, 1980).

## Normative Ethics

Normative ethics is concerned with what people should believe to be right and wrong, as distinct from descriptive ethics, which deals with what people do believe to be right and wrong. Normative ethics is sometimes said to be prescriptive, rather than descriptive. The central notion in normative ethics is that a person's conduct must consider moral issues and that one should act morally by using reason to decide the proper way of conducting oneself.

A key assumption in normative ethics is that there is only one ultimate criterion of moral conduct, whether it is a single rule or a set of principles. Normative ethics is a search for an ideal test of proper behavior. The Golden Rule to do unto others as you would have them do unto you is an example of a normative principle: we should do to others what we would want others to do to us. Since I do not want my neighbor to steal my property, then it is wrong for me to steal his property. Using this reasoning, one can theoretically determine whether any possible action is right or wrong. The Golden Rule is an example of a normative theory that establishes a single principle against which we judge all actions (Rand, 2006).

## Relativism

Do the standards of conduct and the moral ways of doing things differ from society to society? Can there be one standard of conduct for all people everywhere? *Ethical relativism* refers to the approach used by those who feel that standards of conduct and ways of doing things differ from society to society and that there can never be one single standard. *Ethical absolutism* refers to the approach used by those who advocate that one set of standards applies across all societies and that we have an obligation to do what is "known to be right."

According to the relativism approach, what is morally right or wrong may vary from person to person or from culture to culture. Arrington (1983) contended that we cannot state that a certain moral judgment is true for all purposes, persons, and cultures and that we can only assert what is moral for a particular person or social group.

*Cultural relativism* refers to the relativism concept that moral beliefs and practices vary from culture to culture. Those who follow cultural relativism contend that we cannot make judgments as to whether certain choices are right or wrong for another culture but can only note that there are differences. Supporters of cultural relativism argue that every society has a different moral code that determines which acts are moral and which are not. They contend that we cannot consider one moral code as superior to another because of the lack of an objective standard to make a comparison. Cultural relativism is considered by many as an anthropological theory.

## Absolutism

Ethical absolutism is the belief that there are absolute standards against which moral questions can be judged and that certain actions are right or wrong, devoid of the context of the act. Absolutism is considered valid regardless of thought and feeling (Banks, 2004, p. 8). Consider the issue of abortion; a person who argues that abortion is never morally justified would hold this to be an ethical absolutism. A similar situation exists for those individuals who contend that the death penalty is never morally justified. The absolutism concept regarding whether lying is ever justified is discussed in Chapter 7.

## Pluralism

Under the concept of ethical pluralism, there are many different things in life that can be considered as intrinsically good. Are there many truths rather than one single truth? A basic concept of pluralism is that there is a plurality of moral norms that cannot be reduced to one basic norm. Postow (2007) advocated that ethical pluralism is a metaethical view that accepts competing moral views as valid. Joshua Cherniss described ethical pluralism as follows:

> Ethical pluralism (also referred to as value pluralism) is a theory about the nature of the values or goods that human beings pursue, and the pursuit of which make up the substance of their moral lives. Most simply ethical pluralism holds that the values or goods legitimately pursued by human beings are plural, incompatible, and incommensurable. (Chermiss, 2008)

## Standards

There are two fundamental problems in identifying the ethical standards we are to follow:

1. On what do we base our ethical standards?
2. How should those standards be applied to the specific situations we face?

## Five Sources of Ethical Standards

Velasquez et al. (1988) listed five approaches that are used to determine the sources from which we obtain our ethical standards:

- Utilitarian approach: The utilitarian approach is based on the concept that the ethical action is the action that provides the most good or does the least harm. The approach examines the course of action that produces the greatest balance of good over harm. Ethical warfare balances the good achieved in ending terrorism with the harm done to all parties through death, injuries, and destruction. The utilitarian approach is concerned with consequences and tries to increase the good done and to reduce the harm done.
- Rights approach: The rights approach suggests that the ethical action is the one that best protects and respects the moral rights of those affected. The approach starts with the belief that humans have a dignity based on their human nature per se or on their ability to choose freely what they do with their lives. The rights approach holds that with rights there are implied duties and, in particular, the duty to respect others' rights.
- Fairness or justice approach: The fairness or justice approach is based on Aristotle's and other Greek philosophers' concept that all equals should be treated equally. Ethical actions are determined by the duty to treat all human beings equally. If human beings are treated unequally, then the ethical actions are fairly based on some standard that is defensible.
- Common good approach: The common good approach is based on the Greek philosophers' notion that life in a community is a good in itself, and our actions should contribute to that life. The approach suggests that the interlocking relationships of society are the basis of ethical reasoning and that respect and compassion for all others, especially the vulnerable, are requirements of such reasoning. This approach also calls attention to the common conditions that are important to the welfare of everyone.

**Figure 1.1.** A police officer helps a young child, circa 1920. Police work should be a helping profession, and to be part of a helping profession, police officers need to be ethical. Photo from the Collections of the Library of Congress, Washington, D.C.

- Virtue approach: The virtue approach contends that ethical actions ought to be consistent with certain ideal virtues that provide for the full development of our humanity. The virtues are dispositions and habits that enable us to act according to the highest potential of our character and on behalf of values such as truth and beauty. Honesty, courage, compassion, generosity, tolerance, love, fidelity, integrity, fairness, self-control, and prudence are all examples of virtues. Virtue ethics proponents examine actions by asking, "What kind of person will I become if I do this?"

## How Do We Develop Our Ethical Standards?

Most people learn ethical norms at home, at school, in church, or in other social settings. Although most people acquire their sense of right and wrong during childhood, moral development occurs throughout life, and human beings pass through different stages of growth as they mature. Ethical norms are so ubiquitous that one might be tempted to regard them as simple common sense (Shamoo & Resnik, 2003). If ethical norms were nothing more than common sense, then why are there so many ethical disputes and issues in our society?

## Character

Waste no time arguing what a good man should be. Be one. (Marcus Aurelius, as quoted in Hadot, 1998, p. 1)

Character is what you do when nobody is looking. (Anonymous)

Sociologist Amitai Etzioni described character as "the psychological muscle that moral conduct requires to overcome emotional barriers that prevent ethical decision making" (Etzioni, 1998, p. 33). Character has also been described as the ability to motivate yourself in the face of frustration, control your impulses, delay gratification, and regulate your moods (Goleman, 1995).

The Josephson Institute developed a list of six core ethical values that constitute character (Josephson Institute for Ethics, n.d.):

- Trustworthiness: Be honest by not deceiving, cheating, or stealing. Be reliable by doing what you say you'll do. Have the courage to do the right thing.
- Respect: Treat others with respect. Follow the Golden Rule. Be tolerant of differences. Use good manners, not bad language. Be considerate of the feelings of others. Don't threaten, hit, or hurt anyone. Deal peacefully with anger, insults, and disagreements.

---

**ETHICS IN ACTION BOX**

The FBI core values are as follows:

- rigorous obedience to the Constitution of the United States
- respect for the dignity of all those we protect
- compassion
- fairness
- uncompromising personal and institutional integrity

*Source.* New Agents Training Unit (NATU) at the FBI Academy in Quantico, Virginia. Retrieved August 18, 2008, from www.fbi.gov/hq/td/academy/sat/sat.htm. Accessed on August 18, 2008.

---

- Responsibility: Do what you are supposed to do. Persevere: keep on trying! Always do your best. Use self-control. Be self-disciplined. Think before you act, and consider the consequences. Be accountable for your choices.
- Fairness: Play by the rules. Take turns and share. Be open-minded, and listen to others. Don't take advantage of others. Don't blame others carelessly.
- Caring: Be kind. Be compassionate, and show you care. Express gratitude. Forgive others. Help people in need.
- Citizenship: Do your share to make your school and community better. Cooperate. Get involved in community affairs. Stay informed, and vote. Be a good neighbor. Obey laws and rules. Respect authority. Protect the environment.
- Accountability by accepting responsibility for our actions and decisions and the consequences of our actions and decisions.
- Leadership, both personal and professional.

## Moral Identity

Moral identity is how you view and describe yourself in ethical terms—honest, caring, opposed to cheating, committed to doing the right thing, etc. Two business researchers say people with a strong sense of moral awareness can actually become the biggest failures in the face of moral challenges. (McManus, 2008)

The only thing necessary for the triumph of evil is for good men to do nothing. (Burke, *Thoughts on the Cause of the Present Discontent,* as quoted in Ali, 1907, p. 406)

Moral identity has been described as one kind of self-regulatory mechanism that motivates moral action (Aquino & Reed, 2002). How does one develop a moral identity? While there is no agreement regarding the answer to this question, several theoretical models have been proposed. One model holds that identity and morality initially develop as two separate systems in childhood. By adolescence the two developmental systems begin to converge in some individuals, and their sense of morality becomes important to their sense of identity–moral identity. Under this concept, the fusion of morality and identity is enabled in adolescence because it is during this stage that the two systems tend to become more ideological, and people's sense of morality becomes based more on internal moral principles than on external things such as consequences of actions. Similarly, identity is now based more on internal belief systems than on external things such as physical characteristics or typical behaviors. While studies have demonstrated these developmental changes in morality and identity, it is unclear how the two merge to form a moral identity in some people (Hardy & Carlo, 2005).

## Moral Identity and Moral Behavior

Reynolds and Ceranic (2007) looked at the issue of how moral identity affects a person's moral behavior. They used the term *moral behavior* to refer to a wide range of behaviors that was subject to being judged according to generally accepted moral norms of behavior. They concluded that individuals rely on both moral judgments (What is right and wrong?) and perceptions of themselves (Who am I?) in making the decision about choices of behavior.

According to a research study by Blasi, Lapsley, and Narváez (2004), individuals who identify themselves as moral may become the worst cheats. The researchers found that when the line between right and wrong was ambiguous among people who think of themselves as having high moral standards, the do-gooders can become the worst of cheaters. Accordingly, a person who identifies himself as honest might cheat because he could view cheating as an okay thing to do, justifying the act as a means to a moral end. For example, if a student wants to be a doctor, he or she could justify cheating on a test, because he or she could help lots of people by becoming a doctor. Therefore cheating on the examination will benefit society. A similar situation is when a police officer commits perjury on the witness stand to send a known child sexual offender to prison. The researchers concluded that those who believed cheating was wrong and had a strong moral identity were generally the most honest.

## False Moral Behavior

Consider this scenario: you are a police officer in a large city. You see a known drug dealer walking down a local street, carrying a brown paper bag. You stop the dealer and inquire as to what is in his bag. He states that it is personal and starts walking away. You stop him and look in the bag. It contains a large quantity of controlled substances. The dealer is arrested and charged with possession of a controlled substance with the intent to transfer. At the trial, you are on the stand testifying about the circumstances surrounding the stop.

1. If you testify truthfully, the substances will be suppressed as the result of an illegal search. This will result in the drug dealer's being released and being back on the street. But you have acted morally by telling the truth.
2. While testifying, you invent sufficient facts to establish a legal justification for the stop and inspection of the bag. The dealer is convicted and sentenced to a long prison sentence. In addition to committing a crime by giving false testimony, you have lied. The result of your lies is a person is sent to prison. This conduct would probably not be considered as morally acceptable. But on the other hand, you have taken a criminal off the streets and may have accomplished a greater good for the community. (In Chapter 7, we examine the issue of whether it is ever morally acceptable to lie.)

The situation discussed in the second item is what Moshman (2004) and others have considered as a "false moral identity." False moral identity has been described as doing the wrong thing and claiming it's for the right reasons. False moral identity results as a willingness to act immorally because the end result justifies it. As the officer in the second scenario, you see yourself not as immoral by inventing justification for the search but as a moral person because of the good you are doing for the community by getting this drug dealer off the street.

The student who cheats on an exam does not see himself or herself as a morally corrupt person, and neither does the police officer who sends a criminal to prison when he or she lies on the witness stand. Instead, the student or police officer will see himself or herself as a moral person and will justify, blame, and seek some form of absolution from it.

The terrorist who uses prohibited weapons and is indiscriminate in his or her attacks and frequently makes civilians and civilian objects the direct object of attack does not consider himself or herself as a criminal or evil. In defense of the choice of targets, means, and methods, the terrorist argues that the use of force in this manner is the only way he or she can draw attention to the cause and otherwise advance the interests of the political community the terrorist purports to represent. Yet, the vast majority of us would consider the terrorist more immoral than the average criminal.

## Ethical Conduct

> To live ethically is to think about things beyond one's own interests. (P. Singer, 1995, p. 174)

Jeremy Travis (1998), former director of the National Institute of Justice, in his plenary address at the Fourth Biennial Conference: International Perspectives on Crime, Justice, and Public Order, stated,

> These times pose very real risks to democratic policing. The imperative to "do something" can easily be translated into an imperative to "do whatever it takes, without concern for the consequences." It is relatively easy, in established as well as emerging democracies, for police activity to remain hidden from public scrutiny—and for abuses to occur in the name of effective crime control. It is hard, in the face of growing crime rates, to retain allegiance to the principles of transparency, to remain vigilant regarding human rights, to adhere scrupulously to the code of ethics, to enforce the law equitably. Yet it is times such as these that these principles take on added importance.

If you had critical information that could free an innocent man from prison, would you reveal it even if doing so was illegal? That was the question that North Carolina attorney Staples Hughes wrestled with for over 20 years. In the 1980s, one of Hughes's clients confessed to the attorney that he alone had committed a double murder for which another man, Lee Wayne Hunt, was serving two life sentences. Hughes could not reveal the confession because he was bound to secrecy by the attorney–client privilege and thus was prevented from disclosing any confidential information obtained from a client. When Hughes's client died, Hughes decided that he could no longer keep the secret. Hughes explained, "It seemed to me at that point ethically permissible and morally imperative that I spill the beans."

When Hughes attempted to disclose this confession to the trial judge, the judge refused to consider the testimony and then reported Hughes to the state bar for disciplinary action, saying Hughes had violated attorney–client privilege, even though the client was dead. The North Carolina state bar dismissed the judge's complaint against Hughes, but Lee Wayne Hunt remained in prison (Liptak, 2008, p. 2).

## Garrow's Lawyers

In 1973, Robert Garrow was arrested and charged with the abduction and murder of a young girl at Lake Pleasant, New York. At the time of Garrow's arrest, police suspected that he had committed at least two other murders.

Garrow admitted these other murders to his defense counsel, Francis Belge and Frank Armani, and told the lawyers where the bodies were. The victims, Susan Petz and Alicia Hauck, were both teenage girls. The lawyers, following Garrow's directions, found the girls' bodies and photographed them. They did not provide information about their discovery of the bodies to the police.

The father of Susan Petz thought it might be possible that Garrow was involved in the case of his daughter and approached Armani to see if he could obtain information about his daughter. Armani did not reveal to Mr. Petz the information he had learned from Garrow and had confirmed.

Armani attempted to use the information about the unsolved killings in plea bargaining with the prosecuting attorney. Armani suggested leniency in Garrow's sentencing in exchange for information about the location of the bodies. The district attorney, outraged at the suggestion, refused to plea-bargain and threatened Armani with obstruction of justice. After the plea bargain was rejected, Armani called Mr. Petz and told him that he was unable to provide further information about his daughter's fate.

The case proceeded to trial, and Garrow pleaded not guilty by reason of insanity. Garrow's lawyers' strategy was to have Garrow confess to the killing of Petz and Hauck, to convince the jury of his insanity. Garrow admitted to the murder he was charged with and confessed to three additional murders and seven rapes. The insanity defense failed, and Garrow was convicted of murder.

After the trial, it became public knowledge that attorneys Armani and Belge had learned about the fate of Petz and Hauck from Garrow, had known about the location of their bodies for almost three months, and had withheld that information from the police and the young women's parents. During this time, the parents had conducted a very expensive and time-consuming search to find the bodies of their daughters.

The prosecutor brought obstruction of justice charges against the lawyers.

*How would you rule as a trial judge in a case against Garrow's lawyers for failure to disclose the additional killings? Did the attorneys have an ethical duty to disclose the location of the young victims' bodies?*[1]


## Ethics in Practice

### "Perspective Gratuities: Pay Now or Later," by Charlie Sewell*

One morning before reporting for duty as a rookie police officer, I stopped at a local convenience store for a cup of coffee. When I placed the cup on the

---

* Reprinted with permission from *FBI Law Enforcement Bulletin* April 2007, Volume 76 Number 4.

counter and reached for my wallet, the clerk said, "We don't charge police officers for coffee." Not knowing exactly how to react, I thanked the clerk and left the store with what I deemed at the time was my trophy. What I did not realize was the position in which I had unwittingly placed myself.

Today, chain restaurants generally offer the same product, level of service, and cleanliness from one location to another. This helps travelers know what to expect when choosing an eating establishment. In the days before fast food, motorists had little prior information to use in selecting a place to eat when away from home. A parking lot full of automobiles often indicated enjoyable food but was not a sure bet. When I traveled as a child with my family, my father selected a suitable restaurant based on whether a police car was parked outside. He theorized that if the local officers ate there, it must be favorable. In retrospect, I wonder whether those vehicles were parked there because the officers enjoyed the food or because they received a reduced bill. In reality, an officer's choice of restaurant could range from assignment location, restaurant availability, or food preference to choice of employees.

Many business owners regularly employ off-duty law enforcement officers for added security. Resourceful entrepreneurs might analyze that attracting officers to their businesses by offering a free cup of coffee or discounted food might afford them a less costly way of boosting security. This practice can be more attractive for smaller restaurants, convenience stores, or retail businesses, especially those in rural areas.

### Encountering Problems

As a new sergeant, I rode patrol with an officer during his first week with my department. He went into a fast-food restaurant to pick up our lunch while I stayed in the car to monitor the radio. When he returned to the car, he was empty-handed. Naturally, I asked about the food. When it was his turn at the counter, he explained, the cashier had snapped, "I guess you want your policeman's discount." To this he had quickly retorted, "No, ma'am, I'd prefer that you charge me double." The snickers, giggles, and awkward comments from customers embarrassed him and led him to make a face-saving retreat.

Another officer recounted an embarrassing moment to me after his third visit to a local restaurant. The first time he ate there, he said that he received a half-price meal. The next week, he ate for free. On his third visit, the cashier became confused about how to apply the police officer discount using the cash register. While she struggled with the register, the other customers' voice levels grew in proportion to the growing service line. The officer's quiet suggestion that the cashier accept full payment went unheard. Repeated requests led to more frustration as the cashier stated that she was simply following company policy. The officer tried to explain that for him to pay full price this time was only fair, telling her about his first and second visits to the restaurant. By paying full price now, he would be making up for the previous free meal. One free meal and one full-price meal equal two half-price meals, he said. Unfortunately, the officer had a difficult time convincing the cashier, slightly elevating his voice and finally thrusting cash into her hand. His words, of course, were within earshot of other customers, and his demeanor sounded similar to a bossy demand that the cashier do as he said. The officer had not asked for a discount or the embarrassment; he resigned himself never to return to that establishment. By developing policies that restrict acceptance of gratuities, law enforcement agencies can protect themselves from such potential predicaments.

### Evaluating Policies

Law enforcement organizations should evaluate their policies regarding gratuities. Wearing the badge of law comes with a considerable amount of honor and pride. For me, that first free cup of coffee made me feel honored. Now, I wonder whether I was being honored or used. Was the clerk honoring my badge or buying a little insurance? The best intentions can become tainted when circumstances change. I have heard numerous stories over the past 32 years about restaurateurs who presented their local governments with a bill for uncompensated food. Business owners could have felt cheated when their perceived special relationships with the law did nothing to help them when they actually fell victim to a crime.

On the other hand, a blanket policy prohibiting gratuities can have the unintended effect of damaging public relations. Some citizens have positive relationships with their local law enforcement officers and want to show their appreciation. Do we tell the well-respected and well-meaning lady who brings the fruitcake to the station at Christmas that we do not want her gift? There is a contrast between a citizen soliciting a police agency and an officer initiating the contact; we can more easily distinguish the officer's intent if he is not the solicitor. Although the public's expectation of a special relationship might be the same regardless of who solicited whom, in either case, citizens may view the relationship as less damaging if the officer or agency has been solicited.

Solicitation by law enforcement agencies certainly dates back many years. My former agency has been involved in raising funds for events since I can remember. The distinction in the intent of the solicitation is where my experience has shown that lines should be drawn. Is the officer receiving personal benefit, or does a special interest group receive the benefit? Annually, my former department sponsors a 4-mile run to raise money for the Drug Abuse Resistance Education (DARE) program. All funds are directly applied to equipment and supplies for the fifth-grade DARE students, with the officers and agency realizing no profit. Some departments hold fund-raising campaigns because they do not have budgets that support the purchase of bullet-resistant vests for the officers' personal use. However, I believe the vast majority of the public easily recognizes the dissimilarity between donating for a lifesaving device and a gratuity given with the express purpose of receiving a reward or payback.

Discounts that attract law enforcement officers also afford hourly clerks the opportunity to develop relationships with those officers. Does the clerk apply the owner's policy of a discount willingly or begrudgingly? The resentful clerk might smile at the moment of service but say to others afterwards, "Why should this officer get a discount? Cops think they're so special." Further, the clerk may expect the same discount when stopped for a minor traffic violation. In that case, the clerk or owner of the establishment could prompt a public relations nightmare for the local law enforcement agency.

Some departments have policies that regulate the exact dollar amount of an acceptable gratuity. Others forbid officers to accept anything of value for performing their official duties except when given permission by the agency. Furthermore, other agencies require officers to notify their superiors when they receive gifts from individuals, businesses, or organizations with which the agency has a business relationship.

While these policies are steeped in tradition, a more stringent one on the acceptance of gratuities can prevent agencies from finding themselves negatively portrayed on the front page of the local newspaper. It also can help eliminate embarrassing moments before the governing body, in both private and public forums. Every time we receive a freebie, we should ask ourselves, "What service have we provided in exchange for this?" Otherwise, the public may ask what profit or wealth we may have received by accepting it. As one author memorably stated, "What makes a gift a gratuity is the reason it is given, what makes it corruption is the reason it is taken." Convincing someone that you want to pay full price for a meal might prove easier than convincing the public that your motives are ethical.

### Realizing Options

Where do we draw the line between saying no thanks to a complimentary cup of coffee and creating a public scene? Clerks can be gregarious in enforcing company rules. A business owner could become offended when a generous offer is turned down. Some establishments always will offer discounts for law enforcement agencies, but that should not stop officers from always offering to pay full price. If the owner or clerk insists on providing a discount, the officer has the option of leaving the remainder of the full price on the table when served. This amount should not be considered a tip or gratuity to the service staff, as tips are based on the full price of goods and services. If the business has counter service (a cash register) rather than table service, the officer can provide the cash register clerk with adequate change to cover the rest of the bill.

Officers are not expected to bring public attention to their ethical dilemmas regarding gratuities, but they can make a reasonable effort to receive the same monetary consideration as the public. Or they can take their business elsewhere.

But what about discounts offered to the general public? Should law enforcement officers accept a greater discount on top of the one everyone else gets? And how do we differentiate between a well-intentioned gift and a self-serving gratuity? The lines are not always clear, but I believe we must try to make them so. The safest way to do so is to insist on transparency. Corruption is a black-and-white issue that cannot be measured by degrees. Free coffee and donuts may be a joke of the trade, but they should not be viewed as a perk of the job. The practice is quietly diluting our honor. Our basic ethics in law enforcement have not changed, but our integrity must be evident and confirmed in the eyes of the public.

> There is only a small difference between accepting a cup of coffee, accepting a cup of coffee and a donut, and accepting a free meal and only a small difference between that and a gift, and another small difference to accepting a large gift and another small difference to accepting … a whopping great suitcase full of cash in small denominations, non-marked, non-sequential bills. Thus, it could be argued that since there is no clear boundary between accepting a cup of coffee and accepting the suitcase of cash, one ought not to accept the cup of coffee. (Coleman, 2003)

The price of a cup of coffee may be only a dollar, but if an officer patronizes the same business during each tour of duty, the price of coffee could equate to $5 each week. Multiplied by the number of weeks an officer works each year, the gratuity can easily surpass $100. And, for even a small law enforcement agency, multiple officers patronizing the same business can consume free coffee valued in the thousands of dollars. Further, adding a free donut, piece of pie, or sandwich can generate very large expenses in the department's name at the business. I am aware of police officers from other agencies who visited a restaurant in such numbers and with such regularity that the business owner was forced to abandon his free-food policy or face bankruptcy.

### Conclusion

We may know the culture of our own departments inside and out. We may even realize the honor and integrity with which our officers regard one another and the public. But what we hear from the public face-to-face may be self-serving and not the same words they would use in another discussion. Agencies can develop a gratuity policy by seeking the help of many officers and local business owners and by reviewing established policies in other jurisdictions. Such a policy should tie directly with modern law enforcement's strict code of ethics regarding financial gains or rewards. When those of us in this profession conduct our jobs in textbook fashion, we step on toes, as the general public frequently does not understand our procedures. To this end, many agencies offer citizen police academies and other programs to improve their relationships with the public.

If the overall perception of public safety officers has improved, should we not work hard to perpetuate that image of ourselves? I do not want my professional discretion questioned. I will not knowingly place my department or myself in the embarrassing position of having to explain why we received a gratuity to which the general public was not entitled. Granted, we should avoid performing a disservice to the public by issuing a top-down prohibition on accepting gifts of any kind.

But, we can let our actions and those of our fellow officers speak for themselves about whether we can be bought for an annual pot of chili. If gift-bearers want to be heard, an agency's open-door policy should provide a means for that to happen without the necessity of special treatment for departments or individual officers. Every agency should examine their policies on financial gains or rewards. But, just as important, they should analyze the culture of their departments. Pay for that cup of coffee today, or, in one way or another, you will pay for it later.

## Questions in Review

1. It is often stated that the single most important difference between the animal kingdom and human beings is humans' propensity to create moral codes and control natural instincts. If this is true, we could state, "Ethics make us human." Do you agree or disagree with this statement? Why?
2. Explain the differences between ethical relativism and ethical absolutism.
3. Consider the Lee Wayne Hunt case discussed earlier in this chapter. What action would you take if your client confessed to a murder that another person was on death row for?
4. Should police officers on duty late at night accept free coffee from a business establishment?

## Endote

1. The charges subsequently brought against the lawyers were dismissed. Garrow's Lawyers, *New York Times* (June 20, 1974).

# Historical Development of Ethical Reasoning

# 2

## Brief Historical Review

> The difference between good and evil is the difference between order and disorder. (Plato, *Plato's Five Dialogues*)

> The concept of good is the distinguishing feature of any act we call moral, because morality means being guided by goodness. (Souryal, 2007, p. 72)

The first known ethical precepts were passed down by word of mouth from parents and elders, but as societies learned to use the written word, they began to set down their ethical beliefs in records. These records constitute the first historical evidence of the origins of ethics. For example, Greek historian Herodotus (430–420 BC) reported that the Persian king Darius I (550–486 BC) summoned some Greeks before him and asked them how much he would have to pay them to eat their fathers' dead bodies. They refused to do it at any price. According to Herodotus, Darius then summoned some Indians who by custom ate the bodies of their parents and asked them what would make them willing to burn their fathers' bodies. The Indians reportedly cried out that he should not mention so horrid an act. Herodotus used this example to illustrate the concept that each society has its own ideas about what is moral and what is not (Encyclopedia Britannica, 2008). This scenario points out how often our concept of what is right and what is wrong is shaped by our culture.

Some of the earliest surviving documents that concern ethics are lists of precepts to be learned by boys of the ruling class of Egypt prepared some 3,000 years before the Christian era. In most cases, the precepts consisted of advice on how to live happily, avoid unnecessary troubles, and advance one's career. There are, however, several precepts that discuss broad ideas of moral conduct, such as:

- Rulers should treat their people justly and judge impartially between their subjects,
- Rulers should aim to make their people prosperous,
- Those who have bread should share it with the hungry,
- Humble and lowly people must be treated with kindness, and
- One should not laugh at the blind or at dwarfs (Hertzler, 1936).

## Religion

Often we assume that our ethical positions originated as religious concepts. As noted by Porter (1980), ethical questions were being debated long before Moses, Jesus, and Muhammad. Since our sense of morality, fairness, and sociability are strongly related to our sense of religiosity, our ethical concepts are greatly influenced by our religious beliefs. But ethics and religion are not the same. An individual who has no religious beliefs may still be an ethical person. Just as religious beliefs may affect our attitude toward work, the desire to succeed, respect for authority, and compassion for others; those same religious beliefs affect our judgments as to what are the ethical courses of action in any given situation.

### Ethics in the Bible

As noted by Souryal (2007, p. 95), Christianity has its roots in Hebrew teaching, but its moral philosophy goes far beyond the teaching and works of Christ and the apostles who followed him. Souryal noted that the Christian philosophy establishes four major doctrines that characterize ethics in the Bible. The four doctrines are as follows:

- Religion and ethics are indissolubly united.
- Worship should include man's kindness toward his fellow man.
- God's forgiveness of sin requires that we forgive those who have transgressed against us.
- Man should expect God's rewards for being righteous.

Ethical concepts that are taught in the Bible include the following:

- The ruler must be just.
- The path to justice is the shining light.
- Through knowledge, justice shall be delivered.
- It is joy to do justice.
- The just shall be protected from evil.
- The just shall increase in faith.
- All things should be done with charity.

### The Torah

The Torah contains statements or principles of law and ethics. Collectively the laws, generally referred to as the biblical law or commandments, are considered as the Law of Moses. Torah in Hebrew refers to "teaching" or "instruction" or "Law." The Torah consists of the Five Books of Moses (also known as the Pentateuch) and refers to the entirety of Judaism's founding legal and ethical religious texts. The Torah is the primary holy scripture of Judaism. According to Talmudic teachings, the Torah was created 974 generations before the world was created and is the blueprint that God used to create the world. The Talmud states that everything created in the world is for the purpose of carrying out the word of the Torah, and the foundation Jewish belief stems from the knowledge that the Lord is the God Who created the world (Wylen, 2001, p. 16).

## Islamic Ethics

Islamic ethics is based on the notion that every human being is called to command the good and forbid the evil in all spheres of life. The role of Muhammad was to facilitate this submission. Another principle is the belief that mankind has the faculty to discern God's will and to abide by it. Accordingly, humans have a moral responsibility to submit to God's will and to follow Islam as demonstrated in the Qur'an. The moral responsibility is subverted, however, by our focus on material success. Such focus first presents itself as a need for basic survival or security, but it then tends to manifest into a desire to become distinguished among one's peers (Houtsma et al., 1938).

The most important writer on ethics in Islam was Muhammad Ibn Miskawayh. He laid down in his Tahdhib al-akhlaq (The Cultivation of Morals) and other ethical writings that provided the groundwork for a whole tradition of Persian ethical writing. The psychological basis of Ibn Miskawayh's ethics was based on Plato's dialogues. Ibn Miskawayh described justice as a form of moderation (i'tidal) or proportion (nisba) and arises when the parts of the soul are in harmony (Donaldson, 1953).

## Buddhist's Ethics

Buddhism is a religion of over 300 million people. Buddha comes from budhi (to awaken). Buddhism has its origins twenty-five hundred years ago when Siddhartha Gotama, known as the Buddha, was himself enlightened at the age of 35. Buddhism is broader than a religion and is a way of life. It is also a philosophy, since philosophy means "love of wisdom," and the Buddhist way of life can be summed up as follows:

- lead a moral life,
- be mindful and aware of thoughts and actions, and
- develop wisdom and understanding (Keown, 1992).

Ethics are considered Buddhist by the ultimate appeal to the enlightened perspective of the Buddha and his enlightened followers. Moral instructions are either included in Buddhist scriptures or handed down through tradition. According to traditional Buddhism, the foundation of Buddhist ethics for most people is the Pancasila. The Pancasila provided no killing, stealing, lying, sexual misconduct, or use of intoxicants (Harvey, 2000; Keown, 1992).

In Buddhist teachings, the ethical and moral principles are determined by looking at whether a certain action, whether connected to body or speech, is likely to be harmful to one's self or to others and by avoiding actions that are likely to be harmful. In Buddhism, the skilled mind is held in high regard. A skillful mind avoids actions that are likely to cause suffering or remorse to others. Buddhism places much emphasis on avoiding mental anguish such as remorse, anxiety, and guilt in order to cultivate a calm and peaceful mind (Harvey, 2000).

# The Greeks

Ethics is the study of dead Greeks. (Anonymous college student)

Greece is considered as the birthplace of Western philosophical ethics. The ideas of Socrates, Plato, and Aristotle are embedded in our ethical concepts. Socrates (469–399 BC), who is claimed to have stated, "The unexamined life is not worth living," is generally regarded as one of the greatest teachers of ethics. Yet he did not tell his audience how they should live. What Socrates taught was a method of inquiry. When students stated that they knew what justice, piety, temperance, or law was, Socrates would ask them to give an account, and he would then show them how entirely inadequate their beliefs were. Because his method of inquiry threatened conventional beliefs, Socrates was put to death on a charge of corrupting the youth of Athens. This also raises the question: does challenging widely held beliefs, customs, or traditions amount to corruption?

## Socrates, the Philosopher

Socrates' (469–399 BC) formal name was Socratessŏk'rətēz. He viewed philosophy as a pursuit that was proper and necessary for all intelligent men. Our knowledge of Socrates and his teachings are based on the information contained in the dialogues of his disciples and from the Memorabilia of Xenophon. The difficulty created in forming an accurate picture of the historical Socrates and his philosophical viewpoints is problematic. This difficulty is commonly called the Socratic problem. Since Socrates did not write any philosophical texts, our knowledge of him, his life, and his teachings is based solely on writings of his disciples. Foremost among his disciples was

Plato. Other disciples included Xenophon, Aristotle, and Aristophanes. In addition, the task of finding the "real" Socrates is difficult because the works discussing his life and philosophy are basically philosophical or dramatic documents, not historical works. Another problem is that the sources that do mention Socrates don't claim to be historically accurate and are often partisan in nature. Accordingly, historians have had a difficult time trying to reconcile the various works and to create an accurate and consistent account of his life and his works (Navia, 1989).

Socrates lived during the time of the transition from the height of the Athenian hegemony to its decline with the defeat by Sparta. During this time the citizens of Athens were attempting to stabilize and recover from its humiliating defeat by Sparta. At the time, it appears that Athenian citizens had doubts about democracy as an efficient form of government. Socrates was apparently a critic of democracy. Many scholars have interpreted his trial as evidence of the political infighting that existed in Athens at the time. At his trial, Socrates was asked to propose his own punishment. Socrates suggested a lifetime government wage and free dinners for the rest of his life in order to finance the time he spends as Athens' benefactor. He was found guilty of corrupting the minds of the youth of Athens and sentenced to death by drinking a mixture containing poison hemlock. It is generally believed that Socrates had an opportunity to escape when his followers bribed the prison guards. But he refused to escape because he stated that a flight would indicate a fear of death. According to Socrates, no true philosopher should have a fear of death. He also noted that if he fled Athens, his teaching would suffer the same fate in another state since he would continue questioning all he met and undoubtedly incur their displeasure.

Plato is generally considered as the most reliable and informative source of information about Socrates' life and philosophy. At the same time, in some works it appears that Plato pushed his literary version of Socrates far beyond anything the historical Socrates was likely to have done or said (Navia, 1989).

Socrates was apparently convinced that his calling was to search for wisdom about right conduct by which he might guide the intellectual and moral improvement of the Athenians. There is evidence that he neglected his own affairs and spent most of his time discussing virtue, justice, and piety wherever his fellow citizens congregated. He was criticized for neglecting his public duty because he never sought public office, which many at the time felt he had a duty to do, although he was famous for his courage in the military campaigns in which he served (Navia, 1989).

Socrates' major contributions to philosophy included a new method of approaching knowledge, a conception of the soul as the seat both of normal waking consciousness and of moral character, and a sense of the universe as purposively mind-ordered. His method, called dialectic, consisted of examining statements by pursuing their implications, on the assumption that if a statement were true it could not lead to false consequences. While his method may have been suggested by Zeno of Elea, Socrates refined it and applied it to ethical problems (Navia, 1989).

Socrates' doctrine of the soul included the belief that all virtues converge into one, which is the good, or knowledge of one's true self and purposes through the course of a lifetime. Knowledge in turn depends on the nature or essence of things as they really are, for the underlying forms of things are more real than their experienced exemplifications. This conception leads to a teleological view of the world that all the forms participate in and lead to the highest form, the form of the good. Plato later elaborated on this doctrine and made it central to his own philosophy. Socrates' view is often described as holding virtue and knowledge to be identical, so that no man knowingly does wrong. Since virtue is identical with knowledge, it can be taught, but not as a professional specialty as the Sophists had pretended to teach it. Socrates himself, however, gave no final answer to how virtue can be learned (Navia, 1989).

## Socratic Method of Reasoning

The Socratic method of reasoning had two interrelated functions:

- Establishment of the purpose of the phenomenon that is being examined, and
- Demonstration of the goodness of the phenomenon by fulfilling its purpose.

To examine the interrelated functions, Aristotle (384–322 BC) devised three simple questions:

1. What is it?
2. What good is it?
3. How do we know?

The three questions move from the purpose of the phenomenon, which is confirming its goodness, to the fulfillment of its purpose. Souryal used a practical example of gun control to show this line of reasoning. What is gun control? According to Souryal, if the main purpose of gun ownership is to ensure self-defense, and it can be established that gun ownership helped ensure self-defense and did not hinder the purpose by being used as a tool for crime, then we can establish what good is it. The third question is "How do we know?" This question is not easily answered. How do we know that its

goodness (ensure self-defense) outweighs its evil as a tool to commit crime (Souryal, 2007, pp. 8–9)?

## Objectivity of Goodness

Socrates asserted that those who act badly do so only because they are ignorant of, or mistaken about, the real nature of virtue (Hertzler, 1936). The Socratic method of inquiry, also considered as the dialectic method, is still used by most law professors in American law schools.

Socrates' greatest follower, Plato, accepted the Socratic beliefs in the objectivity of goodness and in the link between knowing what is good and doing it. Plato also followed the Socratic method of conducting philosophy, developing the case by exposing errors and confusions in the arguments of others. Plato's writings were dialogues in which Socrates was portrayed as engaging in arguments with others. Plato's early dialogues are generally considered as reasonably accurate accounts of Socrates' views, but the later dialogues, written many years after Socrates' death, appear to be a vehicle for presenting ideas and arguments that were original to Plato rather than Socrates (Hertzler, 1936).

Plato contended that justice exists in the individual when the three elements of the soul—intellect, emotion, and desire—act in harmony with each other. And the unjust person lives in an unsatisfactory state of internal discord, trying always to overcome the discomfort of unsatisfied desire but never achieving anything better than the mere absence of want. According to Plato, the soul of the just person is harmoniously ordered under the governance of reason, and the just person derives truly satisfying enjoyment from the pursuit of knowledge (Hertzler, 1936).

## Nature of Truth

To the Greeks, veritas (the truth) was the focal point of philosophy. They considered truth as the central point around which all intelligible forms revolved, and the difference between humans and livestock was humans' ability to search for the truth. Without truth, living would be random and reasoning would be meaningless because neither the purpose of life nor the goodness of society would make any distinguishable difference. In Chapter 7, the concept of truth and lying will be explored in more depth.

## Plato, the Philosopher

Plato, a Greek philosopher, who, along with his mentor, Socrates, and his famous student, Aristotle, is credited with the establishment of Western philosophy. Plato's dialogues generally consisted of Socrates asking questions of another and proving, through these questions, that the other person had the wrong idea on the subject. The precise relationship between Plato and Socrates remains an area of contention among scholars.

Plato was a mathematician, a writer of philosophical dialogues, and the founder of the Academy of Athens, the first institution of higher learning in the Western world. Plato was influenced by what he saw as his teacher's unjust death. Plato's birth date is unknown. Scholars have estimated that he was born in either Athens or Aegina between 429 and 423 BC. He died in either 348 or 347 BC.

Plato's Academy of Athens was one of the first institutions of higher learning in the Western world. While he lectured at the Academy, the pedagogical function of his dialogues, if any, is not known with certainty. The dialogues since Plato's time have been used to teach a range of subjects, mostly including philosophy, logic, rhetoric, mathematics, and other subjects about which he wrote.

Plato's writings reflect his interest in the father–son relationship and the question of whether a father's interest in his sons has much to do with how well his sons turn out. During his time, a boy was socially placed by his family identity. Often Plato referred to his characters in terms of their paternal and fraternal relationships.

Unlike Plato, Socrates was apparently not a family man and considered himself as the son of his mother, who was probably a midwife. In fact, Socrates, a fatalist, mocked fathers who spent excessive fees on tutors and trainers for their sons. To Socrates, good character was a gift from the gods.

## Plato's Republic

The Republic was the most famous of Plato's dialogues. Plato's Republic centers on the question, is it always better to be just than unjust? The Republic, written in 360 BC, is the longest of his works, with the exception of the Laws. The Republic is one of the most influential works in Western philosophy. In the Republic, Socrates and various other Athenians and foreigners discussed the meaning of justice and whether a just man is happier than an unjust man by constructing an imaginary city ruled by philosopher-kings. The dialogue also includes a discussion on the conflict between philosophy and poetry, and the question of the immortality of the soul.

In the Republic, Plato examined the problem of how to live a good life. To examine this problem, he asked two questions:

1. What is justice, or what would an ideal state be like?
2. Who is a just individual?

Included is a discussion on how citizens of a state should be educated, what kinds of arts should be encouraged, what form its government should take, who should do the governing and for what rewards, what is the nature of the soul, and finally what divine sanctions and afterlife should be thought to exist.

In speaking through Socrates, Plato divided people based on their intelligence, strength, and courage. Those who are not overly intelligent, strong, or brave should be assigned to the professions of farming, building, and so on. Plato felt that the overwhelming majority of the people were the "producers" and were the most suited for productive work.

The middle group of individuals who are of average intelligence, strength, and courage should be selected for the military and policing professions. This smaller group is called "auxiliaries."

Those who are extraordinarily intelligent, virtuous, and brave are the ones best suited to run the state itself. He advocated an aristocracy form of government. Aristocracy is a Greek word that means "rule by the best." This group of the best and the brightest, a very small and rarefied group, are those who are permanently in complete control of the state. He called this group "guardians."

In the ideal state, "courage" characterizes the auxiliaries, and "wisdom" displays itself in the lives and government of the guardians. According to Plato, a state had "temperance" if the auxiliaries obey the guardians in all things and the producers obey the auxiliaries and guardians in all things. To him, a state was intemperate if any of the lower groups do not obey one of the higher groups. A just state existed when the auxiliaries do not simply obey the guardians but enjoy doing so. In other words, they don't grumble about the authority being exercised over them. It is also required in a just state that producers not only obey the auxiliaries and guardians but do so willingly.

The definition of "justice" arrived at in the Republic is the action of doing what one ought to do, or of doing what one does best, according to one's class within society. Accordingly, a just society is one in which the organization of the government mirrors the organization of the tripartite soul. And the three classes in the government correspond to a part of the soul. The guardians correspond to the rational part of the soul. The auxiliaries correspond to the spirited part of the soul. And the working class reflects the desiring part of the soul. Thus, all three classes, according to their engagement in their particular corresponding part of the soul, has a virtue most appropriate to it. The guardians must be wise, the auxiliaries must be courageous, and all three classes must exhibit moderation.

## The Allegory of a Cave

Plato used an allegory of a cave to explain his concept of "forms" as an answer to the problem of universals. He used the allegory in an attempt to justify the philosopher's place in society as king. The allegory is about a group of people who have lived in a cave all of their lives, chained to a wall so they cannot see outside or look behind them. Behind the prisoners is a flame that illuminates various statues that are moved by others. The movement causes shadows to flicker around the cave. When the cave people see the shadows, they realize how imitative they are of human life, and begin to ascribe forms to these shadows, such as either "dog" or "cat." The shadows are as close as the prisoners get to seeing reality.

Plato explained how a philosopher, a former prisoner, after being freed from the cave, realizes that the shadows on the wall were not constitutive of reality at all. The philosopher recognizes that the fire and the statues that cause the shadows are indeed more real than the shadows themselves, and he therefore understands how the prisoners are so easily deceived. Next, Plato explained that a freedman is released into the real world. At first, the prisoner is blinded by the light. As he adjusts to the brightness, he begins to understand that all of the real objects around him are illuminated by the sun. Thus, the sun becomes a form of the good that has caused the brightness. The former prisoner also realizes it is the sun to which he is indebted for being able to see the beauty and goodness in the objects around him. He is finally cognizant that the fire and statues in the cave were only copies of the real objects.

Plato described the former prisoner's stages of understanding as levels on a divided line. The line is divided into what is the visible world and what the intelligible world is, with the sun being the divider. When the prisoner was in the cave, he was obviously in the visible realm that received no sunlight, and outside he comes to be in the intelligible realm.

Plato concluded that the shadows in the cave that the prisoners can see are the lowest level of the line, that of imagination and conjecture. The prisoner reaches the second stage on the divided line when the individual is freed and sees the fire's reflection onto the statues that causes the shadows in the cave. This is the stage of belief, as the former prisoner believes that the statues in the cave are real. After leaving the cave, the former prisoner sees objects more real than the statues inside of the cave. This correlates with the third stage on Plato's line of understanding. Now the prisoner is able to ascribe forms to objects as they exist outside of the cave. Finally, the prisoner sees the sun, which he accepts as the source of truth, or the Form of the Good. This last stage, named as dialectic, is the highest possible stage on the line. At this stage, the prisoner, as a result of the Form of the Good, can begin to understand all other forms in reality.

Plato reasoned that the freedman is a philosopher, and he is the only person able to discern the Form of the Good and thus understand absolute goodness and truth. Plato ended his allegory with the conclusion that it is the philosopher's burden to reenter the cave and educate those in the material world or spread the light to those in darkness. Because the philosopher is the only one able to recognize what is truly good, only he can reach the last stage on the divided line, and consequently only he is fit to rule society.

## Plato's Defense of Socrates

Plato's second most famous dialogue, the Apology, was an account of Socrates' trial. The Apology was written in the early 380s and was the earliest dialogue written by Plato. It may be the oldest extant document of Greek philosophy currently in existence, because everything earlier was lost and is known only through quoted fragments in later works.

The word "apology" is the direct descendant into English of the Greek word apolog'a, but the meaning has changed. Socrates was not apologizing or making excuses. The Greek word apolog'a simply and precisely meant a defense or a defense speech. Note even now, an "apologist" is someone who presents a defense of someone or something, and "apologetics" is the discipline of argued defense of something, generally a doctrine, cause, or institution. Accordingly, the Apology may be translated as the "defense of Socrates."

Socrates' trial for his life is generally believed to have taken place in 399 BC. According to the Apology, Socrates astonished his followers by apparently trying to get the court to find him guilty and condemned to death. There were no Greek court reporters, so there was no official record of the trial. Socrates' words are remembered only by the writings of Plato and Xenophon.

Socrates' trial was held in the court of one of the major officials of Athens, the King Archon. Socrates' prosecutors were three private individuals. At this time in Greece, there were no district attorneys or public prosecutors, and all trials were brought by private citizens. Apparently, if no one cared about the victim, then it was unlikely that the offender would be prosecuted. According to Plato's account of Socrates' trial, Socrates never mentioned the judge; his remarks were all addressed to the jury. In fact, there is a question as to whether a judge was present at the trial.

The Council of the Areopagus, the ancient senate of the aristocracy, undertook to protect the state from vengeful spirits. At the time of the trial, there were nine archons (rulers) in the constitution at Athens. Six were judges, and the other three were the Eponymous Archon, after whom the year was named. The King succeeded to the religious duties of the original Kings of Athens. One of the King's duties was to preside over court cases involving religion. Those cases included murders, which involved the pollution of spilled blood, and accusations of impiety. This was why Socrates was in the King's court: he was accused of impiety.

Most of the power in the Athens courtroom was in the hands of the jury. In Socrates' trial, there were 501 jurors. There was no screening of jurors. The jury consisted of any free adult male citizen who showed up. The jury had all but absolute power. In addition, there were no formal rules of evidence. The prosecution and defense could say pretty much whatever they wanted. Thus, Socrates, who in a sense was put to death for practicing free speech, nevertheless had more freedom of speech at his trial than most defendants do in the present-day courts. Rather than appeal to the jury, Socrates carried out his defense in a manner that was designed to antagonize the jury. Only a bare majority was needed, but the prosecution was fined if it did not get a fifth of the vote. In this case, Socrates was found guilty by 30 votes.

The procedure of the trial was that the prosecutors made their speeches, accusing the defendant of the crimes against him. Next, the defendant made his defense speech. Plato's Apology begins at the point in the trial when Socrates initially comments on what he has just heard from his prosecutors. After the defense, the jury voted innocent or guilty. If there was a finding of guilty, the prosecution proposed a punishment. In Socrates' case it was the death. Then Socrates proposed a counterpenalty. The jury voted to pick which penalty to impose. The jury voted to condemn Socrates to death. In the final part of the Apology, Plato discussed what Socrates had to say after that vote and after he knew that he had been sentenced to die.

Socrates began his postsentencing speech with a bit of irony. He remarked that he did not know how the jury was affected by the speeches of his accusers, but the prosecutors' speeches were so persuasive that he had almost forgotten himself. Socrates then stated, "hardly anything of what they said was true." He indicated that his accusers are liars.

## Plato's Theories

Plato, like most ancient philosophers, subscribed to a virtue-based eudaemonistic ethics. Eudaemonistic refers to the highest goal of moral thought and conduct. Plato's support for an ethics of happiness differs from ordinary views of happiness. He devoted as much time to undermining the traditional understanding of a good life as he did to describing his own concept of a good life. Plato regarded happiness as a state of perfection and one that is based on metaphysical presuppositions that seem hazy and out of the realm of ordinary understanding. Unlike Aristotle, who saw happiness as a self-sufficient state of the active individual, Plato emphasized solving problems and difficulties. In addition, Plato's moral ideals were austere and self-abnegating. To him, the soul remained aloof and separate from the pleasures of the body (Irwin, 1977).

Plato's ethical thoughts were also subject to various modifications during his life. In his early works, the "Socratic dialogues," there were no indications that the search for virtue and the human good should go beyond the human realm. In his middle dialogues, he developed an increasing interest in an all-encompassing metaphysical grounding of knowledge. In his "Forms" he discussed the true nature of all things and stated that the "Form of the Good" was the transcendent principle of all goodness. During this period, Plato contended that moral values must be based on an appropriate political order that is maintained by leaders with a rigorous scientific training (Irwin, 1977).

Plato's late dialogues displayed a growing tendency to see a unity between the microcosm of human life and the order of the entire universe. To him, such holistic tendencies seemed to put the attainment of the requisite knowledge beyond human boundaries. In Plato's late works, he did not appear to display any readiness to lower the standards for knowledge. And in discussion of cosmic order, he provided for conjecture and speculation, which is reflected by a more pragmatic treatment of ethical standards and political institutions (Irwin, 1977).

## Aristotle

Aristotle was a younger contemporary of Plato and his rival in terms of influence on the course of Western philosophy. He was often fiercely critical of Plato. While Aristotle's writing was very different in style and content, there was a considerable amount of common ground between the two. Aristotle agreed with Plato that a life of virtue was rewarding as well as beneficial for the community. Aristotle also agreed that the highest and most satisfying form of human existence involves the exercise of one's rational faculties to its fullest extent. A major point of disagreement between them is based on Aristotle's rejection of Plato's doctrine of Forms. Aristotle did not accept the belief that in order to be good, a person must have knowledge of the "Form of the Good."

Aristotle considered the universe as a hierarchy in which everything has an assigned function. To him, the highest form of existence is the life of the rational being. The function of lower beings was to serve the rational being. Aristotle defended slavery because he considered the slaves less rational than Greeks, and by nature slaves were destined to be "living tools." Aristotle held that all living things had inherent potentialities, which it was their nature to develop. He considered the question, what is the potentiality of human beings? For him, the answer depends on what is distinctive about human beings. To Aristotle this was the capacity to reason. Accordingly, the ultimate goal of humans should be to develop their reasoning powers. When they do this, they are living in accordance with their true nature, and they will find the most rewarding existence possible. Aristotle believed that an investigation of human nature would reveal what one ought to do in a given situation (Barnes, 2001).

While Aristotle agreed with Plato that the life of the intellect is the most rewarding existence, he was more realistic than Plato in suggesting that such a life would also include the goods of material prosperity and close friendships (Barnes, 2001).

## Aristotle's Nicomachean Ethics

Aristotle wrote Nicomachean Ethics (sometimes spelled "Nichomachean"), or Ta Ethika, about 350 BC. Nicomachean Ethics is a discussion on virtue and moral character, both of which play a prominent role in defining Aristotelian ethics. Nicomachean Ethics contains ten books and is based on Aristotle's notes from his lectures at the Lyceum. It appears that the work was either edited by or dedicated to Aristotle's son, Nicomachus (Barnes, 2001).

The work focuses on the importance of always behaving virtuously and developing a virtuous character. Aristotle emphasized the importance of context to ethical behavior. He contended that a virtuous person has the ability to recognize the best course of action. To Aristotle, eudaimonia was the goal of life, and an individual's pursuit of eudaimonia, if rightly conceived, would result in virtuous conduct. Eudaimonia literally means "having a good guardian spirit" along with virtue. Ancient philosophers considered eudaimonia to be the highest human good, and they were concerned with understanding how to achieve it. Eudaimonia is often translated into English as "happiness," but that is not an adequate translation because it means more than just happiness (Barnes, 2001).

Aristotle's ethics may be considered as character-centered ethics. Individuals who do things well and consistently are good people. An act should not be considered as an isolated act but be considered in relation to a virtuous ideal. A person's actions should be considered as to whether those actions make that person better and build better character. According to Aristotle, others will see you as courageous if you generally perform courageous acts when the chance arises.

## Ethics in Practice

The following remarks were delivered by Robert S. Mueller, III, director, Federal Bureau of Investigation, City Club of San Diego, San Diego, California, May 11, 2006.

The vast majority of public officials—both elected and nonelected—are honest in their work and committed to serving their fellow citizens. Unfortunately, a small percentage abuse the public trust. As anyone who follows the news is aware, there are countless examples of corrupt acts around the country.

For a nation built on the rule of law, and faith in a government of the people, by the people, and for the people, we can and should do better.

I want to talk today about how the FBI is engaged in the fight against public corruption, the impact our program is having nationally, and how we can continue to work together toward better government and a more secure United States.

To see how focused the FBI is on public corruption, one need look no further than here in San Diego.

As many of you are no doubt aware, the FBI has played an active role in several recent and ongoing investigations of public corruption. Just last year, a city council member was convicted on federal public corruption charges. A jury found that the politician conspired with an owner of an adult entertainment club to ease restrictions on such clubs.

Also last year, former congressman Duke Cunningham pled guilty to accepting $2.4 million in return for helping defense contractors secure Pentagon contracts.

Even more recently, five members of the San Diego Retirement Board were indicted. As alleged in that indictment, they engaged in a scheme to defraud the citizens of San Diego of their right to honest services.

San Diego is not alone. Philadelphia, Pennsylvania; Chicago, Illinois; Dallas, Texas; Tennessee; and Connecticut are just some of the cities and states in which we have seen significant investigations and prosecutions.

Nor are we in the FBI immune. In 2002, a former FBI special agent was sentenced to 10 years in prison for protecting a source who committed numerous crimes, including murder.

Public corruption is not just an American problem, of course. It plagues many countries around the world.

Although the FBI cannot fight public corruption in other countries, we can help those who do. Our International Law Enforcement Academy in Budapest, Hungary, and our National Academy here in the United States provide critical training to foreign law enforcement officers. That training promotes the growth of stable governments and respect for the rule of law.

It is a struggle for many countries. I recently met with the attorney general of the Dominican Republic, who has made rooting out public corruption in his country a priority. He said that when he first started prosecuting these cases, a defendant approached him. The defendant said, "If you are intent on prosecuting public corruption in the Dominican Republic, you are going to need a stadium to hold all the defendants."

To which the attorney general replied, "I have a stadium, and I am going to do my best to fill it."

We do not need a stadium here in the United States, but the problem of public corruption is significant. And we in the FBI are responding.

Since 9/11, we have had to prioritize how we use our resources, placing our national security programs first. But at the same time, we made public corruption our top criminal investigative priority.

We did this because public corruption is different from other crimes. It does not just strike at the heart of good government—it can strike at the security of our communities and our nation.

Last year, we ran an investigation in Tucson, Arizona, called "Operation Lively Green." The investigation exposed serious corruption along our southern border. Fifty current and former U.S. soldiers and law enforcement officers pled guilty to accepting $650,000 in bribes. They conspired to smuggle cocaine, drug money, and illegal immigrants across our border.

If public officials violate their oath to uphold the law by smuggling drugs or humans, where would they draw the line? For the right price, would they assist terrorists to smuggle a bomb into the country or help terrorist operatives cross the border?

In this way, public corruption can permeate all aspects of society and as well affect national security. Corrupt officials can allow organized crime to operate with impunity, allow drugs to flow into our cities, and even allow terrorists to enter the country.

Public corruption is a betrayal of the public's sacred trust. It erodes public confidence and undermines the strength of our democracy. Unchecked, it threatens our government and our way of life.

That is why I believe it belongs as our top criminal investigative priority. And that is why, more than ever, the FBI must be actively engaged in combating public corruption.

Rooting out corruption is exceptionally difficult, but it is a mission for which the FBI is singularly situated. We have the skills to conduct necessary undercover operations and the ability to perform electronic surveillance. But more than that, we have insulation from political pressure.

Investigating public corruption is an FBI commitment as old as the Bureau itself. When the FBI was founded in 1908, its responsibilities included the investigation of land fraud, which often involved public corruption. The first head of the Bureau, Stanley Finch, took great pride in this line of work. He wrote, "I am always particularly glad to see brought to justice a person guilty of wrongdoing by injuring persons who it was his sworn duty as a government officer to protect."

Given what is at stake, today's FBI must have that same dedication—and we do.

Since 2001, when we marked public corruption as our top criminal priority, we have significantly increased the number of special agents working these cases. As a result, we are seeing tremendous returns on that investment.

We now have approximately 2,200 public corruption cases pending nationwide. Indictments are up 40 percent. And in the last two years, FBI investigations have led to the conviction of more than 1,000 government employees involved in corrupt activities.

Some of these cases are well-known examples of public corruption. The former governor of Illinois, George Ryan, was convicted of a pattern of fraud committed while in office. Former Washington lobbyist Jack Abramoff pled guilty to conspiracy, mail fraud, and tax evasion. He will have to pay more than $26 million in restitution.

For every scheme on Abramoff's scale, there are many more cases that involve less money but are no less a violation of the public trust. In Baltimore, two police officers were convicted of robbing drug dealers. In Alabama, a police chief pled guilty to shaking down motorists.

It does not matter if it is a big city or a small town. It does not matter if it is millions of dollars or just hundreds of dollars. There is no level of "acceptable corruption." The violation of the oath of office is the same.

These investigations do not tell the whole story. The more we uproot public corruption, the more we drive reform throughout all levels of government.

Let me give you a couple of examples. Last year, we arrested five Tennessee state legislators. They were charged with accepting $146,000 in bribes. This investigation spurred sweeping ethics reform in the state of Tennessee.

And in Philadelphia, multiple city officials and contractors were convicted of mail fraud, money laundering, and extortion. In response, the citizens of Philadelphia voted to amend the city charter, enacting some of the nation's strictest ethics laws.

Now is the time to build on this momentum.

Our most important partner in this fight is you the public. The support the FBI receives from our partners in federal, state, and local law enforcement is valuable. But our most important asset truly is the American public.

Many of our investigations start with a tip from someone who encounters corruption. There is a growing intolerance by the American people of public corruption—an intolerance reflected in the willingness to come forward and report abuse of public office. We are always grateful for those who have come forward to report corruption. That information is critical to our work.

Unfortunately, for many reasons, corruption is not always reported. Some may fear retribution at work or in business. Others may be indifferent, thinking that corruption is just the cost of doing business. Still others may not know to whom they should turn.

Because of this, we are working to make it easier for the public to report public corruption.

In the wake of Hurricane Katrina, we set up a telephone hotline to receive tips about public corruption related to the rebuilding of New Orleans. We received 2,500 calls, initiated more than 400 investigations, and have already netted a public official who allegedly extorted a kickback of $100,000.

The tip line was successful because people knew where to direct their information. We want to replicate that success nationwide. We have established a Web site to enable the public to send information about public corruption to the FBI. The Web site is http://reportcorruption.fbi.gov.

When you type in that address, you will see a page that gives you instructions on how to report corruption to the FBI—by phone or through the

Internet. Our analysts will then review that information case-by-case and ensure there is follow-up.

Through this Web site, and with help from the public, we will continue to build on our efforts to root out public corruption.

Theodore Roosevelt once said, "Unless a man is honest, we have no right to keep him in public life." That sentiment is as true today as it was in Roosevelt's time.

We are fortunate to live in a country where public corruption is the exception rather than the rule. But we must never relax our efforts against those who betray the public trust.

Public corruption, unfortunately, will never be totally eradicated. But the will of the American people to fight it, so as to preserve our freedoms and protect our democracy, is strong. And the FBI stands committed to working with the citizens of this great country, this great city, and our partners in law enforcement to ensure that public servants serve the public good.

Thank you.

---

### Classroom Exercise: Ethics Training

---

According to Joycelyn Pollock and Ronald F. Becker (1996, p. 20), the practice of ethical behavior defies universally accepted standards. The authors stated, "Aside from exposing officers to the different philosophical frameworks—including, among others, religious ethics, natural law, ethical formalism, utilitarianism, and the ethics of care—instructors generally focus on practical exercises to reinforce desired behavior." Pollock and Becker recommended that in ethics training, instructors employ ethical dilemmas submitted by class participants as the basis for 50 percent of the course content. The other 50 percent of the course involves discussing the dilemmas within specific ethical frameworks. They recommended that the class be asked to provide ethical dilemmas to discuss. The authors defined the term ethical dilemma as a situation in which individuals

- do not know the right course of action,
- have difficulty doing what they consider to be right, or
- find the wrong choice very tempting.

Class exercise: Have each class member submit an ethical dilemma that the class would like to discuss and then select several for class discussion.

---

## Questions in Review

1. What role should religion play in our ethical decision making?
2. How do the teachings of Plato differ from the teachings of Aristotle?
3. Explain the importance of the cave to Plato's teaching.
4. Do you agree with Robert S. Mueller's statement that the vast majority of public employees are honest in their work and committed to serving their fellow citizens? Justify your opinion.

# Understanding Ethics

3

## Introduction

In this chapter, some of the basic tenets involving the study of ethics are examined. Included are discussions on natural law its effects on ethics, the hierarchical order of virtues, the law of humanity, the ethics of law, philosophical theories of ethics, and moral implications of ethical codes. One central concern that we examine in this chapter is the question of where do we get the ethical principles on which we base our ethical decisions. Many individuals will contend that our ethical principles are given to us by a supreme being. Others will contend that our ethical principles are simply rules based on an implied agreement when we become a part of society.

St. Augustine contended that our principles are given to us by a supreme being and that a person who did not believe in a supreme being could not be an ethical person. Thomas Aquinas also examined this issue in his discussions on the concept of natural law as the eternal law of God (Lynch, 1997).

## Natural Law

Natural law in ethical philosophy is a set of principles, based on what are assumed to be the permanent characteristics of human nature that can serve as a standard for evaluating conduct and civil laws. It is considered fundamentally unchanging and universally applicable. Because of the ambiguity of the word nature, the meaning of natural varies. ("Natural Law (Ethics)," Microsoft® Encarta® Online Encyclopedia 2008, http://encarta.msn.com Accessed on December 31, 2008)

Natural law may be considered an ideal to which humanity aspires or a general fact, the way human beings usually act. Natural law is contrasted with positive law, the enactments of civil society. (Lynch, 1997)

"Natural law" is simply that "unwritten law" that is more or less the same for everyone everywhere. It is the concept of a body of moral principles that is common to all humankind and, as generally posited, is recognizable by human reason alone. Natural law is distinguished from positive law, which is the formal legal enactments of a particular society. Dolhenty (n.d.) described natural law as the disposition of things as known by our human reason and to which we must conform ourselves if we are to realize our proper end or "good" as human beings.

Dolhenty stated that natural law

- is not made by human beings,
- is based on the structure of reality itself,
- is the same for all human beings and at all times,
- is an unchanging rule or pattern that is there for human beings to discover, and
- is a means by which human beings can rationally guide themselves to their good.

The concept of natural law can be traced to the ancient Greeks; Stoicism (one of the philosophical movements of the Hellenistic period in ancient Greece [Dolhenty, n.d.]) provided the classical formulation of natural law. The Stoics contended that our universe is governed by reason, or rational principle. If individuals act in accordance with reason, they will be following nature or natural law. They further contended that all humans have reason within them and therefore should know and obey its law. The Stoics noted that because human beings have free will, they will not necessarily obey the law.

Christian philosophers, such as Thomas Aquinas, adapted the natural law theory and identified natural law with the law of God. Aquinas saw natural law as the eternal law of God ("the reason of divine wisdom") that is knowable by human beings by means of their powers of reason. In contrast, positive law is the application of law to particular social circumstances and is manmade. Both the Stoics and Aquinas believed that positive law that violates natural law is not a true form of law (Dolhenty, n.d.).

The seventeenth-century Dutch jurist Hugo Grotius, who is credited with developing the first comprehensive theory of international law, contended that natural law was based on the rules of human nature there were dictated by both reason and social requirements. He believed that humans by nature are not only reasonable but social. Thus the rules that are "natural" to humans are those dictated by reason and social requirements because of the need to live in harmony with others (Dolhenty, n.d.).

John Locke (1632–1704), an English philosopher and founder of British empiricism, contended that human beings in the state of nature are free and equal yet insecure in their freedom. Under this concept, when individuals become part of a society, they surrender only such rights as are necessary for their security and for the common good. Each individual retains fundamental prerogatives drawn from natural law relating to the integrity of person and property (natural rights). Based on this reasoning, natural law theory eventually gave rise to the concept of "natural rights." The natural rights theory was later used by Thomas Jefferson to justify his "inalienable rights" that were stated in the U.S. Declaration of Independence. Accordingly, the natural rights theory provided a philosophical basis for both the American and French revolutions (Dolhenty, n.d.).

## Thomas Aquinas

Thomas Aquinas has also been referred to as Thomas of Aquin because Aquinas refers to his home rather than his surname. He was born in either 1225 or 1227 and died in 1274. Aquinas was an Italian Catholic priest in the Dominican Order. He was the foremost classical proponent of natural theology and the concept of natural law. Aquinas is considered by many in the Catholic Church to be the model teacher for those studying for the priesthood. His best-known works are the *Summa Theologica* and the *Summa Contra Gentiles*. His father was the Count of Aquino, and his mother was the Countess of Teano. His family was related to the kings Henry VI and Frederick II and also to the kings of Aragon, Castile, and France (Dimock, 2001).

In *Summa Theologica* (*Summary Treatise of Theology*, 1265–1273), Aquinas considered natural law as the rational guidance of creation handed down by God and referred to it as the "Eternal Law." According to him, Eternal Law provides the inclination to those actions and aims that are proper and ethical. Because we are rational creatures, we can direct our own actions and guide the actions of others, thus sharing in divine reason itself. Aquinas concluded that the dictates of natural law corresponded to the basic inclinations of human nature. Thus, according to him, it is possible to distinguish good from evil by the natural use of reason (Lynch, 1997).

Murphy (2002) summarized Aquinas's fundamentals of natural law in the following principles:

- Natural law is given by God.
- It is naturally authoritative over all human beings; to reject it is to be evil.
- Natural law is naturally knowable to all human beings.
- The good is prior to the right.
- Right action is action that responds to the good.
- There are a variety of ways in which action can be defective with respect to the good and a variety of ways to reach the natural, common ends.
- Some of these ways can be captured and formulated as general rules, while some allow for a range of interpretations.

Dimock (2001) added two additional principles to Murphy's list:

- When there is more than one way to reach common ends, human law is rightfully introduced to supplement natural law.
- A human law (positive law) is morally binding only if it meets the following validity conditions:
  - It must be reasonable.
  - It must be made by someone with appropriate authority.
  - It must be directed toward the common good.
  - It must be promulgated.
  - It must be just.

## St. Augustine and Divine Illumination

Divine illumination is a doctrine that holds that human beings are unable to be ethical by themselves and that they require a special divine assistance in their cognitive activities. Under this doctrine, a person who does not believe in a supreme being cannot be ethical. This doctrine is the oldest and most influential alternative to naturalism in the areas of mind and knowledge (Pasnau, 1995).

The early spokesperson for divine illumination was St. Augustine. Throughout his long literary career, St. Augustine stressed the role of divine illumination in human thought. It is estimated that St. Augustine left behind writings with the sum total of over 5,000,000 words that survive today (Portalié, 1907).

St. Augustine argued that even though we can learn things from others, only God can teach us to be ethical. For example, in one of his many writings, he stated, "For he is taught not by my words but by the things themselves made manifest within when God discloses them" (Pasnau, 1995, p. 51).

Aurelius Augustinus (354–430 CE), popularly referred to as St. Augustine of Hippo or Augustine, was a major spokesperson for medieval philosophy. He was born in Thagaste, what is now Algeria, and educated in Thagaste, Madauros, and Carthage (Portalié, 1907).

St. Augustine's followers have disagreed as to the meanings of his teaching. The disagreements can be traced as far back as the Middle Ages. Many contend that St. Augustine saw divine illumination as an influence that we receive in an ongoing way throughout our lives. Others contend that Augustine saw divine illumination as an infusion all at once at the start (Pasnau, 1995).

Many consider Thomas Aquinas as the person largely responsible for ending the theory of divine illumination. Others regard Aquinas as one of the last defenders of the theory (Pasnau, 1995). The reason for this disagreement is that in some of Aquinas's writings, he apparently supports divine illumination, and in other writings, he tended to discredit the doctrine.

## Introduction to the Philosophical Theories of Ethics

In this section, we will examine some of the leading philosophical theories of ethics. In Chapter 4, the more important theories or schools of ethics will be discussed in greater depth.

### Stoicism

One of the earliest philosophical theories of ethics is Stoicism. Stoicism is the philosophy and social movement that took place in Greece around 300 BC. The movement lasted for about 500 years. Stoicism is considered as the ethics of freedom from passion, moral fortitude, and tranquility or as the philosophy of tranquility and indifference to pain (Souryal, 2007). The name Stoicism was based on the location in Athens where it was formed. The movement was based on the teachings of Zeno of Citium. He lectured his followers from a porch. The porch (*stoa poikilê*) was located in the Agora at Athens and was decorated with mural paintings. It was on the porch where the members of the school congregated and their lectures were held. Zeno's philosophy was continued in the writings of Cicero, Epictetus, and Marcus Aurelius.

The Stoics contended that emotions such as fear or envy were false judgments and that a person who had attained moral and intellectual perfection would not indulge the false judgments. The Stoics considered philosophy not as an interesting pastime or a particular body of knowledge but as a way of life. To the Stoics, to be good an action must benefit its possessor under all circumstances. The Stoics saw a distinction between what is good and things that have value. Some things could have value but not goodness. One of the basic principles of Stoicism is to live in harmony with nature: human nature and physical nature (Brennan, 2005).

For a Stoic, the moral purpose or the "will" is the only repository of things that have absolute value. According to the movement, whether things are projected wisely or foolishly, for good or for evil, is up to individual. When a person's will is on the right course, the person becomes good; when it's on a foul course, the person becomes evil. With the right course of action comes good luck and happiness, and with the foul course, bad luck and misery. To the Stoics, bad luck is your fault. It is a sign that you've become addicted to externals (Stockdale, 1993).

James Stockdale was a vice admiral in the U.S. Navy. He led aerial attacks from the carrier *USS Ticonderoga* (CVA-14) during the 1964 Gulf of Tonkin

Incident. On September 9, 1965, he was shot down over enemy territory. Stockdale was the highest-ranking naval officer held as a prisoner of war during the Vietnam conflict. He was awarded the Medal of Honor and four Silver Stars. In the 1970s, he served as president of the Naval War College. In 1992, Stockdale was a candidate for vice president of the United States, on Ross Perot's independent ticket.

During Stockdale's time as a prisoner of war, he credited Stoicism with helping him survive and not succumb to the torture. Stockdale stated that he constantly reminded himself, "I am the master of my fate; I am the captain of my soul." He related that Stoicism taught him that his true business was maintaining control over his moral purpose and that this was his moral purpose and who he was. Stockdale contended that your deliverance or your destruction is 100 percent up to you. Stockdale stated that everybody has to play the game of life. According to him, "You can't just walk around saying, 'I don't care about my health, or wealth, or my reputation, or whether I'm sent to prison or not.' " Stockdale noted that Epictetus, an early Stoic, stated that everybody should play the game of life and to pay it with skill, speed, and grace (Stockdale, 1993, pp. 132–134).

## Hedonistic School of Thought

Hedonism is based on the Greek word *hedoné* (pleasure). Hedonism refers to the ethical systems that advocate that feelings of pleasure or happiness are the highest and final aim of conduct. Accordingly, under this school of thought, actions that increase the sum of pleasure are good or right, and those that increase pain are wrong. Hedonism is considered as the ethics of the pursuit of pleasure. As discussed in Chapter 2, Plato proposed that the state be lead by philosopher-kings and that social justice depended upon the judgment of the philosopher-kings (Fakhry, 1970).

## Virtue School

The virtue school is considered as the ethics of knowledge and moral character and is reflected in the teachings of Socrates, Plato, and Aristotle. The school is reflected in Plato's teaching that knowledge and reason are essential attributes in guiding an individual's behavior. Plato equated knowledge with a "noble" and "commanding" state (Souryal, 2007, p. 141).

## Religious School

The religious school is considered as the school based on the love of God. Its principle spokespersons were St. Augustine and Thomas Aquinas. Under this school, the determination of whether actions are good or bad is based not on the consequences of the actions, but by whether or not they are in line with the will of God (Porter, 1980).

## Natural School

The natural school is considered as the school that advocates the ethics of egoism and power. Its principle spokespersons were Thomas Hobbes and Friedrich Nietzsche. Hobbes was a pragmatic thinker and was suspicious of any exhortations concerning the "shoulds and oughts" of human behavior. Hobbes contended that self-preservation is the primary objective of human beings. His theory of what is right and what is wrong should be based upon the concept of the Golden Rule. Hobbes contended that this rule, "do not do unto others what you do not want them to do unto you," is based on the concept of a social contract. The social contact theory is based on the concept that in order to achieve peace and self-defense, people, by being a part of the society, agree to be bound by the rules of the society. Hobbes contended that merely living in the society evidenced an implied consent to agree to society's rules (Souryal, 2007, p. 167).

Friedrich Nietzsche, a German philosopher of the late nineteenth century, challenged the foundations of Christianity and traditional morality. He believed in life, creativity, health, and the realities of the world we live in, rather than those situated in a world beyond. Nietzsche, like Hobbes, considered human beings as aggressive in nature with a universal desire to dominate. He contended that what is right and what is wrong are established by those in power. A central theme of his philosophy was the idea of "life-affirmation." Life-affirmation involves an honest questioning of all doctrines that drain life's energies, however socially prevalent those views might be (Ferm, 1956).

## Utilitarianism

According to utilitarianism, an act has utility if it produced happiness or prevented pain. Utilitarianism, in its basic form, contends that persons, actions, and institutions should be measured by how well they promote human happiness. Jeremy Bentham and John Stuart Mill defined happiness as consisting in pleasure, and they believed that the ultimate aim of each person is predominantly the promotion of the person's own happiness or pleasure (Masters & Roberson, 1990).

Jeremy Bentham was a prolific writer. He is frequently described as the ultimate "armchair philosopher." In addition to his writing involving utilitarianism, he is considered as one of the founders of the classical school of criminology. He is also noted for the statement that "Only the lawyer escapes punishment for his ignorance of the law." When Bentham died in 1832, in accordance with this will, his body was dissected. His skeleton was dressed in his usual attire and is on display at the University College in London. For over 150 years, the fully dressed skeleton has attended the college faculty assemblies at the college. Speakers at the assembly traditionally first voice recognition to Mr. Bentham and then to the other members of the assembly and the guest (Masters & Roberson, 1990, p. 93).

Bentham, discussing human motivation in his *Introduction to the Principles of Morals and Legislation* (published in 1789) stated: "Nature has placed mankind under the governance of two sovereign masters, pain and pleasure." While Bentham contended that we may be moved by the pleasures and pains of others, he appeared to think that these pleasures move us only insofar as we take pleasure in the pleasure of others. Bentham apparently endorsed a version of the principle of psychological egoism that claims that the person's own happiness is and can be the only ultimate object of his desires (Bentham, 1789, p. 178).

John Stuart Mill (1806–1873) was the most famous British moral philosopher in the nineteenth century. His greatest philosophical influence was in moral and political philosophy, especially his articulation and defense of utilitarian moral theory and liberal political philosophy. His two most popular and best-known works were *Utilitarianism*, published in 1861, and *On Liberty*, published in 1859 (Crisp, 1997).

## Ethics of Duty and Reason

The ethics of duty and reason is the school of Immanuel Kant. Kant was born in the East Prussian city of Königsberg, studied at its university, and worked there as a professor most of his life. It is reported that he never traveled more than fifty miles from home. Kant's central thesis was that the possibility of human knowledge presupposes the active participation of the human mind. Kant argued that moral requirements are based on a standard of rationality he dubbed the "Categorical Imperative" (CI). Kant contended that an analysis of practical reason will reveal the requirement that rational agents must conform to instrumental principles. His argument was based on his doctrine that a rational will must be regarded as autonomous or free in the sense of being the author of the law that binds it. And the fundamental principle of morality, the CI, is none other than the law of an autonomous will (Walker, 1999).

## Existential School

The existential school is considered as the ethics of moral individualism and freedom of choice. "*Existentialism*" is a term whose definition is to some extent one of historical convenience. The term was adopted as a self-description by

Jean-Paul Sartre and his associates, most notably Simone de Beauvoir and Albert Camus. Existentialism is identified with the cultural movement that flourished in Europe in the 1940s and 1950s.

Sartre, an atheist, contended that man was condemned to freedom, a freedom from all authority, which he may seek to evade, distort, and deny but that he will have to face if he is to become a moral being. To him, the meaning of a person's life is not established before the person's existence. Once man acknowledges freedom, man has to make this meaning himself, has to commit himself to a role in this world, and has to commit his freedom. An attempt to make oneself is futile without the "solidarity" of others (Taylor, 1991).

Simone de Beauvoir (1908–1986) was honored as a central figure in the early struggle for women's rights. She was also famous for being the companion of Jean-Paul Sartre. She was active in the French intellectual scene and a central player in the philosophical debates of her time. Beauvoir's argument for ethical freedom is based on analyzing the ways in which a person's existence as a moral agent is conditioned by the fact that we start life in a world already endowed with meaning. Beauvoir noted that we are born into the condition that she labeled the "serious world." And this world has ready-made values and established authorities. It is also a world where obedience is demanded. Beauvoir contended that we are limited by our ability to decide what constitutes ethical behavior by the conditions of our situation (Keefe, 1998).

### Social Justice

John Rawls (1921–2002) is considered as the leader of the social justice school. Rawls was an American political philosopher in the liberal tradition. His theory of justice envisions a society of free citizens holding equal basic rights cooperating within an egalitarian economic system.

Rawls contended that the exercise of political power was proper only when it was exercised in accordance with a constitution that provides that all citizens are free and equal. He contended that power may only be used in ways that all citizens can reasonably be expected to endorse. According to Rawls, ethical conduct includes the promotion of social justice (Pogge, 2007).

## What Makes an Act Unethical?

In determining the implications of ethical decisions, we need to consider that merely living in a society requires us to accept many concepts that are value laden and leaves us with the fundamental question, What is it that makes an act unethical? In attempting to answer this question, we also are faced with the question: are there different degrees of unethical action, and if so, how do we decide the degree?

Richard Hall (2000, p. 290), in his attempt to answer the question, what makes an act unethical, stated that we should look at three characteristics that an act must have in order to be unethical or corrupt. Those were the following:

- The act must involve a misuse or abuse of a duty.
- It must be an intentional act.
- It must be motivated by self-interest.

There are several issues involving Hall's requirements. The concept that there must be a misuse of a duty for an act to be unethical appears to be logical if duty is broadly defined. The requirement could be stated as we have a duty to be ethical. Can you unintentionally commit an unethical act? There may be some argument regarding this requirement. For example, if a person acts negligently, can he or she commit an unethical act? The answer to this question would probably depend upon the definition of what constitutes an unethical act. A similar argument would exist regarding the requirement that the act must be motivated by self-interest. And the answer probably also depends upon the definition of self-interest.

## Ethics in Practice

**Bob Harrison was the chief of the Vacaville, California Police Department when he wrote "Noble Cause Corruption and the Police Ethic," presented below.** *

The City's Guardians must be gentle toward their own people but rough toward their enemies; otherwise, they will not wait for others to destroy them; they will do it themselves first. (Socrates, Plato's *The Republic*)[1]

In Plato's *The Republic*, Socrates and Glaucon discuss the formation of a city that embodies justice. As their dialogue builds this city, the final element involves selecting the guardians. Socrates' guardians would be keen of perception, strong enough to subdue opponents, and high-spirited in temper. At the same time, they would love wisdom and learning so they could treat their own people gently. However, the philosophers failed to address one question. Who would decide which individuals represent the guardians' own and which deserve the rough treatment of an enemy? Today, U.S. society wrestles with the same unanswered question as its contemporary guardians, the police, attempt to interpret and enforce the law.

---

* Reprinted with permission from the *FBI Law Enforcement Bulletin*, 68(8): pp. 1–9, August 1999.

If the law represents an expression of moral sentiment, then police officers stand as instruments of that morality. Although appearing as paramilitary organizations, modern police agencies actually perform specific functions within communities through individual police officers' acting largely without supervision or direct control. Unlike a military unit, which operates cohesively as a team, the cop on the beat is left alone to make decisions regarding who goes free and who becomes subject to closer scrutiny. Society might regard the lone street cop as its single most powerful individual. Consider that the police alone are charged with depriving others of their liberty and that it is illegal to resist their authority to do so. Neither the president nor a Supreme Court justice can issue or execute a death warrant without prior review, yet police officers have the authority to employ readily available lethal weapons to protect themselves and the public they serve. In many cases, little conflict arises with regard to the propriety of police actions. Society generally recognizes the need for public safety, and few would disagree with the removal of murderers, rapists, or other violent individuals. The issue becomes more problematic when an attempt to service that desired end conflicts with the laws and regulations instituted to control the decision of who represents the "enemy" of the law.

Echoing ancient Greek dialogues, those who founded the United States as a constitutional republic in which no person or group could rise to absolute power deliberated at length on the ability of government to engage in punishing transgressors without resorting to tyranny.[2] James Madison, the father of the U.S. Constitution, noted the problematic issues of governance when he wrote, "In framing a government which is to be administered by men over men, the great difficulty lies in this: you must first enable the government to control the governed; and in the next place oblige it to control itself."[3] From Plato to the modern day, this remains a vexing problem. In a democracy, how can policing, as an institution, police itself, and how can police officers maintain an appropriate balance between governing others and controlling themselves?

In contemporary American life, officers commonly face the dilemma between following rules and enforcing the law. Often, the result constitutes an individual utilitarianism, a sense of electing a course of action based on a self-perception of what is good for the greatest number. This personal interpretation of the law inevitably leads to questions of conduct (the means: an officer's methods to elicit cooperation from another) versus a desired outcome (the end: apprehension of the guilty and protection of the community). For example, does an officer have the duty to infringe on an individual's liberty for a laudable outcome? Should society excuse police officers for breaking fundamental laws, not for personal gain but to serve a greater moral imperative? Is this "noble cause corruption"[4] (i.e., illegal actions that violate the rights of citizens for moral considerations) an unstated norm in police conduct, or should an individual's right to freedom from that behavior be society's paramount consideration?

### Policing and the Law in America

The police are the constituted authority for the use of force within society.[5] Although society has recognized the need for a person or group to hold coercive power over others since ancient times, current police practices did not exist at America's founding.[6] In fact, the first professional police agency in the United States, modeled after the London Metropolitan Police, was formed in New York in 1833. Interestingly, the use of the word "police" to describe society's guardians has significant implications. For example, the word derives from the Greek *polis* and *polites*, meaning "city/state" or "citizen." In Scotland, the term *polis* remains in use as a formal title for an officer of the law. Perhaps Ireland has the most descriptive term for a modern police force, *garda siochana*, which translates to "guardians of the peace." In many American communities, the police are legally entitled peace officers, an important distinction when considering the police role in the interpretation and application of the law.

Ideas from Plato and others exerted considerable influence over the education of the Anglo-European culture of America's forebearers and shaped the law that police officers uphold today. Also, Lockean and biblical traditions had a dramatic effect on the framework of American freedom and liberty. For example, Thomas Jefferson wrote in the Declaration of Independence, "We hold these truths to be self-evident, that all men are created equal, that they are endowed by their Creator with certain unalienable Rights, that among these are Life, Liberty and the pursuit of Happiness," a passage strongly similar to John Locke's writings that government should protect "life, liberty, and property."[7] Although Jefferson did not attribute a significant influence from Locke in the development of his writings, the impact of Locke's theories is undeniable.[8]

While Jefferson regarded the Bible as the ultimate source of moral guidelines,[9] he also readily absorbed the ideas of the Enlightenment[10] and of Locke's *Essay Concerning Human Understanding*.[11] In 1769, after being shut out of the Virginia Assembly for his views regarding the immorality of slavery, Jefferson sent to England for a copy of Locke's *On Government*.[12] By 1773, Locke's natural rights theories had become as commonplace for discussions as the Epistles of the apostle Paul.[13]

Jefferson's foundation of Lockean individualism and moral certitude regarding the unalienable rights of the individual over that of the state inadvertently set the stage for the tension between the individual's rights and the public good with which contemporary American police officers must wrestle. Locke's intent can be interpreted to mean that the government assumes the power to decide whom to punish for transgressions to protect property and ensure safety. This inference easily can lead police officers into a dilemma of engaging in extralegal acts to serve their perceived duty to the public good. No matter how mightily society may struggle to develop a legal system that serves justice, occasions inevitably will arise where one undeniable good comes into conflict with another undeniable good, and no amount of effort, negotiation, or goodwill can bring the two into harmony and reconciliation. Officers thrust into arbitrating between these conflicting goods may fall into corrupting the public trust to which they are sworn, not for personal gain or revenge but in an effort to fulfill a noble sentiment arising from the conflict endemic to the human condition itself.

### Societal Ends and Police Means

Imagine working as a police officer assigned to investigate the kidnapping of an "X-year-old girl." Officers have arrested a suspect who may know of the girl's whereabouts. Unless they elicit a quick confession, the girl may die.

Under the law, the suspect has an absolute right against self-incrimination. Officers may adhere to the law and respect the rights of the suspect, or use extralegal measures to coerce the information they need to save a life. The dilemma becomes which course of action better serves the concept of Jeffersonian Happiness—that of respecting the individual arrestee's rights or that of serving the greater good by using formal authority to ensure safety for the community.

Some police administrators would assert that no dilemma exists. Officers are sworn to uphold the law, and illegal activity can never be justified by an emotional argument to the contrary. Other administrators would focus on the act, and not the outcome, as the gauge of desired actions. If the act could not be applied in all circumstances (Immanuel Kant's Universal Law),[14] it should not be performed.

Judging from his writings, John Locke also might have been caught on the horns of this dilemma. On one hand, he asserted that each man has a property in his own person to which no one has a right to but himself, and that the chief purpose of government is to protect that property.[15] For example, Locke maintained that what individuals produced through their own labors belonged to them and that the law must protect this property. At the same time, he also contended that man submits to the authority of the law to ensure that his property is protected.[16] According to Locke's philosophy, officers faced with this dilemma could justify harsh actions against criminals, similar to killing murderers to deter others.[17] Faced with the opportunity to save a life and deter the offender, officers could employ a true Lockean concept of policing to support the mandate of using any means necessary to achieve the desired end. Therefore, officers unilaterally could elect to take any measures necessary to serve the interests of society.

Further, officers who read John Stuart Mill and ascribe to a more utilitarian credo would have little trouble justifying actions that support the greater good.[18] Using the greatest happiness principle, these officers rationally could expect the violation of a single individual's rights (the means) to promote a greater societal end, that of happiness for the greater number of individuals. Of course, a true utilitarian view has little use for the resolution of true moral dilemmas because the rights of the individual always weigh less than those of the larger group. Mill's premise, however, amounts to no more than a justification for any action against individuals who are different, especially if taken on behalf of the societal or cultural majority.

What, then, should police officers do when faced with violating the letter of the law in order to serve a desired moral end? American traditions formed from religious and classical philosophy affirm the principle that each individual has an innate worth and that police officers cannot descend from reasoned persuasion to aggravated coercion without losing a respect for the fundamental rights of freedom and self-determination. The noble cause corruption concept of officers' acting illegally, not for personal gain, but to fulfill moral obligations, stands as a testimony to the difficulties encountered by those entrusted with the public's safety. However, Edwin Delattre contends that ends do not necessarily justify the means and asserts that three basic considerations exist when contemplating actions intended to serve a desired end.[19]

- A good end cannot justify a means in a context that makes it wrong and evil. Violations of civil liberties and laws, violations of oaths of office, and abuses of authority and power—all betrayals of public trust—are wrong and cannot be justified by any end.
- Attempts to revise regulations and rules cannot eliminate a conflict in ideals. Although revisions in the law can alter the mechanics of accountability, they cannot change elements of the human condition.
- Inflicting pain sadistically or without regret can never be excused.[20]

Interestingly, Delattre comments that most thoughtful people will come down on one side of noble cause corruption while expressing a sympathy and respect for those on the other side. He personally would not rule out the use of physical coercion to save a life; however, he then would immediately report his actions to his agency and resign his position of public trust.

Is Delattre's "act wrong, then resign" resolution the best officers can hope for to resolve the issue of achieving desired ends? Does the human condition render some choices as inevitable tragedies for those unfortunate enough to have to make them? Should the difficulty in arriving at a consensus regarding appropriate actions excuse those who have elected to put themselves in positions of public trust? Unfortunately, the problem of ethics in policing is not solved readily by the "silver bullet" approach. Even if officers know what is right, that knowledge remains separate from the question of how much an individual is willing to pay to do the right thing. As appealing as it may be to satisfy the emotional dilemma by choosing the short-term solution, compelling arguments exist in favor of acting only in a manner that serves the long-term interests of society.

### Restoring the Wise Guardian

Although the dilemma of noble cause corruption appears superficially problematic, in actuality, it is not. On the surface, the issue of saving innocent lives and incarcerating those who have transgressed against society seems to constitute ample justification for acts necessary to achieve that noble end. From a relativist perspective, society's guardians could rationalize any circumstance to legitimize the brutalization of another human being. To do so, however, denies basic human rights and the concept of equality upon which police officers base their authority. Once equality and confidence in the institution of policing is eroded in the general community, the ability for government to fulfill its legitimate aims also becomes decimated.

Government refrains from coercion and intimidation to accomplish its ends because the society it serves deserves a legal system that remains consistently just. The convenient deviance from the belief that each individual has worth proves a slippery slope from which anyone concerned with justice may not be able to escape. For every instance where a dilemma may occur regarding competing noble ends, countless examples of police misconduct under the guise of law enforcement exist. In the majority of cases, however, officers committed these acts in the name of law and order.

Unfortunately, contemporary policing in America contains many examples of conduct detrimental to the profession and the community it serves. Because recent law enforcement studies have shown the existence of widespread perjury, brutality, and other forms of corruption, judges, attorneys, juries, and the public sometimes question police courtroom testimony.[21]

For example, in one East Coast city, the term "testilying" is a code word for police perjury to obtain a conviction. Also, excessive force for the purpose of exacting "street justice" is a problem noted in commission reports from New York to Los Angeles. In California alone, the Rodney King incident in 1991 replayed itself in 1996 in Riverside when officers used their batons against defenseless individuals at the end of a high-speed pursuit. On both occasions, the victims received punishment without court review or a legitimate conviction for breaking the law.

When officers use unlawful means to gain a desired end, they damage the system they represent. Beyond the damage to the justice system, however, officers who engage in illegal behavior denigrate not only the uniform of the guardian but also the individual within. The eventual result to society is a loss of confidence in those charged with the protection of others, leading to a fraying of the tapestry of the culture that binds communities together.

What can be done? Socrates' assertion that education of the guardians is essential remains strongly supported by modern law enforcement scholars. A New York commission exploring tactics to combat chronic corruption in their department recommended at least one year of formal, general education beyond the high school level prior to police service. In California, however, of the 800 hours a new recruit spends in basic academy training, only a fraction deals with issues beyond basic skills. Most police training academies devote little classwork to the broader understanding of the police role in society at a philosophical level. Many new officers enter a culture where they are taught to perceive anyone who is not a street cop as the enemy, including top law enforcement managers. Patrolling their beats largely unsupervised, officers can easily develop a sense of being the lone crime fighter—heroes left to rely on their own devices and skills to get the job done. Added to this is the fact that officers work within a system of changing policies, conflicting court rulings, and increasing scrutiny and distrust. Taken together, these factors contribute to the sense that the pedestal upon which society has placed justice is showing cracks and erosion.

Without appropriately educating its guardians regarding their roles and responsibilities to the public they serve, society could see the result of this subtle erosion in the eventual collapse of the American justice system.

And what should this education encompass? Beyond laws and procedures, the modern guardian should possess a sense of integration with the larger fabric of American society. Moving from a sense of individualism to the Stoicism[22] perspective might better reflect the intent of Jefferson and others who founded the American democracy. In other words, an individual who filters events through a Stoic perspective would move from a judgment of how the world should be to an acceptance of events as being a part of the natural course of humanity. It does not mean that external events will go well but that an individual accepts these events, leading toward a fulfilled life. In this paradigm, the individual's motivation and action result from an intrinsic sense of worth, rather than a reaction to extrinsic influences.

Using the Stoic, or solicitous, path over the individualistic path to design the education of police officers will move their attitudes and perspectives from seeing actions as distinct from one another to understanding the civic good from a community perspective. Officers who understand the role of the guardian would prove far less likely to shirk their duty to the longer perspective of upholding the basic tenets of the guardian.[23] This education remains necessary, not only when officers enter the profession but also throughout their careers.

*Conclusion*

Law enforcement officers face difficult decisions on a daily basis. Sometimes situations arise that require them to weigh the laws they are sworn to uphold against the life of an innocent victim. Such incidents force officers to confront the noble cause corruption dilemma of violating fundamental laws to serve a greater moral good. Officers need all of the assistance that police managers can provide to resolve these ethical quagmires.

Without a concerted educational effort to turn the contemporary cop into Plato's "lover of wisdom," society easily can envision the increasing dissatisfaction caused by inappropriate actions by law enforcement as a precursor to the direction of American culture itself. In constant contact with those who commit crimes, officers would do well to heed Friedrich Nietzsche's admonition that "whoever fights monsters should see to it that in the process he does not become a monster" and "when you look long into an abyss, the abyss also looks into you."[24] For society's sake, police officers must take a step back from the abyss to reassess who the enemies of the city are and to ensure gentle treatment of all within the city's walls.

# Questions in Review

1. Why do some individuals claim that a person who does not believe in a supreme being cannot be ethical?

2. What are the key differences between the philosophies of Kant and Mill?
3. What are the key contributions of Thomas Aquinas to the study of ethics?
4. What should police officers do when faced with violating the letter of the law to serve a desired moral end?

## Endnotes

1. Plato, *The Republic*, Book II, *Great Dialogues of Plato*, trans. Philip Rouse (New York: Mentor Books, 1950), 172.
2. Edwin Delattre, *Character and Cops* (Washington, DC: American Enterprise Institute, 1989), 16.
3. Alexander Hamilton, James Madison, and John Jay, *The Federalist Papers*, No. 47, Introduction by Clinton Rossiter (New York: Mentor Books, 1961), 301.
4. Supra note 2, 194.
5. Supra note 2, 197.
6. Plato wrote of the need for the guardians; John Locke asserted that each man had the right in the natural state to enforce conformance upon others who transgressed on his property. Kings, property owners, and appointed servants of a ruler or leader of most European cultures have all asserted the right to enforce adherence to a stated or codified norm. In the nineteenth century, dissatisfaction over the use of the military in England for the role of civil government enforcement led to the creation of the modern police model.
7. Fawn M. Brodie, *Thomas Jefferson—An Intimate History* (New York: Bantam Books, 1975), 145.
8. Charles Maurice Wiltse, *The Jeffersonian Tradition in American Democracy* (Chapel Hill, NC: University of North Carolina Press), 45.
9. Ibid., 48.
10. A philosophical movement of the eighteenth century marked by a rejection of traditional social, religious, and political ideas and an emphasis on rationalism.
11. Leonard Wibberley, *Thomas Jefferson—Revolutionary Aristocrat* (New York: Franklin Watts, 1991), 40–41.
12. Supra note 7, 112.
13. Supra note 7, 113.
14. Alasdair MacIntyre, *After Virtue* (Notre Dame, IN: University of Notre Dame Press, 1981), 42–45.
15. John Locke, *The Second Treatise on Civil Government* (Buffalo, NY: Prometheus Books, 1986), 70.
16. Ibid., 69.
17. Ibid., 12.
18. John Stuart Mill, *Utilitarianism* (Buffalo, NY: Prometheus Books, 1987), 16–17; Mill defines happiness, not in the hedonistic sense but as the pleasures of the intellect.
19. Supra note 2, 193.

20. Supra note 2, 194–195.
21. Commission Report for the city of New York, July 1994, 37.
22. A philosophy begun about 300 BC, Stoicism holds that individuals should be free from passion, unmoved by joy or grief, and submissive to natural law.
23. The most relevant biblical reference is Romans 13:3–4, which reads, "Do you want to be free from fear of the one in authority? Then do what is right and he will commend you. For he is God's servant to do you good. But if you do wrong, be afraid, for he does not bear the sword for nothing. He is God's servant, an agent of wrath to bring punishment to the wrongdoer."
24. Friedrich Nietzsche, *Beyond Good and Evil*, trans. Walter Kaufman (New York: Vintage Books, 1989), 89.

# Ethical Schools

4

## Introduction

In this chapter we expose readers to the foundation and logic of the leading ethical schools of thought. Each school is constructed of different logic, and it is important that one be familiar with each. We urge readers to explore each school with an open mind and consider each of the main postulates. The essence of this chapter is to provide basic points of each school in an attempt to foster critical thinking. In other words, as you review the foundation of each school, ask yourself these questions: Where do I stand? Do I agree with the information contained in this school of thought? If I were on the receiving end of someone's actions, representing each of the different schools, how would I feel?

In addition, it is important to understand that each school and its attendant postulates should not be considered as mutually exclusive. That is, readers may find themselves agreeing with or accepting certain points in various schools, which later compiled may serve as their personal foundation from which they determine appropriate actions in the myriad circumstances faced by criminal justice professionals. For those readers already employed in a criminal justice organization, an interesting question may be related to the ethical code governing the organization. As readers study this chapter, they should review the ethical code and see if they are able to identify the primary school of ethics from which it is drawn. Remember, it may be a hybrid code of ethics incorporating the logic and postulates of several different schools.

## Hedonistic School

Of all the ethical schools, the hedonistic school may be the most misunderstood if not thoroughly explored. Before we discuss the origins of this misunderstanding, let's first review the basic postulates of this school of ethics. First, hedonism is a concept that describes the process of maximizing one's pleasure while minimizing one's pain. Therefore, pleasure is the ultimate virtue, and one should only engage in actions that result in pleasure. It is important to understand that this school of ethics is primarily concerned with action. This makes the hedonistic school a deontological theory of ethics because its

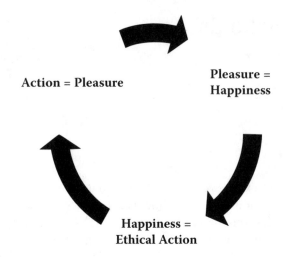

**Figure 4.1** Basic logic of the hedonistic school.

focus is on action as opposed to consequence. Second, if one follows the logic of traditional hedonism, pleasure is pursued because it results in happiness. Happiness is argued to be the state from which good deeds or ethical actions follow. The basic logic of the hedonistic school can therefore be depicted through a sequence of steps illustrated in Figure 4.1 (Hyslop, 1903).

Epicurus (341–270 BC) is widely described as the leading hedonist (Albanese, 2008). According to Epicurus, "The term (hedonism) referred specifically to the pleasures of nobility, tranquility and philosophical reflection" (Souryal, 2007, p. 131). This is an important point to keep in mind and should serve as the original philosophical essence of this school. Throughout history the concept of hedonism has been "massaged" to represent different views. For example, egoistic hedonism describes the process of pursuing pleasure through the form of physical pleasures. And, as noted by Albanese (2008), physical pleasure is the concept commonly associated with hedonism in today's world. This is unfortunate, however, and represents the foundation of the misunderstanding mentioned earlier. The idea of physical pleasure being central to one's happiness is likely to have originated with the Greek philosopher Aristippus (born circa 435 BC) (Hyslop, 1903).

The real irony is that Aristippus' egotistic version of hedonism is what most people think of today, even though his basic postulates of extravagance concerning materials and sexual affairs were largely rejected within the philosophical community of his time. The salient point is that we aggressively assert that hedonism and egoism should not be considered the same and should, in fact, be thought of as independent. The interesting question becomes, how has modern society settled on Aristippus' view of hedonism as opposed to those of Empiricus, Aristotle, or Socrates? Souryal (2007) provided five points that directly address this question. It appears as though the enigma (p. 132) is predicated on perceptions surrounding the concept of PLEASURE. The points are as follows:

1. There is little evidence that pleasure is good in itself; the fact that something is desirable does not mean that it is worthy of being desired. For instance, craving rich foods and exotic drinks can be detrimental to health.
2. Many activities can hardly be classified as pleasures in spite of the obvious happiness they can produce; for example, playing sports and exercising strenuously every day.
3. Some pains are, in essence, also pleasurable; for example, giving birth or conducting arduous work in pursuit of a successful career.
4. It is logically erroneous to divorce the idea of pleasure from the concept of social value; otherwise the pleasures of madmen such as Adolf Hitler and Charles Manson would be considered equal to those of Albert Schweitzer and/or Mother Teresa.
5. Some pleasures may not necessarily be satisfying, as is often the case in sexual pleasures. Schopenhauer noted that sexual pleasures are not fulfilling but only alleviating. Erich Fromm also pointed out that many persons who seek the satisfaction of love confuse it with sex, believing that a sexual experience can fulfill their need for love.

The definition of hedonism has evolved over time. While some believe it is based on material and physical pleasures sought to achieve happiness, others believe it is the good life in terms of material goods.

## Naturalistic School

The naturalistic school approaches the study of ethics from a very different perspective than is normally considered as one ponders the ideals of right and wrong. An analogy may be useful to help create the foundation from which ethical naturalism permeates. When considering the motivation of criminal behavior, there are two extremes that set the boundaries for most practical explanations: on one side is the idea of free will; on the other is the concept of hard determinism. Free will says that all behavior is a result of choice. Hard determinism says that choice is not a relevant factor. Behavior is largely predicated on factors beyond the control of the conscious person.

Within the study of ethics, ethical naturalism could be thought of as an approach representing a particular boundary of the theoretical domain containing all existing knowledge of ethical thought. Ethical naturalism is concerned only with what is able to be observed. John Dewey (1859–1952), a leading ethical naturalist, went so far as to describe ethical naturalism as a school based on the principles of the scientific method of research that is a purely applied discipline similar to that of mathematics or biology. It is important to understand that ethical naturalism is only concerned with objective, measurable, and quantifiable actions, as opposed to subjective reasoning (Garner & Rosen, 1967).

In addition to Dewey, one of the most prominent proponents of ethical naturalism was Thomas Hobbes (1588–1679). Hobbes was certainly not the only proponent of ethical naturalism, but he was arguably the most prolific. He vehemently opposed much of the traditional thought and teachings regarding ethics and wrote about his views at a time when they were not well accepted. In fact, Hobbes, born in England, was once threatened by the English Parliament for publishing his views (Garner & Rosen, 1967).

The essence of Hobbes's work centered on the concept of power and ego. The point at which Hobbes departed from traditional ethics is precisely related to man's motivations for actions. Hobbes did not believe in benevolent and romantic depictions of man's innate goodness, and this was contradictory and alarming to many ethical traditionalists who believed good deeds were the result of kindness. Hobbes believed that good deeds such as charity and pity are centered on the idea of demonstrating one's own power (Williams & Arrigo, 2008). In essence, the charitable deed is an attempt to show not only power, but dominance. As stated by Williams and Arrigo, most people experience a pleasant sensation as a result of giving. Hobbes, on the other hand, felt, "Such a feeling is not one of kindness and concern but one of power—the strength of one's own fortune, ability, status and so forth in operation" (2008, p. 106).

In regard to pity, Hobbes's views were just as grim. Hobbes believed that humans only felt pity for someone's misfortune if they believed there was a reasonable chance they could someday find themselves in the same position. Hobbes believed that one's pity would quickly dissipate if they suddenly came to know there was no chance of them experiencing the same circumstances. As noted by Williams and Arrigo (2008), Hobbes's primary belief is that we are concerned about our own well-being. Through the expression of pity, it may seem that we are genuinely concerned for another who is less fortunate; however, the true feeling, is of concern that we could one day be in the same position and not empathy or compassion for another. Therefore, self-preservation is really the crux of Hobbes's ethical philosophy. And what better way to preserve oneself than to possess power? This is precisely why power is so central to Hobbes's view. It is the one possession that most guarantees one's survival.

The views of Hobbes (and others) are what create the foundation of ethical naturalism. Because Hobbes rejected the traditional explanations of behavior, he felt that "all statements made about moral conduct are descriptive rather than evaluative because they do not have a scientific base" (Souryal, 2007, p.

164). Hobbes was heavily influenced by Galileo, who spent his life working within the realm of science. Accordingly, Hobbes believed that if "it" could not be measured, "it" could not be presented as truth or fact.

## Utilitarian School

Utilitarianism is an interesting concept that is simple in theory. Utilitarianism describes the process of choosing an action that results in the greatest amount of pleasure for the largest amount of people. How do we depict pleasure? Through happiness. Therefore, an action is deemed good when it is capable of producing happiness and bad if the action produces pain or a lack of happiness. The moral utility of a decision is therefore directly related to its ability to create the most amount of happiness for the most number of people. As a result of this foundation, utilitarianism is considered a teleological theory because it decides or guides responses to ethical questions based on the goods that result from the action (Shaw, 1999).

Examining the school from a political perspective, utilitarianism was a movement aimed at extending social reform, expanding political privileges, realizing a higher standard of living for the less fortunate, and correcting the injustices caused by harsh and corrupt penal codes. Clearly utilitarian theory is massive in both breadth and depth. Utilitarian theory describes an attempt to provide support to large segments of the population who did not possess the wealth or political clout of the ruling class (Shaw, 1999). And, similar to today's society, those without wealth and status, at best, had a more difficult time obtaining valued goods (wealth, education, independence, autonomy, etc.) and at worst simply did not have equal access and were unable to obtain the quantity or quality of valued goods as those with wealth and status. Classical utilitarianism can therefore be described with three central postulates:

1. Actions are judged right or wrong only with reference to their consequences.
2. In determining consequences, what is important is the amount of happiness or unhappiness that is brought about.
3. No one's happiness is more important than anyone else's (Williams & Arrigo, 2008, p. 197).

The first two postulates are obviously important. In essence the action is not important, only the consequence is of concern, and as long as the consequence promotes happiness, the action is deemed acceptable. This postulate has often been the source of intense debate concerning a situation where one may tell a lie that brings about happiness for others. The question is, is it ok to lie if it makes people happy? The second postulate is directed at the quantity of happiness. This is a more elusive aspect of utilitarian theory as it can often be difficult to quantify intensity. At any rate, according to the theory, the more intense the happiness, the greater the moral good of the action. The third postulate, however, is critical. In essence, no one person's happiness is of greater importance than his neighbor's, regardless of status. This, in fact, is what delineates utilitarianism from ethical egoism. Ethical egoism suggests that whatever brings about the most pleasure for the individual is what should be done. Utilitarianism holds that the individual is not more important, and what should be considered is what is best for the masses.

Jeremy Bentham (1748–1832) is responsible for creating the theory that became known as utilitarianism. Bentham used five direct postulates to describe the concept of utility:

1. Utility is the foundation of determining morality.
2. Utility is the property of an object whereby it tends to produce benefit, advantage, pleasure, good, or happiness. By the same token, an object that prevents the occurrence of pain, evil, or unhappiness also constitutes utility.
3. The greatest and sole good in the principle of utility is pleasure.
4. All pleasures are of one quality, and one quality only, regardless of their nature or sources.
5. All pleasures are calculable in accordance with a quantitative formula (Shaw, 1999).

In addition, much of Bentham's work involved criminology and the ideal of justice. Bentham never practiced law but spent most of his life forcefully advocating legal reform. Utilitarianism was therefore a major platform from which Bentham and others addressed a brutal penal system that existed in the mid-1800s and operated with little regard for the welfare of inmates. In fact, Bentham's work was primarily aimed at making the criminal justice system more responsive to the needs of offenders as opposed to providing simple brutality as a means of deterring the individual offender, as well as the masses, from engaging in future criminal behavior.

The question then becomes, how can the concept of utilitarianism aid us in making decisions? In other words, how do we operationalize utilitarianism so that we know which decision is capable of producing the greatest happiness? Bentham created what he called the "felicity calculus," which was his method of quantifying perceptions of pleasure and pain in relation to a circumstance. Bentham developed seven dimensions, reproduced by William and Arrigo (2008, p. 201):

1. *Intensity of pleasure:* How strong is it?
2. *Duration of pleasure:* How long does it last?

3. *Certainty of pleasure:* How sure are we that it will be experienced?
4. *Proximity of pleasure:* How soon will it be experienced?
5. *Fecundity:* Will the pleasure lead to or produce other pleasures as well?
6. *Purity:* How free will the pleasure be from pain?
7. *Extent:* How many people are affected?

Not everyone, however, was in agreement with Bentham. In fact, one of his students, John Stewart Mill, set out to alter the essence of Bentham's thesis because he did not believe following Bentham's calculus would always yield the best decision. For example, according to Bentham's calculus, it may be surmised that it would be better to attend a party as opposed to preparing for an exam. Obviously, this is a subjective circumstance that depends on various factors. How important is the exam? Is the exam going to determine whether one graduates or is found eligible to enter a university? On its face, the party may seem to be the obvious choice in relation to yielding the greatest amount of happiness, but Mill was not convinced that this was in fact the best way to make decisions.

According to Mill, it was not sufficient to simply quantify happiness. Mill believed that in order to be more accurate, one must consider the quality of the happiness when deciding which action to take. For example, Mill believed that intellectual endeavors were of greater quality than an afternoon of drinking. He believed that actions that enhanced one's overall physical and spiritual health were of superior value than actions that provided only short, temporary pleasures. In essence, Mill believed that one should choose actions that provided the greatest quality of happiness over the longest period of time, and these actions likely to be contradictory to actions that bring about short-term pleasures of lower quality. According to Williams and Arrigo, "Mill essentially reformulated the Greatest Happiness Principle from greatest happiness for the greatest number of people to the greatest quantity and quality of happiness for the greatest number of people" (2008, p. 204).

The question that remained, however, was, how do we determine which action is capable of producing happiness of the highest quality? Unlike Bentham, Mill did not create a scale to capture what he believed to be paramount in making ethical decisions. Remember, for Mill the greatest decision was one that produced the greatest quality of happiness, not only the greatest quantity. For Mill, the answer to this question was **experience**. In other words, once people had experienced various situations, they would be in the best position to determine the action that produced results of the highest quality. Of course, this is a subjective method of determining the utility of an action. What may be considered a superior result to one may not be to another. For example, one may value a large bank account and the security it provides in times of uncertainty. Another, however, may view a large bank account as useless and be more inclined to use the money to travel and experience people, places, and things. Which is correct?

In addition, there is a substantial lag in Mill's process of determining the best action. If one is to rely on experience, then one is naturally attached to the concept of time. In essence, it can be surmised that there are two categories central to the thesis of Mills. First, we can rely on the information passed on to us by our predecessors. The disadvantage to this category is that we are dependent on the subjective experiences of others. Second, we can rely on our own experience to come to our own conclusions regarding the most utilitarian action. The disadvantage here is that by the time we have figured out the best actions, we are "old." But Mill believed it was superior to Bentham's method of quantification due to the obvious shortcomings of numerically rating an action in the present and not considering long-term effects.

## Existential School

### What Existentialism Is Not

As we began our discussion of ethics you may recall the section in Chapter 1 by describing what ethics is not. Often times it proves easiest to synthesize information and comprehend a concept by first clearly understanding its antithesis. The antithesis of existentialism is *determinism*. Determinism is a concept that describes the process of being bound by events of the natural world. If you are sick it is because you have a virus or an infection. If you remove the virus or infection, you are no longer sick. In this example the virus or infection would be considered causal factors. Therefore, the essence of determinism is that all thoughts and actions are a result of causal factors that permeate the natural world. The natural world is predicated on causal factors. Another example could include rainfall. It rains when the atmosphere becomes saturated with moisture. Once it rains the water begins to evaporate until the atmosphere is once again saturated and causes more rain (Solomon, 1987).

When one considers human behavior, according to determinism, the central thesis is that **all** behavior is a result of some causal factor that we may not even be aware of. We eat because we are hungry. We stop eating because we are satisfied and no longer hungry. We pay bills because we do not want to lose our amenities or possessions. In other words, human beings are creatures of the natural world that exist in a constant state of reaction to biological and environmental factors that cause a response or a lack of response.

### What Existentialism Is

The theory of existentialism completely counters the basic postulates of determinism. According to existentialism, human behavior is a direct result of free will. What is free will? Free will is a concept that describes the process of making choices based on one's own logic or free-flowing thought that leads to the best action concerning some circumstance. Existential philosophers argue this is what separates human beings from animals or inanimate objects who do not possess the ability to reason. Human beings have evolved to the point where we are able to consider multiple factors at once that influence the specific behavior of the present. What is important to understand is that the "best action" is subjective. This is an important point concerning existentialism, and guides the discipline as it sets out to answer three very basic questions concerning existence and choice (Solomon, 1987):

1. What is human freedom, and what limitations restrict its exercise?
2. What is human happiness, and how can it be achieved?
3. What ethic or way of life can emerge from a position that emphasizes individuality?

Early existential philosophers argued that human beings exist in a world largely alone. According to existentialism, many of the decisions humans make are subjective, with only the individual making the decision knowing the reasoning. Therefore, what is freedom to one person depends on how the individual defines freedom. The same is true for happiness and the methods one selects to accomplish happiness. Finally, the way of life that emerges depends largely on one's answers to the first two questions and what one views as important. Determinism, on the other hand, would argue that our world is objective and void of meaningful reason that determines behavior.

One of the leading existential theorists is Jean-Paul Sartre (1905–1980). He was born in Paris to Jean-Babtiste Sartre and Ann-Marie Schweitzer. His father, a naval officer, died before he was two years old. Sartre was heavily influenced by the works of Hegel, Heidegger, and Karl Marx. He began developing his existential views while writing in the cafés of Paris (Souryal, 2007). Sartre was a staunch believer in human freedom and man's ability to exercise choice in making decisions. As noted by Jones and Carlson (2004, p. 34), Sartre articulated his views clearly by stating, "Existentialism's first move is to make every man aware of what he is and to make the full responsibility of his existence rest on him." To bolster this point was the fact that Yves Nizan, a classmate, was one of his closest friends. Nizan was described as having suffered from crippling bouts of depression that seemed to set in for no known reason. During these bouts of depression, it was reported that Nizan was not capable of engaging in any work. Sartre viewed this as a sign of weakness, insinuating that Nizan was free to choose to not be depressed.

For Sartre, we are responsible for everything we do. He believed the views of determinism were predicated on "taking the easy way out." By simply saying, "We are bound to do what has already been decided" was simply ridiculous. Sartre also talked about human consciousness. Existentialists believe everything starts with the state of consciousness. Being conscious is what allows one to be in a state capable of thinking and reasoning. Again, this is what separates humans from animals. Consciousness is a concept that describes the process of being awake and aware of one's surrounding. It provides for the state of actions possessing the concept of intentionalism. Lavine (1984) described seven properties of consciousness:

1. Being conscious of objects and of one's consciousness of them
2. Being able to think of what one lacks, what one's possibilities are, and what one is dissatisfied with
3. Being free from other objects, free to doubt and to say no
4. Being totally free and spontaneous because the past does not determine what people are at present
5. Being responsible for one's own situation
6. Being totally alone and independent
7. Being able to escape self-deception, a condition that presumes that fate exists

Existentialists argue that one must choose his or her path on the basis of this foundation of consciousness. We are not predestined to act in any way. This philosophy was very prevalent within the criminal justice system of yesterday, and it is still very much so today.

Modern criminal justice assumes that people choose their actions. If this were not the case, it would be impossible to justify the imposition of punishment due to the commission of a criminal act. If we were all predestined to act, including carrying out crimes, how could one justify incarcerating someone based on actions that were determined upon his birth? Arrest and incarceration would be unacceptable responses for someone who is acting absent of free will. In order to punish we must assume that one is acting based on choice and rationality.

Rational choice theory is a leading criminological approach to criminality, and it is very existential. Consider the concept of deterrence. Deterrence describes the process of implementing some sanction as a result of a crime being committed in order to reduce one's motivation of committing the crime in the future. Deterrence is aimed at both the individual offender as well as society at large. In essence, the existential philosophy of punishment is to make the punishment harsh enough so that it outweighs any possible benefit one may obtain from the commission of crime. The rationality and utility of such a philosophy is contingent solely upon the criminal deciding to engage in the criminal act based first on consciousness and then free will. Finally, whether one chooses to act in an ethical way is first based on consciousness (the ability to think and reason), the information at hand (awareness), and the perceived consequences of one's actions (free will) (Solomon, 1987).

## Ethics of Duty and Reason

Immanuel Kant (1724–1804) was a German philosopher who has had a profound impact on the study of ethics. All major publications exploring the concept of ethics include the views of Kant. He provided a vital theory of ethics that not all agree with, but most agree that the foundation of his thoughts provide an excellent platform on which to think about and explore the process of making moral decisions. Two of Kant's most influential books include *Groundwork of the Metaphysics of Morals* (1797) and *The Critique of Practical Reason* (1788). These are vital works for any student of ethics, but one should be warned they are not easy to read.

Kant was a firm believer in the fact that ethics should rest on simple concepts that affect ordinary people. Kant's views of simple rationality were probably influenced, at least in part, by his childhood, which was also simple and ordinary. Kant was raised by modest middle-class parents and began his studies in the discipline of theology. This was short-lived, however, as he was much more interested in the natural sciences and philosophy. And although Kant's upbringing and much of his philosophy regarding ethics are based on modest, simple principles, the essence of Kant's views is extraordinary (Gardner, 1999).

From the beginning, Kant rejected determinism. In fact, Kant could be described as very existential in his thinking. His theory of ethics is deontological because in his view the choices one makes should not be governed by the perceived consequences. Kant's central thesis is that moral decisions should be made in accordance with duty. Kant distinguished between decisions that one is inclined to make and decisions that one must make. The decisions that one must make are our duty, and morality is predicated solely on the concept of duty (Souryal, 2007; Williams & Arrigo, 2008). The logical question then is what exactly is meant by the word *duty*?

Duty, according to Kant, is a concept that describes the process of expressing free and autonomous will, self-legislating, and commanding. In other words, being respectful to your boss because you are afraid that if you are not you will be fired is not considered a moral act. Your showing respect to your boss in this case is based solely on the consequences of the possibility of being fired. It is not free or autonomous. Kant spoke in great detail about the concept of goodwill. Goodwill according to Kant is defined in the same manner as duty. Therefore, duty is goodwill and goodwill is duty. Furthermore, duty and goodwill consist of engaging in actions that strictly adhere to moral rules (Gardner, 1999).

At this point it should be clear that Kantian ethics demand one act according to duty. How do we know, however, what is dutiful in the myriad circumstances with which we are faced? Next we discuss several concepts that Kant used to address this question. First, however, let's consider a scenario, the Case of the Inquiring Murderer, by James Rachels, that is very common in much of the literature discussing Kantian ethics. Our version is based on that provided by Williams and Arrigo (2008, p. 217). Suppose you are sitting on your front porch one sunny afternoon enjoying the nice breeze when suddenly a woman comes running past you, dives behind some bushes, and quietly hides herself from view. After a moment, you approach the woman and ask her what she is doing. She proceeds to tell you that someone is trying to kill her and asks if you would please leave so she can remain hidden. After a moment, you return to the front porch and make yourself comfortable again. A couple of minutes later, a man approaches with a gun in his hand and asks if you have seen a young woman. Should you lie to him or tell the truth?

At first blush, the answer may seem obvious. Most would agree that we would simply lie to the man in order to save the woman's life. To do so, however, would be completely contradictory to classical Kantian logic. First, the decision to lie would be based on the perceived consequence of the man killing the woman. This was not acceptable to Kant, who argued that one can never be sure of a certain consequence. Following Kantian logic, consider for a moment you are the person on the porch. What if you lied to the man, and he kept walking and searching? The woman thinks she is safe, comes out from behind the bushes, approaches you on the porch, and asks if she can use your phone to call for help. You agree, and as she is walking up the steps, the man looks over his shoulder and sees the woman. He then begins walking toward the woman now on your porch and points the weapon. The woman sees the man pointing the weapon at her and ducks. The man fires and strikes you in the chest instead of the woman.

Obviously, these scenarios are far-fetched and certainly do not occur every day. They are, however, useful in depicting the essence of Kant's logic that was a rejection of consequentialism in favor of maxims that provide the foundation for what Kant called the "categorical imperative." First, a maxim is a concept that describes a duty or a moral rule. For example, "One should never lie." A maxim therefore is the prerequisite one must identify on the path to making a moral decision. A categorical imperative may be the concept for which Kant is most famous. The categorical imperative is a concept originally stated as "Act only according to that maxim by which you can at the same time will that it should become a universal law" (Gardner, 1999).

Duty, therefore, is acting in a manner that is right for everyone; if it is not right for everyone, then it is wrong for everyone. For example, "We should lie to our best friend about his partner's infidelity because the truth would be too painful." The maxim is that we should lie when the truth about infidelity is too painful. Now, whether this maxim should be a categorical imperative depends on how we answer the question, "Would it be best for all people to always lie to their friends about their partner's infidelity?" If we answer no to the question, then we must conclude that it is never morally permissible for anyone to lie to their friends concerning their partner's infidelity. For Kant it was never permissible to lie. This was a categorical imperative. Therefore, Kant would have rejected the option of lying to the man with the gun (Gardner, 1999).

This is why Kant received harsh criticism regarding his theory. Many of his detractors argued that his philosophy was too harsh and rigid and that the complexities of the real world do not lend themselves to such an idealistic philosophy. For example, maybe you would choose to lie to your friend about his partner's infidelity because he was also just laid off from his job. Once he is able to regain employment, then you would inform him of the unfortunate circumstance. Let's once again revisit the case of the Inquiring Murder. What if you have two categorical imperatives: (1) it is always wrong to lie, and (2) one should never allow the murder of an innocent person (Williams & Arrigo, 2008). How do you choose which to follow?

W. D. Ross (1877–1971) addressed this problem in what he called *Prima Facie Duties*. According to Ross, some categorical imperatives may be overridden by other categorical imperatives in certain conditions or circumstances. For example, it may be better to protect life as opposed to never telling a lie. In criminal justice agencies there will be many circumstances that will dictate that one choose between a number of different options. In policing, for example, faces the option "do I make an arrest, or do I provide a warning?" Circumstances will dictate different responses depending on the conditions. If a father who has been drinking and is disorderly is arrested, he may not get out of jail in time to be at work the following day. If he is unable to attend work, he will not earn money to pay the electricity bill that may already be late. How do you decide the appropriate action to take given the totality of circumstances? For Kant the decision was never predicated on the possible response. The question, though, is whether this philosophy is practical in a real-world setting when dealing with human beings suffering real-world problems.

## Ethical School of Social Justice

John Rawls (1921–2002) was a philosopher who contributed greatly to the field of ethics with his theory of social justice. For Rawls, the essence of justice was predicated on the equal distribution of goods. His theory hinges on the manner in which political, economic, and legal systems function and operate within a society. If every member of a society does not have equal access to the available goods and services provided by its institutions, then there will be a lack of harmony. Sociologists would likely describe these circumstances via the concepts of strain or conflict theories. In essence, everyone must have equal access to the means through which acceptable goals can be achieved. If not, societies' balance will be disrupted through upheavals consisting of rebellion and, in the extreme, violence (Rawls, 1971).

Arrigo (1999, p. 282) defined social justice as a "perspective of justice that evaluates how a society provides for the needs of its members and the extent to which it treats subgroups equally." In essence, all members of a society, regardless of race, status, economic or political influence, should be treated as equals by the various social and governmental entities responsible for the distribution of goods. In the justice system, for example, everyone should be treated fairly and equally. The quality of justice should not be predicated on any demographic factor, including wealth. Obviously, this is not always the case, but for Rawls it is a central postulate and may be why the current system of justice can be described with many adjectives, of which *harmonious* is not likely to be one. When society, as a whole, perceives that it does not have equal access to certain goods, including justice, disruptions will be frequent, and a lack of trust will ensue.

Social justice is meant to describe a macrolevel process of fair and equitable distribution of services to all members of society. In other words, social justice is most concerned with how our political, legal, and economic institutions provide for the well-being of a society as opposed to an individual. According to Rawls, those who are less fortunate or have the least should be able to receive the most from social institutions. This view is not always popular and would not be championed by staunch supporters of capitalism. It is important, however, to consider this point as one begins to understand the central thesis of Rawls's theory of social justice.

Rawls (1971) established three principles of justice that are critical:

1. The principle of the greatest equal liberty: Each person must have an equal right to all liberties available to anyone else.
2. The principle of the greatest equal opportunity: Positions should be open to all, and all who possess similar abilities and skills should have equal access.
3. The difference principle: Maximum benefit should be available to those with the least.

In essence, discrimination, prejudice, bias, and lack of tolerance are concepts that describe actions and ideologies that are completely contradictory to the foundation of social justice. If these concepts are present within social institutions, the equal distribution of goods and services will be disrupted, causing confusion and ultimately anger among members of society. As noted by Rawls, the principle of greatest equal liberty is most paramount. He used the concept of *lexical priority* to make this point. Without equal liberty, Rawls contended that principles two and three would be impossible to achieve. One last point is worthy of mention. Rawls distinguished between the concepts of justice and fairness. For Rawls, justice is a concept that must apply to all persons all of the time (Albanese, 2008). Examples include the freedoms of speech and/or to engage in one's own practice of religion. Fairness on the other hand applies to circumstances where one has the opportunity to not engage or participate. The system of higher education could be said to be fair if everyone has the option of not attending. For example, one could have decided not to go to college and decided instead to work. It would not be fair if only a portion of society had access. As noted in Chapter 3, the ultimate social achievement for Rawls is a society comprised of free citizens with equal rights and opportunities to access all available goods and services provided by the political, legal, and economic institutions with which we must all engage in some capacity.

## Conclusion

We began this chapter by asking that the readers keep an open mind as they review the different schools of ethics. Each school and its respective philosophers have provided critical steps in the foundation of how we exist as humans and together as a society. Of course each school is different, but the clever, open-minded consumer of this information will realize that there is merit in them all. Ultimately, it is up to each person to determine whom they most agree with. Keep in mind that our cultural backgrounds will have a great influence on the direction we lean. And even more important is the fact that we are all different. What may seem intuitive to one may seem ridiculous to another. That is the beauty of diversity. It is only beautiful, however, when one is able to freely explore and intellectualize openly, free of judgment.

## Questions in Review

1. Which school of ethics do you mostly agree with? Why?
2. Compare and contrast the concepts of teleological and deontological approaches to making decisions. Which of these do you think is most appropriate for on a course of action? Why?
3. What would be your decision in the Case of the Inquiring Murderer? On what foundation do you base your decision?
4. If someone who had no knowledge of ethics asked you to describe the concept of social justice, what would be your response?

# Unethical Themes in Criminal Justice

5

## Introduction

After examining the major ethical schools, you should be able to begin formulating your own logic for the manner in which you make important decisions. By important decisions we mean those that will affect the well-being of others. For example, the decision to go to the grocery store today or tomorrow is not likely to be a decision point that requires a great deal of ethical reasoning. It will instead be based on convenience and whether you have minimum goods on which you can sustain yourself. However, important decisions that produce consequences for not only yourself, but also for others are considered to be decisions of a higher order. They demand careful attention and the ability to critically think about the impact. Criminal justice is a discipline that is responsible for providing a service to society. All decisions made by criminal justice practitioners acting within the purview of official duty are important because they are likely to affect others directly or indirectly.

In this chapter we examine the critical process of applying the concept of ethics. We begin with a discussion on why ethics is important and then proceed to two major unethical themes within criminal justice. The two themes that we discuss specifically include the spoils of management and corruption. These two themes were chosen because they are significantly related to each other, and both are capable of immense destruction within the criminal justice system. Two other unethical themes that we will discuss include lying and the abuse of authority. For purposes of presentation, however, and the gravity of these phenomena, we have chose to dedicate an entire chapter to each of them.

The second part of this chapter explores a method of management that is capable of addressing the spoils of management. Specifically, we examine the theory of principle-based management as it is described by its founder, James O'Toole. The chapter concludes with a discussion of the concept of professionalism and how it is critical within the complex enigma of making decisions that are moral, legal, and advantageous to all mankind.

Here is a gentle reminder as we being our journey: open your mind, clear it of distraction, and think about these issues critically. Many students of criminal justice are interested in the exciting aspects of the profession: driving fast with the lights and siren on; fantasizing about pouncing on the suspect as he is fleeing with all of his might with the stolen cigarettes; ultimately "saving the day" and being seen by all as the hero. The truth, however, is these events are rare. The real work of criminal justice is trying to enhance the quality of life for all citizens, and this can only be accomplished through decisions that are made with this goal in mind.

## Why Are Ethics Important?

Consider the following scenario: you have just been hired by a police department with which you applied over a year ago. The hiring process is competitive, and the department only selects 2% of the applicants who apply. After being selected, you attended the training academy and successfully complete all requirements. You then begin the six-month-long field-training phase, where you are assigned to various training officers who observe your actions.

As you begin this process of field training, you are reminded regularly of the importance of this phase of your training. In essence, the training officers decide whether you remain on the force or whether you are fired based on not being able to do the job. Safety is often cited as the major requisite. In other words, training officers want to know that you are capable of safely doing the job and able to physically take care of yourself and also be there in the event other officers need assistance.

On one occasion you and your training officer are dispatched to a disturbance at a local hotel. As you arrive you observe a white, male banging on the door of one of the hotel rooms. He fits the description you were given by the dispatcher as being the individual responsible for the disturbance. You and your training officer then approach the individual, who is unresponsive and appears to be under the influence of some type of stimulant. The individual tells you that his girlfriend is inside the room, and he is going in to get her regardless of what you think you are going to do to stop him. You ask the suspect to move away from the door and walk with you a short distance to try and figure out what has occurred that has him so upset. He begins to walk with you and then suddenly puts both hands in his pocket. You instruct the individual to take his hands out of his pocket, at which time he refuses and states he is going to kill you if you attempt to place him under arrest. He states that he has been to prison and will never return.

Recognizing the immediate danger, your training officer physically grabs the individual and places him on the ground, at which time you remove his hands from his pocket. As you remove his right hand, you find it clutching a small caliber revolver that is found to be fully loaded. At this time the suspect is placed under arrest, handcuffed, placed in the back seat of the police unit, and transported to the local jail. The suspect is booked into the jail, and you return to the station to write your report. As you complete your report, you give it to your training officer for review. The training officer states that you did a good job of writing the report, but you forgot to include a very important detail. You did not include that you advised the suspect of his rights as required by the Miranda rule. You inform your training officer that in the intensity of the circumstance, you failed to advise the suspect of his rights. Your training officer turns to you and says, "Whether you did or not, put it in the report."

Answer the following questions:

1. What would you do?
2. What are the possible consequences of your choice?

In Chapter 1 we described the concept of ethics and what ethics is not. Recall the working definition: "For the purpose of our discussions on ethics, ethics will be used to refer to the study of the standards of behavior that tell us what choices we should make in the many situations in which find ourselves as criminal justice professionals. In other words, ethics is the study of morality." It is a philosophy that is meant to inform or describe the process of making moral decisions. The next logical question then may be, what is a moral decision? This is a very difficult question to answer and precisely why the different characterizations of the phrase "a moral decision" are legion.

Moral decisions are those decisions that are based on honesty and purity. Purity in this context describes a decision that is just and made free of toxins such as emotion, ego, or power. It is a decision that is right, and when delivered appropriately the response is usually unanimous acceptance even for those who may not benefit. Moral decisions made by leaders of criminal justice agencies are vital to the health of the organization. A healthy organization may be described as being made of workers who are reasonably satisfied to very satisfied with most major governing parameters of the organization such as management, immediate supervisor, equipment, pay, and so on. In essence, ethics is important because it is the philosophy that provides the foundation for making moral decisions.

## Spoils of Management

The concept of "spoils of management" is used to describe unethical management practices that stifle productivity and leave workers exhausted. Their energy is spent struggling to make sense of an organization's professed values and those that are actually carried out. The use of the word spoil is important. Spoil describes the process of damaging, decaying, or reducing the value of something. Here we are specifically aiming at describing management practices that are damaging to the organization and result in a service that is delivered in a decayed state. Of course the service that we are interested in is justice that is supposed to be the end product of the criminal justice system. When justice is delivered in a decayed state, however, the damage to a community is significant. There is an immediate loss of trust that is followed by a lack of respect that ultimately manifests as anger.

What is unethical management? How is it described? Can you see it or smell it? Unethical management describes the process of managers' making decisions that are based on ego, power, insecurity, greed, selfishness, retribution, and emotion. They are decisions that erode the foundation from which purity and justice can resonate. They reduce perceptions of satisfaction and also reduce trust not only in a supervisor but also in the organization as a whole.

One example is based on an incident that occurred in a correctional facility. A newly hired correctional officer was told by her immediate supervisor to place an inmate in a different cell block. The young officer, of course, complied and moved the inmate. What the officer did not know was that she was moving a sex offender from solitary confinement into a general population unit. Within two hours the sex offender had been beaten so severely that it took six hours in an emergency room to save his life. When questioned about why she had transported the inmate, she replied, "Because that is what my supervisor told me to do." The supervisor was then brought in and questioned about the transfer. He completely denied, in front of the young officer, having had instructed her to take such action. Did the supervisor know the inmate was a sex offender? Was the supervisor afraid to own up to his mistake? Was it a planned event in which the actions were premeditated? Regardless of the answers to these questions, the reality remains. The organization now employs at least one officer who is shocked, disgusted, confused, and angry.

It is important to note that unethical management practices do not have to be those that are considered illegal. Using the previous example above, the supervisor may have made a genuine mistake in directing the young officer to transport the sex offender into the general population. He may not have had any malicious intent and could have simply been trying to make room in an overcrowded facility. What is unethical, however, lies in the fact that he was not willing to be truthful and instead chose to protect his own self-interest at the expense of the young, inexperienced officer. The ramifications of such an incident are legion. Let's briefly consider one possible result that is not uncommon. Let's assume the young officer is fired for making such a critical mistake. Based on the firing, a report is written and placed into her file. With this official documentation in her personnel file, how likely do you think it is that she will be able to obtain employment in her chosen profession?

## Authoritarianism and Fear

Many criminal justice agencies operate from a strict hierarchical design with clear channels of communication that are congruous with a strict chain of command. An authoritarian style of management is common among criminal justice organizations. Authoritarian management, or authoritarianism, is a concept that describes strict, rigid, and inflexible rules that one must obey or else face harsh consequences. This style of management is also common in the military. The important point, however, is that the military operates from a different perspective and with a wholly different mission. In civilian organizations such as criminal justice agencies, the idea of managing people based on authoritarianism is not always beneficial, efficient, or effective (Robbins, 2005).

Within an authoritarian style of management, the consequence of disobedience is usually punishment. Punishment is meted out based on power, which results in compliance predicated on fear. The logical question at this point may be, "Is authoritarian management unethical?" The general answer is NO. Within the military, especially in wartime, there are rules and protocols that have been developed over time that are specifically aimed at saving lives and successfully carrying out missions critical to our security. The same is true in criminal justice organizations; the nature of some criminal justice operations certainly entails danger that demands strict adherence to policy and procedure. Therefore, it is not the concept of authoritarianism that is unethical but the manner in which it is sometimes applied. When one uses the guise of an authoritarian style of management to "massage" his or her ego, damage will be done to the individual receiving the order as well as to the organization. And within criminal justice agencies, the damage can be far-reaching (Robbins, 2005).

## Consequences of Unethical Management

The ultimate victim of unethical management is often the society in which the organization was designed to serve. Souryal (2007) described this as the "Harvest of Shame." In essence, some important characteristics are suffocated and forced into repression. Among one of most important of these stifled characteristics is creativity. Creativity is a vital concept that possesses an enormous potential for developing enhanced methods of delivering the product of justice. When one is able to exercise and voice creative energies, a productive spirit usually resonates that fosters excitement, a feeling of importance, and self-worth. When one's creativity is suffocated, these vital feelings and perceptions are destroyed (Robbins, 2005).

Closely related to the concept of creativity is morale. Morale is generally considered a concept that describes a state of mind of an individual or group and expresses their level of confidence, cheerfulness, and overall happiness. Simply stated, morale is critical to an organization. High levels of morale foster creativity, which leads to effective solutions to complex circumstances and problems. There is a trust between all levels of an organization that embodies cooperation, communication, and confidence in one's ability to do the best job for the organization and society.

Unethical management destroys morale and creativity and ultimately leads to a pathologic organization. When unethical management is allowed to operate, workers quickly become disenfranchised and lose all motivation to provide their best effort. The energy and spirit of the workforce is depleted and in some cases destroyed. Workers begin to perform their duties based on completing a transaction with the organization or supervisor as opposed to doing what is right because it is the right thing to do. Unethical management quickly demonstrates that what is important is not the quality of one's product but rather not being a nuisance to the supervisory chain of command. Doing a good job often goes unnoticed while making a mistake receives an inordinate amount of attention followed up with punishment. The decaying nature of unethical management will ultimately drive out of the organization the exact workers most capable of providing a quality product (Robbins, 2005).

## Corruption

Unethical management is also the platform from which corruption often germinates. Corruption is a concept that is closely associated with the word spoil. Corruption describes the process of immorality, decay, bribery, and, of course, dishonesty. Before we delve too deeply into the concept of corruption within criminal justice agencies, a few qualifiers are in order. First, our discussion is mostly aimed at those organizations that have traditionally possessed management practices that a reasonable person would describe as unethical. Of course, not all agencies have unethical management, but corruption still exists. Therefore, it is possible that corruption can stem from either personal and individual characteristics as well as be a result of unethical management. The difference, however, can often be gleaned from an agency's response to corrupt practices. Agencies with a healthy management system will react immediately and swiftly to the first sign of corrupt activity. The message sent by the response is one of disgust and absolute condemnation. In addition, and critically important, the response of an ethical management system to reports of corruption will be open and transparent for all to observe.

Unethical management systems will often look the other way or tolerate corrupt practices until the issue becomes so large they have no choice but to address it. In such circumstances where the pressure from the community is overwhelming, unethical management will usually engage in actions that create an appearance of addressing the issue, but the engagement is "surfacy." The real intent is to appease an alarmed community in order to reduce the pressure and scrutiny. In many cases harsh action is taken, and punishment is delivered to the employees responsible. This type of managerial response is meant to "look good," but it further erodes the stability of the organization as workers are left confused due to being punished for behaviors that are acceptable when not found out. In reality, there is no real intent to change the basic fiber of the organization, and therefore corruption continues. Our purpose in this section is to address those agencies with pathological management and discuss how this can influence, create, and provide shelter for corrupt practices.

Much of the literature delineates between levels of corruption within an organization. For example, Schmalleger (2008) distinguished between grass eaters and meat eaters. Grass eaters are those forms of corruption commonly thought of as not being very serious. Accepting a free meal, for example, is commonly associated with the corruption characterized as grass eaters and often thought to be one of the perks of the job. Meat eaters on the other hand represent corrupt activities of a much more serious nature. A police department in the southeastern United States serves as a great example for what is considered to be a meat eater. In this particular department, an internal investigation uncovered several police officers being hired by narcotics traffickers to guard warehouses containing their stashes of narcotics. All of the officers involved were fully aware of what they were guarding and the nature of the business being conducted by their off-duty employer. Certainly, this type of corruption is classified as a meat eater.

## Premeditated Corruption

Consider the following two examples of murder:

1. A man and woman married for the last twenty years have decided it is now time to divorce. They have tried to reconcile their differences, but both agree it has become impossible. The couple is in possession of substantial wealth as a result of the husband's successful career as a financial planner. The wife, a homemaker, has never earned money as a result of employment but has diligently contributed to the couple's success through carefully and meticulously attending to all household affairs, including caring for the couple's three children. As a result of the impending divorce, the wife hires an attorney and plans to ask for half of the estate, which includes the

couple's home. When learning of this request, the husband becomes irate and cannot understand how his wife could feel entitled to half of the estate when she had never earned a penny of the amassed wealth. After considering all options, the husband decides to have his wife murdered in lieu of giving up his hard-earned money and possessions. In order to carry out this plan, the husband locates an individual willing to kill the woman for $10,000. The deal is agreed upon and finalized.

2. Two business partners meet for lunch in a busy downtown café to discuss the latest happenings within the company. They have successfully built one of the most profitable real estate businesses in the area. They handle both commercial and residential properties with a specialty in high-priced waterfront locations. During the luncheon one partner makes a statement that is contrary to what had been discussed previously in regard to a particular transaction. As the conversation continues, one partner begins to piece together the sad reality that the other has actually been skimming money from the business. There had been signs in the past, but there was a strong trust between the partners, who had known each other since childhood. At this point, however, the obvious could no longer be denied. As the partner being cheated begins the painstaking process of confronting the situation, he quickly notes that his colleague has no interest in being honest and admitting his shortcoming. As tempers begin to flare, a physical struggle ensues, at which time the cheated partner, in a state of rage, grabs a knife from the table and begins to attack the other. Before the two partners can be separated, the man is stabbed in the chest and dies suddenly before first responders have any chance of delivering medical assistance.

As you consider these two examples, the question to ponder is which is more egregious? Which would be considered more heinous? Most would probably agree that the first scenario is most shocking. They are both tragic, and certainly both could have been avoided. The principle ingredient, however, that often serves to shock the conscious of reasonable people is the idea of premeditation. The fact that someone takes the time to consider, plan, and carry out some event that is known to be criminal, wrong, and immoral. The willful intent to engage in criminality when one is fully aware of the unethical nature of the action is very difficult for most people to cognitively align in a manner that makes sense.

The second scenario, although brutal and unfortunate, is likely to be seen by most as being less heinous than the first. The primary ingredient that is lacking is premeditation. There was no contrived plan to kill the other person. It was an act that occurred as a result of extreme emotion and passion that ignited within the context of the situation. The lack of premeditation, although not excusable, may serve to preserve a slight degree of humanity that is swallowed up in premeditation. One may describe the second scenario with reactions such as, "That is unbelievable, so tragic, and so unnecessary, but I can understand how someone may get so angry when having to confront the painful reality of being betrayed, abandoned, and rejected by someone they trusted their entire life."

Corruption often occurs as a result of careful planning and detailed thought. This premeditated aspect of corruption, similar to that in the examples above, is what often makes this type of criminality so heinous. It is hard to imagine a more heinous event than a serious criminal act planned and carried out by a criminal justice employee who is supposed to be working to better protect society. The exact, precise, and specific nature of premeditation is often what is most shocking. And it is the serious premeditated forms of corruption within the criminal justice system that most damage the relationship between communities and their criminal justice representatives. Imagine a scenario where a police officer is found guilty of violating the same laws which were instrumental in his sending others to prison. Further imagine that this officer entered each tour of duty with the sole purpose of seeking out incidents in which he could exploit others through various means of criminality for his own gain. This type of corruption results in a sudden and immediate loss of respect and confidence in the police department. Premeditated corruption usually occurs in those agencies with management practices that are historically unethical. The culture of the agency is one that tolerates corruption as being inconsequential or necessary to get the job done.

## Three Explanations of Corruption

Generally, there are three types of explanations that attempt to describe the origins of corruption. Albanese (2008) and Delattre (2002) both provided discussions centered on the three common explanations and provided the foundation for much of what we provide below. The three explanations are typically characterized in the following manner:

1. Corruption is a result of the individual officer, often called the "rotten apple" theory.
2. Corruption is a result of the department, commonly referred to as "structural theory."
3. Corruption is a result of society, commonly depicted as the "society at large" theory.

## Rotten Apple Theory of Corruption

The central thesis of the rotten apple theory is that corruption is a result of individual officers who engage in corrupt practices that in turn casts a negative perception of the entire agency. In relation to the rotten apple theory, recruitment practices generally receive the most attention. In other words, corrupt individual officers were not adequately screened or investigated during the hiring process and should never have been hired in the first place. And, as is often the case with social science theories, there are proponents and detractors of the rotten apple theory. On one side, there are those who vehemently disagree with the idea that corruption is a result of individual characteristics brought to the job. The argument is that powerful socializing factors within the organization are ignored. On the other hand, there are those who provide solid support for the rotten apple theory and highlight that several departments ravaged by corruption can point to massive and sudden increases in the number of personnel hired as the point in which serious corruption became an issue. Delattre (2002) used the case of the Miami Police Department as a good example. In the early 1980s, Miami was experiencing rapid change. It was undergoing a period of significant transition from a quiet peaceful town to one of violence. It was becoming dangerous and violent as a result of the cocaine traffickers' intense struggle for control. Millions and millions of dollars were at stake as much of the cocaine was introduced into the United States via Miami.

Murder rates skyrocketed, and crime in general significantly increased. The citizens of Miami quickly grew frightened and gravely concerned as they witnessed tranquility be exchanged for turmoil. As a result of the drug wars and other volatile circumstances with the city, the decision was made that the police department needed to expand. Specifically, officials in Miami agreed to double the size of the department, which meant nearly 200 officers were hired in just two years. This immense expansion that took place so rapidly overwhelmed the department's ability to properly screen applicants. In addition, these officers were not properly supervised. Many of the rookie officers hired at the end of the two-year hiring cycle were being supervised by fellow rookie officers hired at the beginning of the expansion. The result was that the department received a large number of complaints, and the complaints were overwhelmingly related to the officers hired during the rapid expansion who were not properly screened or trained to handle the complex issue of providing quality criminal justice services.

Regardless of how one views the rotten apple theory, it is clear that it must be considered in some cases of corruption. Prior to the massive hiring, the Miami Police Department, albeit not perfect, was not generally viewed as a corrupt or troubled department.

## Structural Theory of Corruption

The structural theory of corruption focuses on the social processes within an organization (Albanese, 2008; Delattre, 2002). These processes are often considered the norms of an organization and have a tremendous influence on behaviors. Many organizations contain at least two types of values: (1) professed values, such as to protect and serve, and (2) actual values that are commonly carried out when not under direct scrutiny, such as earning money or carrying out favors for something in return. The structural theory describes a phenomenon where corruption is part of the fabric of the entire organization. Corruption is widespread and in many circumstances considered normal.

Take for instance the words of a training director of a large metropolitan police department. The director was addressing a new class of recruits as they settled in for their first day at the academy. The director welcomed the class and then immediately transitioned to the issue of pay. "Don't worry," he stated, "I know your starting salaries are pathetic, but as soon as you get out of the academy, you will have many opportunities to supplement your income. The veteran officers will show you how to do it. There is a lot of opportunity out there." Consider that this statement was made to a class of recruits by the director of training and that the statement was in direct relation to being paid off for not taking certain actions, being paid to provide confidential information, or engaging in certain practices to earn money all in the name of supplementing one's income. This describes a very severe and profound stage of corruption that is now part of the structure of an organization. This is a form of corruption that is extremely complex and very difficult to combat because deviance in this setting would be considered not engaging in corrupt practices.

As an example, consider the "Mama Rosa's Test" of Crank and Caldero as noted by Ruiz and Bono (2004, p. 49):

> A new recruit and his training officer are eating at Mama Rosa's café. Soon they are joined by other officers. At the end of the meal, they prepare to leave; the rookie has his money in his hand and asks how much should he leave. The veterans tell the rookie to shut up and put his money away. It seems the cops have been eating free forever, and the place has never been held up, unlike other restaurants in the neighborhood. Mama Rosa is very appreciative of this. The rookie insists that he wants to pay for the meal, but he is told to shut up and not jeopardize a good thing.
>
> Here is the test: if the rookie goes along, he is tainted. He loses his virginity. If he doesn't play ball at Mama Rosa's he won't be trusted as a team player. If he does go along the next step will be to test him in the field. This might include "dropsy" testimony or backing up another officer in court that makes an honest mistake by supporting his partner's version of events. This is how it happens; a test at the restaurant, then a test in the field.

## Society at Large Theory of Corruption

The third explanation of corruption is aimed at many of the common expectations and perceptions of society in general as well as some of the laws created by government that the police are responsible for enforcing. First, Delattre (2002) noted that one of the common public perceptions is that gratuities are expected within many of the service-related occupations. For example, taxi cab drivers, delivery personnel, waiters, and waitresses all work for and expect gratuities for the services they provide. In fact, gratuities are often directly related to the quality of service one can expect to receive. And, as noted by O. W. Wilson, the former superintendant of the Chicago Police Department, it was very easy, almost a natural progression to extend the concept of gratuities from service providers or servants to law enforcement personnel (Smith, 1974).

This gradual shift starts with the infamous accounts of the free cup of coffee and then leads to more direct, specific, and premeditated acts of corruption that jeopardize the basic mission of criminal justice agencies. Wilson also explained how he viewed this process of corruption as a slippery slope. Here, Wilson's analogy is similar to that of the Mama Rosa's story. First, the public believed that it was necessary to give gratuities in order to receive a decent service. Second, this perception was transferred from servants to the police. Third, the concept of gratuity was extended to include not only the free cup of coffee or free meal but also cash or favors in return for not receiving a ticket or some other enforcement action. Fourth, officers then began seeking out opportunities to make money or earn favors. For example, officers would intentionally make traffic stops that were no longer in the spirit of protecting motorists or maintaining the integrity of safe streets but instead were a way to collect money for not issuing a citation. In essence, the shift had been made from a single cup of coffee to outright premeditated and predatory acts of criminality.

Following this logic, corruption begins with seemingly inconsequential acts of accepting gratuities and quickly escalates to actively seeking out opportunities to make a profit. Oftentimes, officials will justify these actions by noting, "What is the difference, they pay me for not issuing them a ticket or they go to court and pay the court a fine and then it goes on their insurance. I am actually doing them a favor and saving them money in the long run." This is the central foundation on which most criminal justice leaders argue that it is never acceptable to accept gratuities and that even the most minor engagement constitutes an act of corruption.

The order in which these explanations of corruption may occur is arguable. For example, does corruption begin with the individual officer, who possesses certain characteristics that make it acceptable to engage in corruption? Or is corruption the result of a corrupt organization that eventually wears down otherwise moral officers? Or, finally, is corruption a result of society at large that possesses a certain ideology that depicts a necessity to give gifts for a service that has been extended to criminal justice organizations? Our response is that it is likely a combination of all three factors. There is support for each postulate. What is important to understand, however, is that corruption does not occur in a vacuum. A single corrupt officer will not last very long in an organization that does not tolerate corrupt activities. And, unfortunately, the same is true for the officer who refuses to engage in corruption yet is employed with an organization that culturally accepts the ideas of receiving gratuities.

What is the ultimate consequence of corruption in criminal justice agencies? The basic answer to this question is a profound decaying or erosion of the concept of justice. Simply stated, if one must purchase justice and if justice is treated as a commodity to be delivered based on the highest bidder, the entire philosophy of criminal justice is turned upside down. Justice describes the idea of fairness. This is not amenable to capitalistic processes that are predicated on the concepts of supply and demand. In this context, what separates the concept of justice from any other product such as narcotics, weapons, or stolen merchandise that is sold to the highest bidder? In order to function properly, justice must be delivered equitably, fairly, and free of prejudice.

## Principle-Based Management

After examining the basic tenets of unethical management and some of the consequences of unethical management, it is time to now shift our attention to appropriate methods of combating these issues. In the remaining portions of this chapter, principle-based management will be examined. Principle-based management is a philosophy of management created by James O'Toole (1995). In his book Leading Change, O'Toole described the basic tenets of what he believes is lacking in management practices throughout all industries. Principle-based management was not developed specifically for criminal justice agencies but is applicable to criminal justice because its essence is grounded in making decisions that are morally correct.

As noted by Souryal (2007, p. 209), "Ironically, the most notable weakness in criminal justice management today is its most rudimentary: failure to understand the true role of management." This is a critical point that must be understood if we are truly interested in transforming criminal justice, as an entire discipline, into one that is capable of effectively functioning in the manner in which it was designed. The goal of criminal justice is to effectively and efficiently serve all members of society through enforcing the laws designed to protect our rights and liberties. The bulk of this work is carried out by practitioners at the lowest levels of all criminal justice agencies. In order for these line workers to effectively perform their duties, they must be managed, led, and guided by supervisors and management personnel who are moral, honest, and in possession of high degrees of integrity. If management practices are unethical, the product of justice will in most cases be unethical. By simple logic, one can therefore deduce that quality and ethical management must be present if an organization is going to be capable of producing and delivering moral justice.

The foundation of principle-based management rests on what O'Toole called "Rushmorean management." Rushmorean management is a concept that was developed based on the four former presidents memorialized on the face of Mount Rushmore. Each of the presidents is noted for their extraordinary accomplishments in light of the difficult times in which they served. What they appear to have in common is a resolve to do what was best, right, and morally correct for citizens of the United States of America. Their conviction appears to be based on values, not on the color of one's skin, the amount of money they had, or their political ideology. Their integrity was representative of the adage "A person's character is best judged by the way they treat someone who can do nothing for them." The four leaders who provide the foundation for principle-based management are as follows:

1. George Washington: The founding
2. Thomas Jefferson: Political philosophy
3. Abraham Lincoln: Preservation of the union
4. Theodore Roosevelt: Expansion and conservation

Principle-based management is a theory that is based on integrity, trust, listening, and respect. These four constructs are central to the idea of fostering a work environment that produces workers who are motivated and enthusiastic about delivering quality justice. These constructs are in direct opposition to more common forms of management in criminal justice agencies that are based on authoritarianism, fear, and egoism (Stark, 2005).

Integrity within a management context describes practices that are strictly honest, congruous with what is right, and authentic. This means that individual managers and supervisors must communicate and engage in actions that are transparent and honest. Their policies must pertain to all workers and not just a chosen few. This is not meant to imply that Rushmorean management cannot make a mistake. Of course, this would be unrealistic. The nature of the mistake, however, must be based on good faith and moral righteousness. Even though a manager's decision can be later found to be flawed, it can still maintain integrity if the purpose was meant to extract goodness (O'Toole, 1995).

The second foundation of principle-based management is trust. Workers must be trusted to do the right thing. If managers do not trust their subordinates, they will likely engage in micromanagement practices that snuff out all creativity and energy among the workforce. Managers should not be on the lookout to catch workers doing something wrong. Instead, they should provide the necessary environment for workers to do something right and for which they should be commended. Trust is a powerful motivator to do the right thing. When one feels trusted, they are more likely to do what is right, as compared to the opposite, where one may conclude, "who cares what I do, management doesn't trust me anyway, all they do is look for the mistakes I have made so they can punish me" (Robbins, 2005).

Principle-based managers listen to their employees. Managers are concerned with their employees' needs and concerns and overall well-being. Ethical managers understand that they can also learn from their employees. Because they trust their workers, they are open to new ideas and are willing to hear them out in open and honest discussions. Listening is one of the most important skills a manager can posses. All humans have a basic and very powerful need to be heard. Rushmorean leaders recognize this and capitalize on it. Within the fields of psychology and counseling there is a phrase that is used in part for humor but also to illuminate the most basic skill needed to help others, which is simply to listen: "How do you treat depression? You need a good listener. How do you treat anxiety? Well, for this too, you need a good listener." The therapeutic technique is not what is most important; the most important skill is being able to provide an atmosphere where one feels genuinely heard free of rejection and judgementatlism.

Respect is the final element of principle-based management. Similar to listening, respect is fundamental to the well-being of all human beings. You cannot expect someone to act ethically if they do not feel respected by those asking or demanding them to act ethically. In this regard it is critical that management be authentically respectful to all workers. To not demonstrate authentic respect will create an environment in which workers become confused and disenfranchised. Respect for employees can be described as sort of the culmination of management:

1. Conducting all actions with integrity
2. Trusting that their workers will do what is right
3. Listening to their worker's ideas and concerns

Cumulatively, these attributes demonstrate respect. There is no need for management to tell their workers they respect them; the respect is felt; it is intuitive, and it serves as a motivator to do what is right and conduct oneself with professionalism. This respect is predicated by management's actions, not words, and is therefore lasting.

Principle-based management is therefore a theory pertaining to a style of management that is aimed at encouraging workers to put forth their best effort based on their own desire to do what is morally correct for those they serve. The desire to do what is right is intrinsic. Its foundation is respect. Simply put, if criminal justice employees are expected to deliver justice that is equitable and fair, then they must be guided by leaders who are equitable and fair. We cannot have it both ways. We cannot have management practices that are ethical only when it is convenient or when someone is looking. It is too late for a department to talk about ethical management when the community is outraged as a result of unethical practices. Moral justice cannot be delivered under such circumstances. Instead management must be Rushmorean. Managers must be willing and dedicated to always doing what is right even when what is right is complex and difficult. Remember that what is at stake is the most fundamental requirement of any civilized nation: JUSTICE.

## Implementation of Principle-Based Management

Unfortunately, we must conclude this chapter with a word of caution. Implementing principle-based management in traditional criminal justice agencies is not easy. Consider the theory of community-oriented policing. This is a philosophy that describes the process of criminal justice agencies working together with the citizens of their community to figure out their needs and concerns and also to strategize on the best methods to achieve the goals. The theory is well grounded and makes sense. Its implementation, however, has been difficult. Much of the problem with implementing community-oriented policing lies in the hands of traditional police officers who do not feel it is their responsibility to do anything but enforce the law. As many officers profess, "I am not a social worker. I don't care what their problems are. If they break the law, I will take them to jail." This authoritarian attitude does little to resolve difficult issues in a community. It may serve to temporarily solve a conflict or disturbance, but this is much different from resolving a problem. Principle-based management is likely to be faced with the same implementation challenge.

First, human beings do not like change. So any change is going to at least initially be faced with some resistance. Second, similar to the analogy of community-oriented policing, authoritarian styles of management often think the basic tenets of principle-based management are foreign and naïve. Authoritarian managers will often profess, "What do you mean, trust our officers? Are you crazy? If I don't watch every step they take, they will get us all fired or killed." In essence, these managers fail to realize the true purpose of management as being a vehicle with which to help workers grow, mature, and learn. An authoritarian leader in a position of authority is not likely going to be very willing to give up such power. For leaders who lack a moral grounding and internal ethical compass, the concept of power can be intoxicating. It temporarily reduces the powerful pangs of insecurity.

Ultimately, the effective implementation of principle-based management demands not only a change in management practices but also a fundamental shift in culture. The culture of the agency must become grounded in always doing what is right for those it serves. This type of shift requires strong leadership that is prepared and capable of staying the course through the difficult period of transition. Principle-based leaders must also be capable of devising strategies that target each of the proposed explanations of corruption. In other words, they must be able to identify and remediate unethical individuals as well as the organization and society at large. Principle-based managers will need to reeducate the public as to the destructive nature and slippery slope of gratuities and aggressively discourage any continuance of practices that jeopardize the moral fabric of the organization. And just as resistant as the authoritarian managers will be in giving up their power, so too will be some members of the community who have benefited greatly from the spoils of management. The bar owner who pays the officers to allow him to operate beyond legal hours will not be overly excited about this new idea of moral management. The same will be true for the politicians and executives who enjoy perks based on payoffs and favors.

The task of transforming management in any agency is monumental. It requires Rushmorean courage, fortitude, and discipline. The payoff, however, is worth every drop of sweat.

## Conclusion

Recall the scenario presented at the beginning of the chapter. The training officer tells the recruit, "Whether you advised the suspect of his rights or not, put in the report that you did." We hope that by now you are able to understand that this training officer's command is unethical. As inconsequential as it may seem at the time, it sets a dangerous precedent that is likely to be expanded as one continues their career. Criminal justice is a difficult business. The problems of people and the ills of humanity can weigh heavily on one who chooses this profession as a career. Cynicism is common among veteran criminal justice practitioners, and the pull to bend the rules can be powerful. The justifications for small infractions initially set the stage for later transgressions that significantly interrupt and counterbalance the scales of justice.

Unethical management spoils the concept of justice. When workers do not feel as though they are respected by management, based on unethical practices and policies, they will not consistently deliver justice in the form in which it was designed. They may provide justice when the public is scrutinizing their actions, but in other cases they will rebel as a result of dissonance and anger. It is critical that management consists of leaders who are ethical, honest, and in possession of unwavering integrity. They must conduct themselves with professionalism that resonates with their subordinates in a manner that manifests into the fair and equitable distribution of justice.

## Questions in Review

1. How would you handle an incident where you felt pressure to falsify a report?
2. Why is the idea of premeditated corruption so damaging to the integrity of an agency?
3. What is the basic foundation of principle-based management?
4. Why would it be difficult, in most cases, to implement principle-based management?
5. What steps would you take to replace a corrupt culture with an ethical culture?

# Abuse of Authority and Power

$6$

## Introduction

In this chapter the basic tenets surrounding the issue of the abuse of authority and power are examined. The frame within which this chapter should be considered is an extension of the previous chapter's description of the "spoils of management." The abuse of authority and power within criminal justice agencies can take place in many different forms. The abuse may take place within criminal justice agencies in the form of unethical managers abusing subordinates. It may also take place between criminal justice officials and members of the public. Regardless of the circumstance, the abuse of authority is a process that is extremely damaging to whoever finds themselves on the receiving end of this wrath.

One of the goals of the chapter is to explore the various ways in which abuse of power and authority occurs. The chapter starts by defining some of the basic concepts that provide the structure for this phenomenon. It is important to understand precisely what each term means in order to properly synthesize the various manifestations of the abuse of authority. Next, the three types of abuse of power and authority will be examined. When considering the concept of abuse within the criminal justice system, we often think of physical abuse; however, as you will see, there are other types of abuse that can be just as damaging if not more so.

The remaining sections of the chapter are aimed at several critical issues related to the abuse of authority. They include a discussion of a very basic question regarding abuse: how do you know if an action constitutes abuse? In addition, the causes and consequences of abuse will be explored and the chapter concludes with possible responses to abuse. Consider the following questions:

- What is the end result when a member of the criminal justice system abuses his or her authority and power?
- How do these actions affect the concept of justice?

## Defining the Concepts

In order to understand the idea of abusing one's authority and the various contexts in which this may occur, it is critical that each component be defined. For example, how do you know if authority has been abused without first defining abuse? Second, in order to understand and identify the abuse of authority, we must define authority and its attendant concept of power. Often, authority and power are used interchangeably. This is a mistake and should be avoided in order to properly conceptualize the true essence of what the phrase "abuse of authority" is meant to capture. For the definitions of authority and power, see David Weisburd, (2001) *"The Abuse of Police Authority: A National Study of Police Officers' Attitudes."*

First, however, let's consider the concept of abuse. In general terms the concept of abuse describes the process of using something wrongly or improperly. It is also used to depict such concepts as maltreat or attack with insults (American Heritage Dictionary, 1983). Therefore, for the purposes of our discussion, the idea of abusing one's authority and power describes the process of using that authority and power wrongly or improperly. In essence, any use of authority or power that is not within the scope of one's duty is likely to consist of abuse. And when the abuse is intentional, the circumstance is considerably aggravated. The intentional abuse of authority and power is among the most heinous miscarriages of justice that take place within criminal justice. Intentionality incorporates and depicts awareness of what one is doing and therefore results in an officer consciously abusing another, gravely harming, if not completely destroying, the process of cooperation that is necessary for justice to be effectively carried out.

Authority is one's right to control the behavior of others within legally determined parameters. One's authority is based on their official position and the legal parameters that govern their position. For example, a police officer has the authority to place a suspect under arrest for the violation of a law. This authority is granted in legal statutes that describe the official meaning of a duly sworn police officer and their responsibility for maintaining order and protecting society. A correctional officer has the authority to control inmates based on similar legal parameters defining the duties and responsibilities of the position and the circumstances in which behavior is legally controlled. For example, a correctional officer has the authority to move inmates, separate inmates, handcuff inmates, and restrain inmates based on the authority vested in the official position. Therefore, criminal justice practitioners have the full authority of their position legally granted through laws and codes of procedure at all times while considered to be acting within their official capacity (Weisburd et al., 2001).

Power is the means for controlling the behavior of others beyond the standards of authority (Robbins, 2005). Authority provides the legal foundation for taking action; however, if we stop at authority, no action has taken place. For example, a police officer is on routine patrol when the dispatcher announces that a truck driver headed south in the downtown area reported seeing a suspect breaking into a vehicle parked in a used-car sales lot. The police officer begins heading toward the downtown area, when two blocks away from the car lot in question he observes a male suspect, with no shirt on, jogging away from the lot and obviously straining to hold on to various objects while he is running. The police officer stops to talk to the individual and finds him to be extremely nervous, bleeding from his right hand, and holding a car radio and speakers. Immediately the officer advises the suspect of his Miranda rights and asks where he got the radio and speakers. The suspect is truthful and states he had broken into a vehicle, which is how he cut his hand and stole the items. Obviously, the officer has the authority to place the suspect under arrest. The actual act of placing handcuffs on the suspect, however, is the result of power. In this case, it is the physical means through which the suspect has his hands placed behind his back and the handcuffs applied.

Before examining the different types of abuse, we believe an important note is warranted. As you have noticed, the title of this chapter is "Abuse of Authority and Power." This is different from the titles of chapters in most other books or academic articles discussing this topic. The most typical title is the "abuse of authority." In most circumstances this title is fine, the points are made, and the discussions are clear. In order to fully explore the concept of abuse in criminal justice organizations, however, one must consider the different definitions of authority and power. The difference may be subtle but important nonetheless. For example, an officer arrests a combative suspect, and in the process of handcuffing the suspect, the officer squeezes both cuffs with all his might to punish the suspect for having the gall to challenge him. In this circumstance what has been abused? By overtightening the handcuffs, has the officer abused his authority? Has the officer abused his power? Has the officer abused both his power and authority? One final question to ponder: is it possible to abuse one's power but not one's authority or to abuse one's authority but not one's power?

## Three Types of Abuse

When discussing the abuse of authority in a criminal justice context the most common perception for most people is physical abuse. Most people think of police officers and correctional officers physically beating a suspect or inmate beyond that which is necessary or reasonable. In fact, we often use the emotionally charged concept of "brutality." Brutality describes the process of treating (beating) someone savagely with no mercy or pity, and lacks any notion of humanity. As we will discuss below, however, this is only one aspect of abuse. In fact, there are at least three types of abuse that take place in the criminal justice system. Carter and Radelet (1999, p. 289) provided good depictions of each.

The first type of abuse is that related to physical force. Physical abuse describes the process of "any officer behavior involving the use of more force than is necessary to effect an arrest or search; and/or the wanton use of any degree of physical force against another by a police officer under the color of the officer's authority" (Carter & Radelet, 1999, p. 289). In this definition, Carter and Radelet were speaking specifically in relation to police officers. Know, however, that this definition applies to any criminal justice official, including correctional officers, judges, attorneys, probation and parole officers, as well as any others acting under an official capacity vested in them by law.

Physical abuse is certainly the most overt. It is the type of abuse that often takes place out in the community for members to see and feel. Beginning with the Rodney King incident, communities have become much more aware of the scope of physical abuse, largely as a result of enhanced technology. Today, the market is filled with recording devices that are small, efficient, and able to be deployed at a moment's notice. Based on this technology, many incidents of physical abuse have been recorded that previously would have remained unknown.

In addition, physical abuse is often a very heinous event for a number of reasons. First, the physical abuse clearly demonstrates and depicts the very damaging emotion of anger in addition to judgmentalism and physical treatment that damages the idea of dignity and humanity. The important distinction each reader should consider as this discussion develops is the clear difference between the use of physical force and physical abuse. We are clearly concerned with physical abuse that when applied has the tendency to shock the conscious of those who observe the abuse as well as the individual(s) directly receiving the abuse.

In one circumstance, a child who witnessed her father being physically abused by police officers became so distraught that she had to be rushed to the hospital for hyperventilation. As investigators spoke with her later, she claimed that she thought the police were supposed to protect people. She further noted that she was not sure how she could ever look at another police officer and not mentally recount the incident of her father being struck repeatedly as several other officers stood around and did nothing. The fact that other officers who were present did nothing is an important note. A law enforcement officer who does not intervene in a situation where a reasonable person would conclude that the actions of other officers constituted abuse can be held liable both civilly and in criminal proceedings.

Even more distressing is the fact that many law enforcement agencies have unwritten rules, passed down through various forms of socialization, that demand physical abuse under certain circumstances. Take, for example, the common unwritten and informal policy of "if they run, they get beat." This is a very troubling phenomenon where police departments have decided that suspects need to be physically punished for having the audacity to run from officers. In essence, the rule states that anytime a suspect flees from the police and gets caught, they should be beaten, first, just for the simple fact that they dared to run away, and second as payback for the officers having to run after them. Some officers have claimed that it is best when the suspect gives up and stops running, usually due to fatigue. In many of these scenarios, suspects will stop and turn to face the chasing officers with hands up and verbally state, "I give up, officer. Please do not beat me." Instead of simply handcuffing the suspect, however, the rule states these suspects must be taught a lesson.

Punishment for running must be meted out. Some officers will reason that suspects who are not taught their lesson will simply run every time. If there are no consequences to running from the police, why would suspects not take the chance anytime they are confronted for illegal activity? Therefore the officer, before handcuffing the suspect, engages in what is commonly referred to as "stick-time." Stick-time describes the process of repeatedly striking a suspect with one's baton. Readers should clearly understand that the physical force used in these types of events is a clear breach of the law and is abuse. Even if a suspect runs from the police, the same rules of engagement apply; only the necessary force can be legally applied. When a suspect turns to the police and gives up, the only legal course of action is to affect the arrest with only the amount of force necessary. In this case, the amount of force necessary is none.

This same type of phenomenon is also common in correctional settings. Correctional officers will often state that they must maintain authority at all costs. This often means that they will use physical abuse if their authority has been challenged. In essence, they must save face or bear the perceived consequences of being seen as weak and continuously preyed on thereafter.

These justifications, however, do nothing to change the simple fact that physical abuse is always wrong, it is always illegal, and it always damages the image of criminal justice. At no time and under no circumstances is it beneficial for law enforcement or correctional officers to decide that they must mete out punishment for what is in essence a perceived lack of respect for their authority. Criminal justice is not a discipline that is served well when practitioners allow their emotions to govern their actions. The professional police officer who eventually catches the fleeing suspect who ultimately gives up will simply handcuff the suspect, advise him of his rights, transport him to the local jail, and accurately report the incident, including the appropriate charges.

In such cases where physical abuse takes place, another very troubling act often accompanies the abuse. Consider the fleeing suspect who turns to the police officer and gives up. Instead of the officer simply handcuffing the suspect, he first decides he must punish the suspect and engages in stick time. How is this officer going to write the report? If the officer accurately depicts the circumstances, he would be forced to articulate that he struck the suspect for no legal reason. Simply running from the police does not provide an officer with probable cause to beat a suspect. Therefore, this officer could be liable for engaging in excessive force. What the officer is more likely to do, however, is articulate in the official report that upon reaching the suspect, the suspect assumed a combative stance and attempted to strike the officer in order to not be arrested. The officer may further embellish the report by stating that while trying to handcuff the suspect, the suspect began violently struggling with the officer and even attempted to remove his firearm. If these statements were true, the officer would certainly be justified in using physical force to affect the arrest, as it could be argued his life was in danger. There is one little problem, however: it is not the truth. Therefore, one act of physical abuse leads to another act of legal abuse to cover up the original act.

The second type of abuse is verbal and psychological abuse. Verbal and psychological abuse describes the process of officers

> relying on authority inherently vested in them based on their office to verbally assail, ridicule, harass, and/or place persons who are under the actual or constructive dominion of the officer in a situation where the individual's esteem and/or self image is threatened or diminished. Also included in this category is the threat of physical harm under the supposition that a threat is psychologically coercive and instills fear in the average person. (Carter & Radelet, 1999, p. 289)

We want to aggressively assert that verbal/psychological abuse can be just as damaging if not more so than physical abuse. At its foundation the consequences are the same; one's dignity and self-respect are destroyed. Think back to the example used above where the little girl witnessed her father being abused by the police. As the officers were physically abusing the father, they were also verbally and psychologically abusing him. They stated on numerous occasions, "Put your hands behind your back," or "You don't have to if you don't want to; this is fun. I am enjoying the opportunity to beat on you. Keep resisting. That way I can keep hitting you." Another officer stated, "We are going to be here a while. This guy needs to learn something about respect. This ain't stopping until I get tired." At this point, stop and ask yourself, is this really about respect or is this really about fear? Consider the officer who tells the individual "not moving fast enough" he better hurry or there is a nice jail cell for him at the local jail. Certainly, the individual may figure out how to move faster, but is this based on a newfound respect for the officer or fear that he will be jailed by an overzealous officer? The basic question is, what is more conducive to the overall function and goal of criminal justice: to be respected or feared? Our answer would be unequivocally respected.

The third type of abuse is legal abuse and violation of one's civil rights. Carter and Radelet (1999) noted that this type of abuse is likely to be the most frequent. They described legal abuse as "any violation of a person's constitutional, federally protected or state protected rights. Although the individual may not suffer any apparent physical or psychological damage in the purest sense, an abuse of authority has none the less occurred" (p. 289). As noted, legal abuse is likely to be the most common type of abuse, and although it may not leave physical marks or bruises it is extremely damaging to the overall mission of criminal justice.

Legal abuse can take place in a myriad of ways, but what all forms of legal abuse have in common is an action taken by an officer without legal justification. Most common to this form of abuse is performing traffic stops without probable cause, arresting someone based on their race or gender or lack of respect without probable cause, as well as searching and seizing property without probable cause (Carter & Radelet, 1999).

## How Do You Know if an Action Constitutes Abuse?

Ascertaining whether the action of a criminal justice officer constitutes abuse is seldom an easy task. This is because actions do not occur in a vacuum. There are often many circumstances, feelings, and emotions that provide both a push and pull within an officer's intellectual framework used to make important decisions regarding possible responses to a circumstance. Further adding to the confusion is the fact that officers are often responsible for dealing with situations that have become emotionally charged long before the officer has arrived. Therefore, police officers, correctional officers, and even judges are responsible for making decisions that affect and involve people entangled in conflict, abuse, and neglect.

One of the best ways to know whether an action constitutes abuse is by employing a simple test of reasonableness. Remember, what makes these circumstances difficult is the atmosphere of highly charged emotion. But, in order for a test of reasonableness to be valid, it must be administered and answered free of emotion and instead based on professionalism. This is what makes working in the criminal justice system very difficult in many circumstances. Criminal justice practitioners are, in essence, expected to handle complex, emotionally charged circumstances without allowing their own emotion to seep into the equation. This is a tall task for even the most psychologically and emotionally well-balanced officers. But it must be accomplished. Justice depends on it.

There are several guiding questions of which officers should always be cognizant. In regard to physical force, officers should ask the following questions:

1. Were my actions reasonable?
2. Could I have achieved the goal with less force?

3. Did I disengage the use of force precisely at the time it was no longer necessary?
4. Did I carry out the task with only the amount of force that was absolutely necessary?
5. Did I carry out the task in a manner that best served the individual, the community, and humanity?

These questions can also be applied with slight variation to questions of verbal and legal abuse. For example,

1. Was the language used reasonable?
2. Was the language used the least intrusive necessary?
3. Did the language used serve to preserve or erode one's feelings of dignity and self-respect?

In relation to legal decisions, the same concept of reasonableness applies.

1. Was the reasoning to engage in an enforcement action based on a legal violation of which the facts can be articulated, or was the reasoning based on personal mannerisms deemed disrespectful or a result of bias or discrimination?

Finally, as noted earlier, it is important to once again recall that an act of abuse does not occur in isolation. When officers abuse their authority and power, they are then in a position where they often must fabricate facts to support their actions. It is never justifiable to intentionally falsify an official report or statements made to a supervisor concerning the events of a circumstance. A common reason to falsify an official report or statements made to a supervisor is that the original actions were not legal. If an officer is caught falsifying a report, the consequences are of the severest order. In essence, the credibility of the officer caught lying is destroyed. Therefore, the officer's testimony becomes suspect from that moment forward. Consider the likely line of questioning from a defense attorney aimed at an officer found to be lying in a report or on the stand: "Officer, since you have been caught lying in an official report, how do we know you are not lying now?"

## Common Causes of the Abuse of Authority and Power

Certainly, the causes of abuse of authority and power are legion. And we certainly will not exhaust the various causes or their variations in this limited space. For example, causes of abuse may be specific to the individual officer or a result of individual characteristics combined with pressures from a corrupted organizational culture. Regardless of the cause, however, engaging in the abuse of authority and power is a decision made by individual officers or groups of officers. The literature is replete with various discussions regarding the troubling enigma of why some officers abuse their authority and others do not.

There are three possible causes or influences that appear to be very salient factors that need to be explored. First, the concept of egoism is examined. Second, will be various personal and organizational stressors, and finally, a brief discussion relating to arguably the most basic concept concerning this issue: communication skills. What is the foundation of abusing one's authority and power through physical force, verbal language, or legal issues? Is there an inverse relationship between one's overall psychological and emotional health and abuse? The better adjusted the officers are psychologically and emotionally, the less likely they probably are to abuse their authority and power. One's mental health is directly related to each of the three areas that follow.

## Egoism

Egoism may be described as an exaggerated concern for self-love or an infatuation with one's official position. If one delves a little further into this definition, another idea that should resonate is the fact that an officer who is functioning from an unrealistic view of himself or reality is not well equipped to provide quality policing. Narcissistic individuals are much more concerned with how they look, appear, and sound than they are with the well-being of others. In addition, many officers of both law enforcement and correctional agencies feel as though they must appear tough at all times. In fact, the culture of criminal justice is one that shows little tolerance for someone who is not tough and physically able to handle oneself as well as assist fellow officers. Therefore, an ego-driven officer functioning in an environment that demands toughness, coupled with frequent highly charged emotional situations involving suspects or inmates, sets up a situation where the abuse of authority and power is not only possible, but extremely likely to happen.

Egoism is a concept that is describes the characteristics of a person who suffers from a fractured ego and overall is not psychologically or emotionally well adjusted. These officers will perform "well" only under certain conditions; namely, when they feel as though they are in total control. They have very little tolerance for any person or circumstance that challenges their authority. In essence, their psychological depth is so shallow that they do not have the capacity to effectively deal with conflict and will usually respond with the only mechanism they know: power. Power in this case may be the use of harsh verbal language meant to demean the person and quickly and definitively reestablish control. This is abuse. The harsh language was directly related to the officer's exaggerated view of himself and his authority being threatened (Miller, 1987). Consider the following scenario to illustrate this point:

> An officer responds to family disturbance. When the officer arrives, he finds a husband and wife engaged in a verbal argument. When the couple notices the police presence, the wife permits the officer to enter the home and demands that the husband be arrested. Then, the husband accuses the wife and demands that she be arrested. While the officer is questioning the wife, the husband is directed to move away and be silent. The husband reacts to the wife's answers to the officer's questions and screams that she is lying. He also states that the officer is not doing his job. The husband then states loudly that the police never believe the man and always end up arresting the man when the woman is also guilty.

As the senior officer on the scene, how would you handle this situation? Obviously two people are distraught; they are angry and emotionally hurt. Many things are on the line in these types of circumstances. For example, if the husband is arrested, he will not be able to show up on time for his next shift at the factory. If he misses work, they will not be able to pay the month's mortgage. If the wife is arrested, there will be no one to care for the couple's infant daughter while the husband is at work.

What needs to happen in this circumstance? First, the intense emotion needs to be reduced. When people are screaming, it is not possible to understand the circumstances of an incident. Second, once the emotion has been calmed, the officer needs to ascertain the facts. In some instances an arrest may be mandatory depending on what has transpired. Regardless, the officer needs to be able to quickly and accurately decipher what has transpired. How is this best accomplished? By an officer who is stern, empathic, and respectful. The officer may say, "Sir, I understand you are very upset. But I cannot help you if you continue to scream. I am here to help you, but in order for me to help you, I must be able to find out what happened." This is one of the many ways in which a volatile situation is deescalated. Let's consider another type of response, one that is based on ego, control, and fear and unfortunately is very common. Under the same circumstances, this officer responds in the following manner: "Shut up. Everyone shut up right now, or I will take you both to jail. I don't care what happened, you are either going to shut up, or I am going to put handcuffs on you. Do you understand? I am going to tell you what to do, when to do it, and how to do it. From this point forward, if I hear someone say something who has not been asked a direct question by me you are going to jail. Period."

The framework in which this example is placed could also be used to depict an example of physical abuse. Remember, physical force is any force that goes beyond what is necessary to achieve a lawful objective. The case of Rodney King provides a great case in point. The Rodney King incident consisted of several uniform police officers beating him with sticks. The case became famous because it was among the earliest incidents involving abuse that was actually caught on tape. In the video it became clear that regardless of the circumstances in which the police contacted King, the amount of force used was nothing short of abuse. The essence of the King beating is this: there were more than enough uniformed police officers present to physically control King and achieve the objective of getting him handcuffed and secured without the repeated strikes he was forced to endure.

## Personal and Organizational Stressors

Experienced pilots often say that what usually leads to a crash is not one system failure but the sequence of several failures that overwhelm the physical and mental capabilities of the crew. Most professional aviators have sufficient training to deal with an emergency in flight so long as the emergency can be isolated and the remaining systems and equipment continue to function. This same analogy can be applied to the personal and organizational stressors experienced by criminal justice professionals.

The essence in which stressors are correlated with abuse is represented in the same inverse relationship we discussed with one's overall psychological health. The more stressors one must deal with at a given time, the greater the likelihood of being psychologically and emotionally overwhelmed, which ultimately leads to greater chances of reacting in an abusive manner.

Stress is toxic and if not properly dealt with can literally destroy the body over time. It is the manner in which stress is dealt with that is central to this discussion. Stress that is not properly released via exercise or counseling often manifests itself in various ways, including the tendency to overreact in circumstances where additional stress is added to an already saturated criminal justice official. For example, consider the judge who is in the middle of a painful divorce. Would you argue that she is more or less likely to disproportionately sentence an offender for a relatively minor crime who happens to display a verbal characteristic similar to that of her spouse?

Carter and Radelet (1999, p. 292) provided seven stressors that do a great job of capturing the essence of this phenomenon and also how each contributes to the breakdown of personal resources needed to function in a professional manner. We have clearly stated that we believe the most professional officers are those who are most balanced psychologically and emotionally. Stress, however, erodes this balance and increases the likelihood of abusing one's authority and power. The seven stressors are discussed in the following sections.

## Life-Threatening Stressors

These stressors constitute the constant potential for injury or death experienced by criminal justice practitioners, especially law enforcement and correctional officers. Carter and Radelet (1999) provided a great point regarding life-threatening stressors and the fact that this type of stress is significantly aggravated based on the fact that violence directed at officers is often intentional as opposed to accidental. Souryal (2007), for example, pointed out that several occupations are statistically found to be more dangerous than law enforcement. Statistically, there is no doubt that this is accurate. What cannot be captured statistically, however, is the constant threat or perception of threat of violent acts where the officer would be targeted based on his or her position or occupation. The intentional aspect of this type of violent act significantly elevates the levels of stress as soon as one puts on the uniform and before ever coming into contact with a troubled citizen of the community. In essence, the officer is starting from an elevated level of stress.

## Social Isolation Stressors

Stress from being socially isolated has a tendency to build as one traverse their career. The nature of criminal justice and its mission provides officers with very difficult circumstances in which they must balance their social activities and their profession. Officers often find it very difficult to engage in meaningful conversations with those who are not employed in law enforcement. Take, for example, the officer who responds to a hanging. He arrives and finds a seventeen-year-old boy hanging in his bedroom with a note under his feet. In the note the boy stated that he no longer wanted to live because his girlfriend decided to end the relationship so that she could date his best friend. These types of incidents are very personal, and the rawness of human nature is fully experienced. After such exposure it can be very difficult for this same officer to find much stimulation among a group of people discussing their latest round of golf. The stress, therefore, is a result of losing vital contacts with one's community through which important social connections are fulfilled.

## Organizational Stressors

These types of stressors are very significant and have been found to be closely correlated with perceptions of job satisfaction (Miller, Mire, & Kim, 2009). Organizational stressors consist of variables such as autonomy, feedback from supervisors, equipment, work schedules, as well as policies and procedures. Unethical management practices are also considered organizational stressors and can have a significant negative impact on an officer's overall sense of well-being, especially if management practices are such that favoritism is shown to a select few who are most loyal to the goals of an individual supervisor.

## Functional Stressors

Functional stressors represent those types of stresses caused by the actual job of an officer. Such examples may consist of having to be able to handle conflict. One class of cadets was told by the instructor, "Who are you going to call if you are involved in an incident that you and your fellow officers cannot handle? Are you going to call the army, the National Guard, or the governor? No, there is no one to call. You are the police. You must figure out a way to handle any situation that presents itself." Consider a typical shift of police officers in a medium-sized town with a population of about 150,000. The night shift is made up of 15 officers dispersed throughout the town, with eight officers assigned to the areas with the highest volume of calls. It is a Saturday night, and the local university's football team is playing for the conference championship. So a town of 150,000 now contains a population of about 225,000 people. In addition, the shift of 15 is short five officers. Two officers are out on sick leave, and the other three are participating in mandatory in service training. Therefore, the reality of this circumstance is that ten officers are responsible for maintaining the safety and security of 225,000 people dispersed throughout a town consisting of approximately 50 square miles. The realization of such a responsibility can be overwhelming and certainly contributes to greater levels of stress.

## Personal Stressors

We alluded to personal stressors in the example of the judge embroiled in a bitter divorce. Personal stressors are very serious issues that significantly contribute to the stress of officers. Personal stress is so powerful because the source of the stress is often those most closest to us: our families. Financial pressures are also considered to be personal stressors. Especially in the economic turmoil of today's economy, financial worries are very prevalent as many people battle to maintain their homes and possessions.

## Physiological Stressors

Among the most salient physiological stressors common to many officers of criminal justice especially those of police and correctional is the constant state of fatigue. Fatigue can be a result of many circumstances including but not limited to the constant rotations of shift work and having to go back and forth between night and day shifts as well as to not being physically fit. The long hours of shift work and the rotating schedules make it very difficult to establish regular routines of healthy eating and exercise. In addition, the low pay inherent in criminal justice often requires off duty work to supplement incomes. Therefore, many officers have little time off to fully rest and rejuvenate their body and mind before having to return to the stressors of the job.

## Psychological Stressors

Psychological stressors can be described as the culmination of stress due to all of the factors associated with working in criminal justice organizations. In addition, certain incidents can be traumatic and cause long-term psychological damage if not treated. Officers responding to car accidents where an entire family has violently perished as a result of a drunk driver or the experience of handling a murder investigation where a husband has killed his wife and children are common examples of the types of incidents law enforcement officers face on a daily basis. The same is true for correctional officers who are responsible for dealing with large-scale acts of violence, many of which are random and lack any connection to reason or the concept of humanity. It can be very difficult to persistently deal with human conditions and circumstances that can only be described as animalistic in nature.

As one reflects on each of these stressors it is important to do so within the framework of each having a negative pull on one's energy, vitality, and emotion. Each of these stressors affects the decision-making abilities of criminal justice practitioners as well as their ability to tolerate the behaviors of others. The more of these stressors an officer is experiencing, the less likely he will be to act in a manner that is most conducive to the well-being of others, including being able to display appropriate levels of compassion and empathy.

## Communication as a Cause of Abuse

In addition to egoism and the various stressors associated with abuse, we believe the style and method of communication is also important. The manner in which one communicates significantly influences the types of responses generated by the receiver of communication. For example, one officer may arrive at the scene of a request for service and ask the caller, "Good afternoon, ma'am. How may I help you?" A second officer may arrive and instead state, "What is it this time? There is always a problem around here, and I am beginning to get tired of coming down here every day." Obviously, these two methods of communicating are likely to illicit very different responses from the callers.

Generally, people want to be reassured; people want to be heard, and they want to feel as though they are important. In essence, all human beings want to feel respected. The method of communication greatly influences the degree to which people realize each of these factors. Appropriate and professional methods of communication are critical and will usually have a direct impact on the manner and methods used to handle a particular incident. We would argue that the more professional the communication patterns, the less likely an officer will be to engage in not only physical abuse but even physical force. Most people, with the exception of those suffering from serious psychological disorders and delusions, will respond positively to officers who engage them in respectful communication that signifies respect, dignity, and humanity.

## What Are the Consequences of Abuse?

The consequences of the abuse of authority and power are felt throughout the entire system of criminal justice and the communities in which they serve. In this section we discuss a few of the critical elements that are likely to result from the abuses of authority and power, especially when the abuse is persistent and has been displayed over long periods of time. First, the concept of spoiled justice is examined and then the destructive emotion of anger, followed by discussing the community's loss of respect for their criminal justice organizations.

### Spoiled Justice

As noted in earlier chapters, the concept of spoiled justice describes the process of justice becoming decayed. In essence, justice is reduced to a process that in its final form is nowhere near the form in which it originated. When agents of criminal justice abuse their authority and power, they are not delivering justice. In most cases what they are delivering is punishment and fear, neither of which they are commissioned to administer.

### Anger

When authority and power are abused, the eventual response from the community will be anger. Even if a citizen who finds himself on the receiving end of abuse initially reacts with fear, the fear usually subsides after a short time and is then replaced with anger. The anger is in relation to being shocked by what is quickly realized as unfair and heinous treatment by the exact people who are supposed to be protecting them from such circumstances. The shock of being on the receiving end of abuse by a criminal justice official can be profound. In fact, in some cases it is traumatic. Underneath it all, the abused citizen is left to grapple with a question that is impossible to answer: "How could they have done this to me?"

**Respect Is Lost**

Closely aligned with spoiled justice and anger is the fact that the abuse of authority and power quickly and decisively erodes the respect individuals may have once had for their criminal justice representatives. Most people are not interested in working with or even being affiliated with those they do not respect. Respect for someone is a concept that generally describes seeing one in a positive light or having high regard for them. People we respect we pay close attention to, and we value their input and knowledge regarding some subject. If, however, we are taken advantage of or abused by a person we respect, the respect is lost. And, instead of the positive feelings of regard, we immediately begin to feel the opposite. Instead of being respected, the person is seen as a phony or as a joke. Their credibility is lost.

When the community loses respect for its criminal justice practitioners, it becomes very difficult to provide quality justice, primarily because the community is no longer interested in participating in the partnership. And when there is a lack of participation from the community, the system of criminal justice suffers greatly. In order for criminal justice agencies to adequately serve their communities, they must have the participation and cooperation of its citizens.

Finally, an important note to conclude this section is the fact that spoiled justice, anger, and a loss of respect are very difficult to overcome. The truth is that many agencies and their officers take the idea of abusing authority and power very seriously. Many of the more progressive and professional agencies take deliberate steps to ensure that abuse is minimized if not eliminated all together. Once respect is lost and anger sets in, it takes years maybe even complete generations to reverse it. Consider the automobile industry. American-produced products were so lacking at one time that even though today's products are much better, the initial reaction for most is to first consider foreign vehicles. This is because they are known for their quality, unlike their originally shabby American counterparts. American vehicles have been greatly enhanced over the last several years, but the quality of the product is still nowhere near being able to overcome the negative perceptions ingrained in people's minds.

## Responses to Abuse

There are at least four specific objectives that must be present and carried out when attempting to rectify a troubled agency or maintain and further establish trust and respect.

1. *Ethical management:* As discussed earlier, ethical management is critical. Managers must be operating from the foundation of honesty

and moral ethicality. This is in essence the bedrock of ethics. Ethical behavior must originate from management, and within management the ethics of the chief, warden, judge, or highest-ranking official must be impeccable. If this is not the case, it becomes foolish to think lower levels of management and line workers will be concerned about ethical behavior. If management is abusing its authority and power, it is extremely likely that practitioners are doing the same.

2. *Training and education:* How do we know what a business is serious about? By the way it spends its money. The same is true for criminal justice organizations. All employees must undergo continuous, professional training regarding ethics. Remaining with the idea of money, the payoff for criminal justice agencies that provide quality training and education on ethical behavior is likely to be realized through reduced liability claims. Of course, this is in addition to the most basic construct of ethical behavior: treating people with respect regardless of how difficult they make it Is simply the right thing to do.

3. *Definitive policies:* How do we know what a criminal justice organization is serious about? By its policies and the degree to which they are enforced. In essence, any report of abuse must be addressed immediately, and the more transparent the findings the better. Even in cases where the findings may not be what the public wanted or expected, it is always best to be honest and make them known.

4. *Sustained persistence:* Criminal justice agencies must be vigilant in maintaining ethical standards. Even when it may appear that regardless of what we do the community is never satisfied, the fight must go on. This is why ethical conduct is not only for the community we serve, but it is also right and just. In this case righteousness and justness trumps even the community. Therefore, even if the community did not care, it would still be wrong for criminal justice agencies to abuse their authority and power.

## Conclusion

The abuse of one's authority and power is among the most heinous acts one can commit. It is also a direct attack on humanity. It serves to erode one's perceptions of dignity, self-esteem, self-respect, and confidence in our fellow man. When there is abuse, there cannot be justice. These two concepts cannot purely occur in tandem.

In the beginning of this chapter, we explained why we chose to include the concept of power in the title of the chapter. We also posed several questions pertaining to whether one can abuse authority and not power or abuse power and not authority. The purpose of this was to invoke critical thinking. The answer is when a person abuses their authority, they are also abusing their power. And when a person abuses their power, they also abusing their authority.

## Questions in Review

1. How would you describe "the abuse of authority and power"?
2. Discuss the different concepts of abuse, authority, and power. What is the difference between authority and power?
3. Discuss the three types of abuse.
4. How do you know if an action constitutes abuse?
5. Discuss the various causes of abuse. Which is the most problematic?
6. Discuss the consequences of abuse. What is the ultimate cost?
7. If you were in charge of a criminal justice organization, how would you ensure that ethical behavior is being carried out?

# Lying and Deception

# 7

## Introduction

False words are not only evil in themselves, but they infect the soul. (Socrates, quoted in Brun, 1978, p. 31)

St. Augustine observed that he had "known many who wished to deceive, but none who wished to be deceived." (Rotelle, 1997, p. 257)

I hate being lied to. Short of violence, it is the worst thing you can do to me. Not because of God, or the Ten Commandments, or any universal moral precepts. The reason that I hate lies is because, like you, I wish to navigate carefully through life, and to do so I must be able to calculate my true position. When you lie to me, you know your position but you have given me false data which obscures mine. (Wallace, 2000)

The architecture of leadership, all the theories and guidelines, falls apart without honesty and integrity. It is the keystone that holds an organization together. (Phillips, 1992, p. 52)

The fascinating study of lying and deception in the criminal justice system will be discussed in this chapter. Is it ever justifiable to lie? Sissela Bok (1999) pointed out that the basic tenet that lying is wrong seems to be universal to all cultures, probably because humans are social animals.

Eugene R. Milhizer (2006) contended that there are several conclusions regarding "truth" that can be deduced. Milhizer saw the desire for truth as the result of human beings' natural desire for knowledge and that truth is a relationship of conformity between the human intellect and the object of intellect reality. Milhizer noted that the relationship of truth and reality necessitates that truth is determinate and as such that the same thing cannot be affirmed and denied at the same time.

Milhizer (2006) pointed out that the opposite of truth is falsity or, when a voluntary act, lying. He stated that falsity is a lack of conformity between one's thoughts and reality, while lying is a lack of conformity between what one does or says and what one believes. Lying is nothing less than the intentional obstruction by another of each person's natural inclination to know.

According to him, truth, which is the correspondence between thought and reality, is needed both to satisfy our innate desire for knowledge and to enable us to make accurate judgments about reality. It is therefore essential that an ardor for truth be considered as the heart of any system of justice.

The *Stanford Encyclopedia of Philosophy* (2008) provides that issues central to a philosophical discussion of lying and/or deception may be divided into two types. Questions of the first type are definitional. They include debates on how lying is defined, how deceiving is defined, and whether lying is a form of intended deception. Questions of the second type look at the morality of the act. They include the questions of whether lying and deceiving are always morally wrong and if either lying or deception is morally obligatory and not just merely morally permissible.

As noted by the *Stanford Encyclopedia of Philosophy*, there is no universally accepted definition of lying to others. If we define lying as the making of a false statement with the intention to deceive, there are several issues with this approach. What if the person who makes the false statement actually believes that the statement is not false? Does lying require the knowing utterance of a false statement?

Another definition of lying is "a person lies when he asserts something to another which he believes to be false with the intention of getting the other to believe it to be true" (Kupfer, 1982, p. 104). What if a person makes a statement that he or she believes to be false, but the statement is in fact true? Is it a lie? For example, two individuals are arrested for a rape. Each suspect is being questioned at the same time by different investigators. One investigator states to one of the suspects that he might as well confess, as his buddy has already confessed. At the time, the investigator did not know that the other suspect had in fact confessed. Is the statement by the investigator a lie?

According to the *Stanford Encyclopedia of Philosophy* (2008), there are at least four commonly accepted conditions for lying:

- A person makes a statement.
- The person believes the statement to be false.
- The untruthful statement is made to another person.
- The person intends that the other person believe the untruthful statement to be true.

There are several problems with the above definition. Can a person commit a lie without making a statement? In a situation where a person would normally be expected to make a statement, can the failure to make a statement ever be considered as a lie? Would it be a lie to tell someone that he or she looks good today when you know that the other person will not believe you? Apparently, the encyclopedia definition of lying does not require that the statement be untrue but only that the person who makes the statement believes it to be false.

## Are Some Lies Justified?

The nineteenth-century author Samuel Johnson once stated, "The general rule is that truth should never be violated; there must, however, be some exceptions. What if a murderer should ask you which way a man he is trying to kill has gone?" (Bok, 1999, p. 40). You visit a longtime friend in the hospital. Your friend looks very unhealthy. Your friend questions you about his or her looks. Is it justified to tell a lie and indicate that your friend looks great, or are you morally required to tell the friend that he or she looks very unhealthy?

In the criminal justice profession, are lies justified in detecting criminal conduct? For example, an undercover police officer is generally lying about his or her identity, motives, and occupation?

Immanuel Kant contended that each of us have a moral duty to everyone to be truthful. Kant contended that the duty to be truthful in every statement cannot be avoided, however great the disadvantage may be. According to him, the duty to be truthful is absolute. Kant stated, "By a lie a man throws away and, as it were, annihilates his dignity as a man" (Kant, 1797/1967, p. 123). If we accepted Kant's standard, undercover police work would never be justified.

Sissela Bok (1999) contended that there are two conceptual domains: the abstract question of truth and falsity and the moral question that examines the intended consequences of the truthfulness or falsity of the statement. Her definition of a lie is "a statement, believed by the liar to be false, made to another person with the intention that the person be deceived by the statement" (Bok, 1999, p. 17). According to this definition, a statement is not a lie if when you make it, you do not think that the other person will be deceived. For example, a classmate asks you whether you have studied for the forthcoming ethics class exam. You reply, "Yes, I have studied 60 straight hours without taking a break." Since you have no intention to deceive your friend because he or she will not believe you, under Bok's definition this is a false statement but not a lie.

Bok does not accept Kant's moral duty to always tell the truth. In determining whether it is permissible to lie, she developed the "principle of veracity," which establishes a strong presumption that lying is immoral. She discussed what it would be like to live in a world where there was no presumption of truthfulness. According to Bok, we benefit enormously by living in a world that condemns lying. She defended the principle in two steps:

first, each of us benefits from a system that we want others to do their part in maintaining, and second, a principle of reciprocity that requires each of us to do our part in maintaining the system of truth telling (Bok, 1999, p. 14).

According to Bok, her strong presumption against lying can be overcome. She developed a mechanical procedure for deciding whether or not the presumption has been overcome. First, there is an introspective part in which you must ask the following questions:

- Are there alternative statements that are true that could be used?
- What is the context of the lie, that is, the relationship between the liar and the person being lied to?
- What are the effects of the lie? Both the good and the bad?
- What are the arguments for and against telling the lie?
- What are the effects on the practice of veracity itself?
- When you weigh the considerations and decide on a conclusion, how would your conclusion and the reasons you made it impress other reasonable persons?

After considering the introspective part, you then need to see how an actual audience responds to your reflections. Would others agree with your conclusions? Your aim should be to arrive at a decision that would be accepted by a reasonable public. To Bok, the active part is a check on the introspective part. She noted, however, that in most cases the active part is impracticable to carry out, so you must fall back on your judgment as to how an actual audience would respond to your conclusions (Bok, 1999, pp. 14–15).

## Perjury by Law Enforcement Personnel

How prevalent is police perjury? Morgan Cloud (1994, p. 1311) stated,

> Police perjury is a "secret" in the obvious sense that the liar tries to keep the lie hidden from public knowledge. It is a "little secret," but not because it is unimportant either morally or practically. Police perjury is always ethically wrong, and often these lies are told about issues that are outcome determinative in the litigation. In a prosecution for drug possession, for example, if the drugs seized from the defendant are suppressed because the police violated the Fourth Amendment, the case is likely to be dismissed. If officers lie about their search and seizure methods to avoid exclusion of this evidence, and their lies are accepted by the court, this perjury has altered the outcome of the lawsuit.

Cloud noted that despite its ethical and practical importance, police perjury is aptly labeled a "little" secret because it is so poorly kept by the regular participants in the criminal justice system. According to him, judges,

prosecutors, defense lawyers, and repeat offenders all know that police officers lie under oath. Cloud noted that the empirical studies on the subject
suggest that perjured testimony is common, particularly in drug prosecutions. He stated that these studies indicate that police officers commit perjury
most often to avoid suppression of evidence and to fabricate probable cause,
knowing that judges "may 'wink' at obvious police perjury in order to admit
incriminating evidence." Cloud wondered if we should expect legal decision
makers to construct rules designed to discourage such official misconduct.
One anomaly of contemporary Fourth Amendment case law, according to
Cloud, is that judges have created interpretive rules permitting them to avoid
confronting the issue of police perjury when they rule on the constitutionality of searches and seizures. These rules create functional—if unintended—
incentives for law enforcers to lie.

Cloud contended that this does not mean that all police officers lie under
oath, or that most officers lie, or that even some officers lie all the time. But these
empirical studies, according to him, substantiate the subjective belief common
among lawyers, judges, and police officers that police perjury occurs—and frequently enough to be a significant problem for the justice system. As he noted,
it is impossible to determine how often it occurs or how often officers "get away
with it." Cloud noted that by their very nature, successful lies will remain unde-
tected, and it is expected that a perjurer conceal his or her crime.

Police officers have been prosecuted for perjury, and when convicted
they are punished. These cases, Cloud observed, are unusual, however, and
undoubtedly represent only a fraction of the cases in which perjury has
occurred. Reported cases involving claims of police perjury support this
conclusion. He also noted that penalties rarely are imposed on the officer or
the government, even where the perjury is clearly established.

Not only are penalties uncommon, but a mere discussion of the problem
rarely escapes the confines of the criminal justice system. Defendants and
their lawyers often are willing to accuse officers of lying, but these claims
typically receive little attention beyond the lawsuits in which the accusations
are made. Judges and prosecutors will discuss the existence of police perjury
candidly in relatively private settings, but rarely in public fora.

When ex-football great O. J. Simpson was tried for the murders of Nicole
Brown Simpson and Ronald Goldman, a detective testified under oath at
trial that the detective had not used a certain derogatory word in the past
decade. Tapes and assorted other witnesses made it clear that this statement
was not true. This proof of perjury, together with the defense's innuendo that
the detective had planted a glove smeared with Nicole's blood on Simpson's
property, damaged the prosecution's case and were probably key factors in
the jury finding Simpson not guilty.

In a 1968 study by Columbia law students, the students' goal was to
study the impact the *Mapp v. Ohio* case had on the investigation of narcotics

offenses. The *Mapp* case applied the exclusionary rule mandatory to state prosecutions. The study compared data for arrests from pre-*Mapp* and post-*Mapp* decisions. One interesting finding concerned police officer accounts of the location of narcotics seized during the course of an arrest. In the pre-*Mapp* period under study (1960–1961), narcotics were found on the arrestee in 34.7% of all narcotics arrests. After the *Mapp* decision, the figure dropped to 3% in 1961–1962. In addition prior to *Mapp* in 1960–1961, narcotics were reported to have been found after being discarded in close proximity to the arrestee in 16.8% of all arrests. After *Mapp*, in 1961–1962, that figure rose to 43.2%. Was the nearly threefold increase in the number of arrests based upon "discarded" narcotics the result of police officers tailoring their testimony or their police reports to comply with their understanding of what the law permitted after the *Mapp* decision? Note under *Mapp*, if the drugs have been discarded or abandoned, it is not a violation of the Fourth Amendment to seize them. No other rationale has surfaced that would explain the apparent behavioral changes by narcotics defendants (Chase, 2001).

In a study based upon a questionnaire sent to Chicago-area judges, public defenders, and prosecutors indicated that they believed that police officers prevaricated their testimony in an effort to avoid suppression of evidence. A majority of judges and public defenders felt that police officer perjury was a major factor in limiting the deterrent effect of the exclusionary rule. Eighty-one percent of respondents expressed their belief that the possibility that evidence would be suppressed caused police officers to change their testimony rather than their behavior during searches. Also 38% indicated that they believed supervising personnel in the police department "encouraged" police officer perjury, and 67% believed that the supervising personnel tolerated it. Nine of eleven judges, nine of fourteen prosecutors, and fourteen of fourteen public defenders held the opinion that judges sometimes fail to suppress evidence even when they know the searches were illegal (Chase, 2001).

A similar questionnaire was sent to law enforcement officers in Chicago. The officers were asked if they had ever heard of law enforcement personnel misrepresenting or failing to fully disclose information concerning a search or seizure to avoid having evidence suppressed. Of the responding officers, 17.4% acknowledged that this happened during in-court testimony, while 24.2% acknowledged that they knew of this happening in police reports. Some of the officers acknowledged having observed this phenomenon in excess of ten times. Several officers stated that they had observed it at least fifty times (Chase, 2001).

In March 2000, the Los Angeles Police Department's (LAPD's) Board of Inquiry (2000) issued a report titled "*Rampart Area Corruption Incident.*" The Rampart Division of the LAPD is the police patrol area that covers the communities to the west and northwest of downtown Los Angeles. The name is derived from Rampart Boulevard, one of the major streets in the Rampart's patrol area. The 2001 Hollywood film *"Training Day,"* which starred Academy Award–winner Denzel Washington and Ethan Hawke, followed a single day in the life of a young LAPD officer as he was subjected to a single-day evaluation by a highly decorated detective with the LAPD narcotics division to see if he had what it takes to be a "narc" (narcotics officer). The film takes place over a single, intense 24-hour period in Los Angeles. It was partly based on and heavily influenced by the Rampart Division unit and the surrounding scandal.

The report stated that the Rampart scandal was the worst scandal in the history of Los Angeles. The report found that L.A. police officers framed innocent individuals by planting evidence and committing perjury to gain convictions. The report concluded that: "Nothing is more inimical to the rule of law than police officers, sworn to uphold the law, flouting it and using their authority to convict innocent people. Innocent men and women pleaded guilty to crimes they did not commit and were convicted by juries because of the fabricated cases against them." The report concluded, also, that many individuals were subjected to excessive police force and suffered very serious injuries as a result.

The report found that the culture of the LAPD encouraged the misconduct and that the LAPD destroyed honest cops who questioned abuses and reported the misconduct. And the report concluded that in this culture, police lying was accepted. Examples of police actions that reflected upon the culture of the department include the following:

- A female police officer who called the police when she was physically abused by her husband, also an LAPD officer, was subjected to reprisals within the department, while her husband was retained and promoted.
- An officer who reported that a suspect was beaten was forced out of the department, and no action was taken against the cops who did the beating.
- An officer who filed a complaint against a fellow officer for excessive force was given the choice: file the complaint and get marked as an outsider or resign. She resigned. Nothing ever happened to the officer she accused of using excessive force.

As noted by Christopher Slobogin (1996), police perjury can cause systemic damages to the profession. For example, the loss of police credibility on the stand diminishes law enforcement's effectiveness in the streets. Most significantly, to the extent other actors, such as prosecutors and judges, are perceived to be ignoring or condoning police perjury, the loss of public trust may extend beyond law enforcement to the criminal justice system generally. Slobogin noted that both lying to convict the innocent and lying to convict the guilty deserve condemnation. Lying to convict the innocent according to him, is undoubtedly rejected by most police, as well as by others, as immoral and unjustifiable. In contrast, lying intended to convict the guilty—in particular, lying to evade the consequences of the exclusionary rule—is common and so accepted in some jurisdictions that the police themselves have come up with a name for it: "testilying." According to Slobogin (1996, p. 1044), testilying can occur at any stage of the criminal process, including trial, but it usually takes place during the investigative and pretrial stages, since it is most frequently an attempt to cover up illicit evidence gathering.

Alan Dershowitz, a noted defense attorney, stated that "almost all" police officers lie to convict the guilty. In one survey, defense attorneys, prosecutors, and judges estimated that police perjury at Fourth Amendment suppression hearings occurs in 20% to 50% of the cases. Jerome Skolnick, a veteran observer of the police, claimed that police perjury of this type was "systematic." Slobogin claimed that few knowledgeable persons are willing to say that police perjury about investigative matters is sporadic or rare, except perhaps the police (Slobogin, 1996, p. 1043).

Judge Milton Mollen (1994, p. 42), who led an investigation into corruption in the New York City Police Department, stated in the official report on New York City police corruption:

> Officers reported a litany of manufactured tales. For example, when officers unlawfully stop and search a vehicle because they believe it contains drugs or guns, officers will falsely claim in police reports and under oath that the car ran a red light (or committed some other traffic violation) and that they subsequently saw contraband in the car in plain view. To conceal an unlawful search of an individual who officers believe is carrying drugs or a gun, they will falsely assert that they saw a bulge in the person's pocket or saw drugs and money changing hands. To justify unlawfully entering an apartment where officers believe narcotics or cash can be found, they pretend to have information from an unidentified civilian informant or claim they saw the drugs in plain view after responding to the premises on a radio run. To arrest people they suspect are guilty of dealing drugs, they falsely assert that the defendants had drugs in their possession when, in fact, the drugs were found elsewhere where the officers had no lawful right to be.

Slobogin stated that the most obvious explanation for all of this lying is a desire to see the guilty brought to "justice." He noted that the police do not want a person they know to be a criminal to escape conviction simply because of a "technical" violation of the Constitution, a procedural formality, or a trivial "exculpatory" fact.

Jerome Skolnick (1982, p. 42) stated that an officer "lies because he is skeptical of a system that suppresses truth in the interest of the criminal."

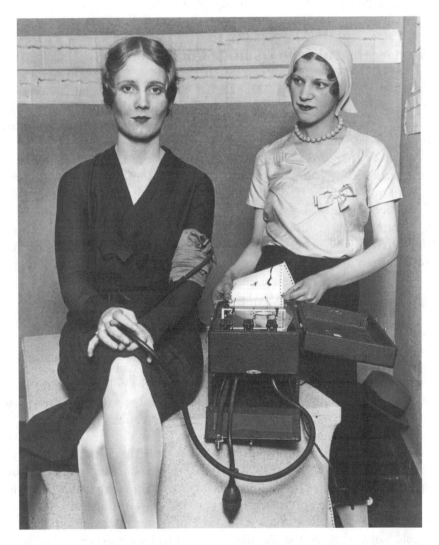

**Figure 7.1** This picture demonstrates the administration of a lie detector examination in Chicago, Illinois, on May 17, 1930. The polygraph in the picture was one of the first that recorded both blood pressure and galvanic skin response. It was invented in 1921 by Dr. John A. Larson of the University of California and first applied in law enforcement work by the Berkeley Police Department under its nationally renowned police chief August Vollmer. (Photo courtesy of U.S. Library of Congress.)

Skolnick contended that police perjury is "systematic" and that "police know that other police are perjuring themselves."

Should police officers be routinely required to take a polygraph test? While polygraphs have advanced significantly in the past 50 years, there are still concerns regarding their accuracy (see Figure 7.1).

## Lying by the Police to Obtain a Confession

In *Frazier v. Cupp* (1969, p. 739), the U.S. Supreme Court stated, "While a lie told to the detainee about an important aspect of the case may affect the voluntariness of the confession, the effect of the lie must be analyzed in the context of all the circumstances of the interrogation."

In the *Frazier* case, Frazier was arrested in connection with a murder and was questioned by police. He admitted being with his cousin Rawls on the night in question, but he denied being with any third person. In the midst of questioning, he was given his Miranda warnings, after which questioning became more vigorous. The officer questioning Frazier then told him, falsely, that Rawls had been brought in and had confessed. Shortly thereafter, Frazier began to confess and eventually he signed a written confession (pp. 737–738).

The Supreme Court rejected Frazier's claim that his confession was involuntary and should have been excluded from evidence. The Court noted the fact that a suspect was given warnings of his constitutional rights prior to making the incriminating statement is "quite relevant to a finding of voluntariness." The Court looked at the age, intelligence, maturity, and length of detention of Frazier and concluded, "The fact that the police misrepresented the statements that Rawls had made is, while relevant, insufficient in our view to make this otherwise voluntary confession inadmissible" (p. 739).

The *Miller v. Fenton* (1986) case involved the voluntariness of a confession made by Miller, a murder suspect. Miller was given his Miranda warnings and was then interrogated. The interrogating police officer employed an approach that involved befriending and sympathizing with Miller. In addition, at the beginning of the interrogation, the officer informed Miller that the victim was still alive, which was false. During the interrogation, the officer told Miller that she had just died, when in fact she had been found dead several hours earlier.

The appellate court concluded in the *Miller* opinion that the lie about the timing of the victim's death, by itself, did not constitute sufficient deception to overcome Miller's will. The court noted, that "because the officer never suggested that the time of the victim's death might be relevant in linking Miller to the crime, the only possible effect of his initial statement that she was alive, followed by his report that she had just died, would be an emotional response in Miller" (p. 601).

The court stated that "Manipulation and lies may play a part in the suspect's decision to confess, but so long as that decision is a product of the suspect's own balancing of competing considerations, the confession is voluntary." The court noted that the test was whether the detective's statements were the cause of Miller's confession or whether those statements were so manipulative or coercive that they deprived Miller of his ability to make an unconstrained, autonomous decision to confess. This test is known as the "voluntariness test." The court admitted the confession. The court held that the emotional response, if any, did not cause the confession to be involuntary. The court stated that a totality of circumstances test should be used to determine if the police deception produced a forced confession (p. 602).

## Using Lies to Obtain a Waiver of Miranda Rights

In determining whether a confession should be excluded because of lies and deception by the police, the courts use the "voluntariness test." The voluntariness test looks at whether or not the deception resulted in an involuntary confession. Under this test, a certain amount of trickery is allowed. As noted in *Jackson v. Litscher* (2002), under the voluntariness test the courts have struggled to distinguish "big lies" that would make a confession involuntary from "little lies," which are considered as harmless. The *Jackson* court also noted that deception by the police has created difficult decisions for courts and provides little guidance to police officers, who are often trained to use deceptive tactics in the interrogation room.

The courts have been uniform in prohibiting false and misleading statements to secure a waiver of the defendant's right to counsel under the Miranda rule (*United States v. Orso*, 2001). Thus, lies, tricks, or misleading statements may not be used to obtain a Miranda waiver. However, there are some cases that have allowed waivers that were induced by police lies concerned lies about the status of the evidence but not about the defendant's rights themselves (*Collazo v. Estelle*, 1991).

In *United States v. Velasquez* (1989, p. 1088), the appellate court held that a lie about a codefendant's statement concerning the crime did not invalidate a waiver. In *Shedelbower v. Estelle* (1989, pp. 572–574), the court held that a lie about the identification of the suspect by the victim did not render the waiver invalid.

In *Collazo v. Estelle* (1991, p. 471), the court held that a police statement, following a suspect's request to talk to a lawyer, that this was the "last chance to talk to us" and that it "might be worse for you" rendered the Miranda waiver and confession made by the defendant involuntary. In *United States v. Anderson* (1991, pp. 97–100), the federal appellate court held that an officer's statement that "this is the time to talk to us, because once you tell us you want an attorney we're not able to talk to you and as far as I am concerned, we probably would not go to the U.S. Attorney or anyone else to tell them how much you cooperated with us" was false and misleading and undermined the effect of the Miranda warnings.

## Counsel's Opinions Regarding whether the Police Are Lying

The Supreme Court noted in *United States v. Young* (1985, p. 6) that a defense counsel also has the same obligation as the prosecutor not to "misstate the evidence or mislead the jury as to the inferences it may draw."

In *Bates v. United States* (2000), a federal appellate court stated that a defense counsel may not call upon a jury to discount the testimony of the police officers because the police are "lying" and committing "perjury." The court stated that it was for the jury, not for counsel, to decide whether a witness is telling the truth. An attorney may not divert the jurors from this task by injecting his personal evaluation as to a witness' veracity.

## Civil Remedies for Perjury by Police Officers

*Should individuals harmed by a police officer's perjury in a criminal case be allowed to sue the officer for civil damages (money) in civil court?*

If a police officer commits perjury (false statement under oath), he or she generally may not be sued in civil court for damages. Supreme Court associate justice Thurgood Marshall stated his disapproval of this rule in his dissent in *Briscoe v. Lahue* (1983, p. 357): "I cannot agree that police officers are absolutely immune from civil liability for testimony given in criminal proceedings." In the *Briscoe* case, a suit for civil damages was filed against several police officers who allegedly had given perjured testimony during the course of criminal trial.

Justice Marshall noted that police officers and other government officials differ significantly from private citizens. A police officer comes to the witness stand clothed with the authority of the state. His official status gives him credibility and creates a far greater potential for harm than exists when the average citizen testifies. The situation is aggravated when the official draws on special expertise. A policeman testifying about fingerprint identification or a medical examiner testifying as to the cause of a death can have a critical impact on a defendant's trial. At the same time, the threat of a criminal perjury prosecution, which serves as an important constraint on the average witness' testimony, is virtually nonexistent in the police-witness context. Despite the apparent prevalence of police perjury, prosecutors exhibit extreme reluctance in charging police officials with criminal conduct because of their need to maintain close working relationships with law enforcement agencies. Justice Marshall concluded that the majority's decision forecloses a civil sanction in precisely those situations where the need is most pressing.

The Court's majority decision in *Briscoe* noted that the probable frequency of such suits would have likely imposed significant burdens on the judicial system and on law enforcement resources.

## Ethics Practicum

In which of the following situations should police be permitted to willfully make false statements?

1. The officer is questioning a suspect, and to induce a confession, the officer tells the suspect that she has proof that he committed the crime.
2. An officer tells a suspect that his friend has confessed and named him as the one who planned and carried out the murder.
3. The officer tells the suspect that if he confesses, the officer will ensure that the suspect does not go to jail.
4. The suspect is informed that unless she confesses, the police will also arrest her husband for the same offense.
5. The police officer makes a false statement in the arrest report, indicating that the vehicle was stopped because it appeared that the driver was drunk.
6. An officer testifies in court that the defendant admitted that he committed the murder.
7. An undercover officer tells a suspect that he needs to buy drugs for personal use.

## Ethics in Practice

### Criteria-Based Content Analysis

Matthias Gamer (2009), a psychologist at the University Medical Center Hamburg-Eppendorf in Germany, contended that finding out who is telling the truth does not require fancy machinery. According to Gamer, a criteria-based content analysis method may be used. The method relies on evaluating the retelling of an incident for a set of defined narrative features that hint at whether it is a true account. The method was developed based on a 2005 analysis by psychologist Albert Vrij of the University of Portsmouth in England. The method suggests that descriptions of actual experiences have the following properties that are generally not present in fabrications:

- Actual descriptions are coherent and consistent but not generally in chronological order.
- They contain a lot of detail and include unusual and superfluous elements.
- They depict personal interactions and reiterate speech and conversations.
- They describe feelings and thoughts.
- They contain spontaneous corrections and the admission of memory gaps and doubts about the believability of the story.

Gamer noted that some studies indicate that the error rate of this method may be as high as 30 percent.

Pair up with a friend who has not read the above material. Ask the friend to tell either an actual experience or a fabrication without telling you whether the material is an actual experience or a fabrication. Using the above guidelines, make an educated guess as to which it is.

## Excerpts from Actual Court Cases

Excerpts from actual court cases on police deception and lying are included in this section.

### *People v. Lawery* (43 Misc. 2d 1084, 1085– 1086, N.Y. City Crim. Ct. 1964)

*Is it legal for a police officer to pose as a gambler in order to get admitted to an apartment where an illegal poker game is being held?*

A police officer had obtained unverified information that an illegal card game was in progress in a private apartment. He proceeded to the apartment and knocked at the door. To the female defendant, who opened the door, he did not disclose his identity as a police officer. Instead, he gave her an assumed name and told her that a supposed mutual acquaintance had directed him to the apartment. The female defendant questioned the officer and then, apparently satisfied that he was "all right," admitted him. Once inside, the officer, after observing and participating in a card game, arrested the defendants and seized some playing cards.

The defendants have moved to suppress the evidence obtained by the officer in the apartment. The evidence comprises the officer's observations as well as the playing cards. The defendants argued that the officer did not enter the apartment with their consent because he did not tell them he was an officer. They contended that he was a trespasser and accordingly that the evidence was illegally obtained.

It is my view that the officer was not a trespasser when he obtained the evidence. That the officer did not make known his true identity before being admitted did not affect his status as an invitee. In this area of law enforcement neither precedent, public policy, nor logic bars the use of deception to gain peaceable entry into a private habitation. Indeed, it is a compelling circumstance that without resorting to such subterfuge, officers would find it virtually impossible to penetrate the facade of respectability that hides such activities as gambling, prostitution, A B C violations, and narcotics. This is so, of course, because these criminal operations are conducted behind closed doors, and if police officers could not conceal their identities to gain entrance, the burden of gathering evidence would have to be sustained by the uncertain efforts of reluctant civilians.

It may be pointed out, parenthetically, that a search warrant would have been useless here, since the criminal activity, illegal card playing, would have stopped the moment the officer announced his authority and purpose. All that the warrant would have reached was an innocent deck of playing cards.

It has been recognized that the police, in order to obtain evidence, must at times use artifice, stealth, and strategy. Of significance is the decision by the U.S. Supreme Court in *Lopez v. United States* where a police officer carrying a concealed recording device gained entrance to the defendant's private office by pretending to be amenable to the offer of a bribe. In that case, the Court found that the officer had not invaded the defendant's office, even though the officer had given a false reason for his presence there.

Directly in point is *People v. Nunn* (1964). There, the highest court of California upheld the conviction of a doctor who prescribed narcotics in his home as well as in his private office for a police officer posing as a narcotic addict.

The defendants were operating an illegal card game, open to anyone who could pass their screening test. The police officer evidently met the defendants' requirements for entrance into their apartment. They accepted him as a card player whose participation would enable them to cut into (take a share of) every hand played. Thus, it must be held that the officer was in the premises with the defendants' consent and that the challenged evidence was gathered without violating the defendants' constitutional rights. The motion to suppress the evidence is denied.

### *People v. Harrell* (2002 Cal. App. 2nd Dist.
### Unpub. LEXIS 8647, 6-8, 2002)

*Does deception by a police officer violate a defendant's due process rights?*

[Excerpts from the court's opinion. Harrell had claimed that lies by the undercover officer amounted to outrageous misconduct and violated his right to due process.]

Due process may require the dismissal of criminal charges when the police have engaged in sufficiently gross or outrageous misconduct relating to the defendant's case. This court has enumerated four factors relevant to determining whether the police have committed misconduct amounting to a violation of due process:

1. Whether the police manufactured a crime that otherwise would not likely have occurred or merely involved themselves in ongoing criminal behavior;
2. Whether the police themselves engaged in criminal or improper conduct repugnant to a sense of justice;
3. Whether the defendant's reluctance to commit the crime was overcome by appeals to humanitarian instincts such as sympathy or past friendship, by temptation of exorbitant gain, or by persistent solicitation in the face of unwillingness; and
4. Whether the record reveals simply a desire to obtain a conviction with no reading that the police motive is to prevent further crime or protect the populace.

These factors do not support a finding of outrageous conduct by the officers on the buy team. Though Officer Williams initially approached the defendant, the defendant took an active role in procuring drugs from a third party. Assuming that Williams approached defendant more than once and offered to buy him $10 worth of drugs before he agreed to get Williams a "twenty," this was neither an appeal to humanitarian instincts nor a promise of exorbitant gain. Williams broke no laws himself, and his conduct was not "repugnant to a sense of justice." Subterfuge is an element of any sting operation, but the danger posed by street dealers justifies a certain degree of deception by police officers who are attempting to make arrests before illegal substances are sold to the public. The police conduct in this case was not so overbearing as to infringe on the defendant's right to due process.

## Smithson v. State (275 Ga. App. 591, 594, 2005)

*Can an officer pose as an insurance agent in order to obtain permission to enter a home?*

*[Excerpts for court's opinion]*

Hall v. State stands for the proposition that there is nothing illegal in the use of deception by police officers in the obtaining of evidence for the purpose of criminal prosecutions. In that case, however, the officer posed as an insurance agent to gain entry to a home but revealed shortly thereafter that he was in possession of a valid search warrant. Here, at the time of the officer's search, no warrant had been obtained. The officer entered defendant's home with another person, who represented that the officer was a contractor with whom he was working. The officer testified that the sole reason for his entry into the home was to search for evidence of a crime. Without more, even probable cause to believe that a crime has been committed or is being committed does not authorize a warrantless search of one's dwelling. The court noted that if had held that consent which is the product of coercion or deceit on the part of the police is invalid. The court held that the officer's search of the home was illegal, but it did not invalidate the search warrant.

## United States v. Heath, 58 F.3d 1271, 1276, 8th Cir. Minn. 1995)

*The* United States v. Heath *decision points out problems that an appellate court has on appeal and there is a question as to whether the police lied.*

Heath was arrested for possession with intent to distribute crack cocaine. He was indicted by a federal grand jury. Heath filed a motion to suppress evidence and statements arising from entry into, and search of, his motel room by Hennepin County sheriff's deputies. Three hearings were held on the motion to suppress. Hennepin County sheriff's deputies Christopher Omodt and Chester Cooper testified at all three hearings, while Heath testified only at the last hearing.

*The deputies' testimony:* On September 3, 1993, Omodt received information from a confidential informant that a male staying in 114 at the Econo Lodge Motel in Minneapolis, Minnesota, was involved in drug trafficking. Omodt contacted Cooper to assist in the investigation.

When Cooper arrived at the motel, Omodt and Deputy Sheriff Erickson were speaking with a motel employee, who said the man renting room 114 had presented an Indiana driver's license with the name "Otis McDuffey" and registered under the same name. The man paid for the room with cash each day and extended his stay day by day. Another person had been paying cash for the numerous telephone calls made from the room.

The deputies decided to attempt a "knock and talk." There was no answer when the deputies knocked on the room door, so they returned to their cars. The deputies met with others and decided to conduct a surveillance of the motel. When Omodt observed a car pull into the parking lot near room 114 and two males exit the car, one carrying a shoe box, he and Cooper decided to try another "knock and talk" at the room. Cooper testified that a "knock and talk" is a casual conversation between the deputies and the target of an investigation, with no show of force.

When the deputies arrived at the room and knocked, the door was opened a crack. Heath answered the door and identified himself as "Otis McDuffey." The deputies identified themselves as law enforcement officers. Omodt told Heath that he was aware of possible drug activity in room 114 and asked if the deputies could come into the room. According to Omodt, Heath opened the door all the way and said, "Come on in."

Mark Wynn (not a party to the appeal) was also present in the room, sitting in a chair near a bed. Omodt told Heath and Wynn that they did not have to speak with the deputies or consent to any searches and that they were free to tell the deputies to leave at any time. Wynn nodded affirmatively; Heath replied that they did not have anything to hide and would speak with the deputies. Once again, Omodt told Wynn and Heath that he and Cooper were deputy sheriffs. Cooper reiterated the same warnings Omodt had given to Heath and Wynn earlier.

Cooper noticed Wynn attempt to slide a shoe box under a bed. Omodt asked if he could look inside the shoe box. Heath said the new shoes he was wearing came in the box, and consented to the search. Omodt opened the shoe box and found a substance the officers believed to be crack cocaine, rubber bands, packaging materials, a scale, a razor blade, and a quantity of U.S. currency.

At this point, Heath and Wynn were arrested and handcuffed. Three other deputies who had been standing in the hallway entered the room. After a pat-down search, Omodt took Wynn and Heath into the bathroom and informed each of his Miranda rights. Each stated he understood his rights and was willing to talk to Omodt.

Omodt made no threats or promises to either Heath or Wynn. Cooper was outside the partially open bathroom door. Although he did not hear the entire exchange between Omodt and Heath, Cooper heard the Miranda warnings and Heath's subsequent waiver. Omodt asked Heath for consent to search the motel room. Heath gave oral consent to do so. Heath also signed a Hennepin County sheriff's department consent to search form. After Heath signed the form, Cooper and the other deputies searched the room.

While searching the room, Cooper found two bags. In one of the bags, a pair of shorts was found which that contained a quantity of U.S.

currency. During a second pat-down search, more crack cocaine was discovered in Wynn's shirt pocket.

*Defendant Heath's testimony:* Heath's version of events is much different. Heath testified at the hearing on February 16, 1994, as follows. When Heath and Wynn returned to the motel on September 3, 1993, Heath did not carry a shoe box with him. When the deputies knocked on his room door, Heath stuck his head out to inquire who was at the door, and Omodt asked if he was "Otis." Heath replied that he was "Otis." Omodt asked if he was the occupant of the room, and Heath responded affirmatively. Then, the deputies identified themselves as law enforcement officers.

Omodt asked Heath what was in the shoe box, and Heath replied that the box was empty. Omodt told Heath that he had reason to believe someone was selling narcotics from the room, and Heath asked how Omodt had made such a determination. Omodt replied that a lot of phone calls had been made from the room, and he had "probable cause" to believe drugs were being sold from the room. Heath asked if a large number of calls constituted "probable cause," and Omodt answered "Yes." Cooper told Heath the deputies wanted to go home to their wives, it was near the holiday weekend, and they were tired. Cooper stated they needed to check things out and report to their boss that everything was all right. At this point, Omodt's voice turned harsh, and he told Heath "If you don't let me in, I am going to get a f...... search warrant and tear your room apart." Heath then let go of the door and pulled back his head. Because of the way Omodt was acting, Heath feared Omodt would grab him. Then Omodt pushed open the door, and he and Cooper entered the room.

Once in the room, the deputies did not tell Heath he had a right to refuse their entry, to refuse to talk to them, or to refuse consent to a search. Omodt presented Heath with a piece of paper that he demanded Heath sign. Omodt told Heath that the paper said the deputies could search his room, but Heath was not allowed to read the paper. Heath did not know he could tell the officers to leave. Heath testified that in Jamaica, where he grew up, it was not a good idea to resist police officers, and it was best to comply with their demands. Heath signed the consent form using the name "Otis McDuffey."

Omodt again asked what was in the shoe box. Heath said nothing, and Omodt opened the box. Then Heath and Wynn were placed under arrest. Cooper called for other deputies to enter the room. A report came across a deputy's radio that an African American male had just pulled up in a black Cadillac. Omodt asked if Heath knew who this was and threatened to make a report to the judge if Heath did not cooperate. Cooper then stated that the deputies would protect themselves if the man came into the room, but he did not know if they would be able to protect Heath and Wynn.

*The deputies' rebuttal testimony:* Deputies Omodt and Cooper testified in rebuttal to Heath's testimony. Omodt and Cooper testified consistently with their prior testimony and contradicted Heath's testimony that they used coercive tactics to gain entry into the motel room and search it and the shoe box without Heath's consent. The deputies testified that (1) they did not use the phrase "probable cause" during their initial encounter with Heath, (2) Heath gave them oral and written consent to enter the room and search it and the shoe box, (3) Heath was advised of his rights at least twice, (4) Heath was not threatened, and (5) they did not threaten to decline protection of Heath and Wynn from a third party. Both deputies expressly denied that Omodt said, "If you don't let me in, I will get a f......search warrant and tear your room apart."

*District court's findings:* The district court adopted the magistrate judge's finding discrediting Heath's testimony and crediting that of the deputies. Based upon those credibility findings, the district court concluded that Heath voluntarily consented to the deputies' entry into the motel room and to the search of it and the shoe box. Accordingly, the district court denied Heath's motion to suppress.

The district court discredited Heath's testimony because (1) he lied to the deputies about his identity; (2) it was incredible that "Heath would challenge Omodt's claim that he had probable cause to believe drugs were being sold there prior to the sheriffs' entry into the room, but then become too timid to ask questions or resist signing a document he knew to be a consent to search form"; and (3) while Heath testified that he did not carry the shoe box with him from the car on September 3, 1993, and asserted the shoe box had been in the motel room since September 1, 1993, he also testified that one of the first questions Omodt asked when Heath opened the door only enough to stick his head out was about the shoe box.

*Discussion by appellate court:* Heath argued the district court erred in finding that he voluntarily consented to the deputies' entrance into the motel room and to their subsequent search of it and the shoe box. Heath contended that the district court's credibility determination, on which its finding of consent to search is based, is erroneous and not supported by the record.

The determination is erroneous, Heath argued, because the deputies' testimony was incredible and inconsistent. Heath contended it would be incredible that he would willingly agree to let the police search the shoe box when he knew crack cocaine was inside. In support of his argument, Heath cited his testimony regarding the coercive tactics used by Omodt to gain entry to the room. We note, however, that Heath did not cite any evidence other than his testimony to challenge the deputies' version of events.

Heath also noted that he has an eleventh-grade education and is a foreign national and argued that the entire nature of the deputies' confrontation with him had an inherently coercive effect.

Heath further argued that the determination is not supported by the record because the facts on the record are unclear as to whether he knew why the deputies were knocking on the room door, whether he voluntarily consented to their entrance into the room, whether he consented to the search that followed, and whether the search was conducted prior to or after he signed the consent to search form.

The government contended that the only issue before this court is the credibility determination of the district court, which the government asserted is virtually unreviewable on appeal. In the alternative, the government argued that the search of the motel room was a valid search incident to arrest.

*Credibility determination:* We must affirm the district court's denial of the motion to suppress unless it is not supported by substantial evidence on the record; it reflects an erroneous view of the applicable law; or upon review of the entire record, we are left with the definite and firm conviction that a mistake has been made.

A district court's determination as to the credibility of a witness is virtually unreviewable on appeal. The assessment of a witness's credibility is the province of the trial court. A district court's decision to credit a witness's testimony over that of another can almost never be a clear error unless there is extrinsic evidence that contradicts the witness's story or the story is so internally inconsistent or implausible on its face that a reasonable fact-finder would not credit it.

We have considered the district court's credibility determination and, applying the deferential standard for reviewing such a determination, conclude that clear error was not committed. The district court was faced with two different versions of the events and chose to credit the deputies' version. There was no extrinsic evidence to contradict the deputies' story other than Heath's own testimony. Further, while the deputies might have made some inconsistent statements, their stories were not so internally inconsistent or implausible that a reasonable fact-finder would not credit their testimony.

*Consent to enter and search:* A search based upon an individual's consent may be undertaken by law enforcement agents without a warrant or probable cause, and any evidence discovered during the search may be seized and admitted at trial. To justify a consensual search, the prosecution has the burden of proving that an individual voluntarily consented to the search.

A district court's finding that an individual voluntarily consented to a search by law enforcement agents is reviewed for clear error on appeal.

Examining the totality of the circumstances, we conclude the district court's determination that Heath voluntarily consented to the deputies' entry into the room and their search of the room and the shoe box was not clearly erroneous. The deputies testified that prior to their entry into the room, Heath was told they were investigating possible drug activity; he was advised of his Miranda rights at least twice; he was not threatened; and he gave the deputies oral permission to enter the room, search it and the shoe box. Heath conceded he signed the consent form after Omodt told him it would permit the deputies to search the room. Moreover, the deputies testified Heath signed the consent to search form without threats or coercion.

*Conclusion:* For the foregoing reasons, we are not left with the definite and firm conviction that a mistake was made by the district court in its finding of consent to search. Therefore, we conclude Heath's motion to suppress was properly denied. We need not reach the government's alternative argument that the search of the motel room was a valid search incident to arrest. Accordingly, we affirm the judgment of the district court.

*McMillian, circuit judge, concurring specially:* I concur only because it is not the province of the appeals court to make credibility assessments. The police officers' saccharine account of the events of September 3, 1993, ironically leaves a bitter aftertaste. Rarely, if ever, have I encountered a case in which the police conduct was so mild-mannered and the suspect so acquiescent. The "fact" that Heath would so willingly consent to the search of his motel room and, more specifically, the shoe box, which he knew contained drugs and drug paraphernalia, is surprising, to say the least.

---

### Civil Service Charges and Specifications v. Hunt
### (Ohio App. LEXIS 103, Ohio Ct. App., 1993)

Former police officer Terry Hunt appealed from a judgment of the Montgomery County Court of Common Pleas that affirmed the police chief's decision to discharge Hunt from his position as a police officer. Hunt was discharged from his position as a police officer following an investigation by the Department of Internal Affairs into allegations that certain police officers had used excessive force while interrogating David Greer during a drug raid on January 12, 1990.

On January 12, 1990, Hunt was one of two uniformed police officers who, along with members of a drug unit task force, participated in the execution of a search warrant at 3308 McCall Street in Dayton, Ohio. Greer was one of four occupants of the house.

During the search, the police found guns, drugs, and money in the house. According to Hunt's version of the incident, after he entered the premises, he proceeded upstairs to search for drugs. While upstairs, Hunt observed Greer lying on a mattress with his hands handcuffed behind his back. Officers Norton and Gamble were also in the room. According to Hunt, Gamble was facing Greer and had his back to Hunt who was standing in the doorway. Hunt saw Gamble drop an object, later identified as a clothes iron, either onto the mattress or Greer's stomach. Hunt stated that he could not see whether the iron had hit the mattress or Greer. Hunt remarked that it was a good thing that the iron was not on. Hunt then observed Gamble plug the iron in and turn it on. Hunt yelled at Gamble to stop and told him that he "couldn't do that." According to Hunt, Gamble stopped. Hunt then left the room, believing that he had prevented Gamble from using the iron on Greer. Greer remained handcuffed on the bed in the presence of Norton and Gamble. Hunt testified that he did not hear any screams or shouts after he left the room. Hunt did not tell his superior officer about the incident.

Greer's version of the incident differed somewhat from that of Hunt's. According to Greer, Hunt escorted him upstairs to the rear bedroom. Officers Gamble and Norton were already in the bedroom. Greer stated that Norton slapped him in the back of the head and he fell on the bed, landing on his stomach. When Greer rolled over onto his back, Norton grabbed his face and starting asking him questions concerning the drugs that had been found in the house. Greer claimed that Norton held his left arm down and Hunt held his right arm down while Gamble applied the iron to his chest and stomach several times. The burning stopped when Greer cooperated and answered their questions.

Greer was arrested that night. He did not request medical treatment nor did he inform any of the officers at the jail that he had been burned. On January 24, 1990, Greer was interviewed by Sergeant Ron Wright of the Department of Internal Affairs ("Internal Affairs"). According to Wright, Internal Affairs became involved after receiving a phone call from Greer's mother in Detroit. Mrs. Greer notified the police that Greer had been burned with an iron during the drug raid on January 12, 1990. During the interview, Wright observed what appeared to be iron burns on Greer's chest and stomach.

It was undisputed that in late February of 1990, Hunt's superior officer, Sergeant McCume, informed him that Internal Affairs was investigating allegations that Greer had been burned. Hunt admitted that he still did not inform McCume as to his observations on January 12, 1990. According to Hunt, he was under no obligation to disclose what he had seen because his superior officer informed him of the allegation of the use of force. Hunt stated at the November 16, 1990, hearing that it was his understanding that he only had to inform his superior of the use of force when the superior was not aware of it. Hunt testified that his policy obligation was fulfilled because his superior informed him of the use of force.

On April 5, 1990, Hunt was interviewed by Wright regarding Greer's allegations that he had been burned three times with an iron during the interrogation on January 12, 1990. During the interview, Hunt was asked if he knew anything about Greer's burns. Hunt denied any knowledge. He was asked if he had seen an iron and ironing board in the room. Hunt stated that he could not remember seeing them.

Hunt was again interviewed by Internal Affairs on April 25, 1990. He was questioned again concerning his knowledge of Greer's burns. Hunt stated that remembered seeing the iron and the ironing board but he deliberately withheld the information that he had seen Gamble with the iron.

On June 7, 1990, Hunt voluntarily came forward to Internal Affairs. He admitted that he had lied during the April 25, 1990, interview with Internal Affairs when he stated that he could not remember seeing an iron and ironing board in the bedroom. He told Wright that he had seen Gamble drop the iron, pick it up, plug it in and turn it on. He told Wright that he had yelled at Gamble to stop and that he thought that he had stopped Gamble from burning Greer. He also told Wright that he had not reported the incident because he had not actually witnessed the use of force nor had he heard any screams indicating that Greer had been burned or injured after he, Hunt, had left the room.

On June 22, 1990, Hunt was charged with failing to report the use of force to his superior officer, and with lying to Internal Affairs during the April 5, 1990 interview. On July 2, 1990, Terry Pearson, Hunt's F.O.P. representative, met with Police Chief Newby and Lieutenant John Krug, the department advocate and commander of Internal Affairs, to discuss the possible penalty Hunt faced. On July 11, 1990, Hunt appeared before Police Chief Newby and pleaded no contest to the charges. On July 19, 1990, Hunt was found guilty of the charges and specifications and discharged from his position as police officer, effective July 20, 1990.

Hunt appealed his discharge to the board. Four hearings were held between September 7, 1990, and March 25, 1991. The board affirmed the dismissal. Two members voted to affirm, and one dissented. Hunt appealed the board's decision to the Montgomery County Court of Common Pleas. The trial court affirmed. Hunt appealed the trial court's judgment affirming the board's decision affirming Chief Newby's decision to discharge him.

*Decision of the court:* "We are unpersuaded by Hunt's argument that he was not guilty of failing to report the use of force because he did not actually see Gamble burn Greer with the iron." Hunt admitted that he saw Gamble drop the iron onto or near Greer. He also admitted that he saw Gamble turn the iron on, apparently in preparation for burning

Greer with it. While Hunt also testified that he thought he had stopped Gamble from using the iron on Greer, it is undisputed that Hunt left Greer in the room with Gamble and Norton less than a minute after Hunt told Gamble not to use the iron on Greer. Given that Hunt saw Gamble drop the iron onto or near Greer, and that Hunt subsequently learned of Greer's allegations, the trial court could have reasonably concluded that Hunt was on notice of the use of force which he was required to report to his superior officer.

Finally, the trial court could have reasonably concluded that Hunt's discharge was not disproportionate to the punishment meted out to other officers guilty of similar violations. In support of his contention that he was unfairly disciplined, Hunt directed our attention to fifteen other cases involving officers who lied to Internal Affairs, but nonetheless were not discharged. However, none of these cases involved an officer who had used force against a citizen and then lied about the incident to Internal Affairs. The one documented case in which an officer had used force and then lied about it resulted in the officer's discharge. The judgment of the trial court was affirmed.

## Questions in Review

1. What lies should a police officer be allowed to use when questioning a suspect?
2. Is it ever permissible to lie under oath?
3. How is lying to convict a guilty person similar to noble cause, as discussed in Chapter 3?
4. What restrictions regarding false statements should be placed on undercover police officers?
5. Does Circuit Judge McMillian indicate in his concurring opinion in United States v. Heath indicate that he believes that the police officers were lying on the stand? If so, why wouldn't he vote to reverse the case?

# Prejudice and Discrimination

# 8

## Introduction

> Everyone is a prisoner of his own experiences. No one can eliminate prejudices—just recognize them. (Edward R. Murrow, December 31, 1955)

Why is a chapter of prejudice and discrimination included in a text on ethics in policing? Most ethics textbook authors do not include this subject in their text. Our approach is that wrongful discrimination and prejudice are two of the most unethical types of behavior in today's world.

A common tool used to simplify and make sense of a complicated world is by dividing people and things into classes. The division reduces the amount of information that we need to collect, maintain, and consider. It is a fallacy to believe that classification itself, or discrimination, is inherently undesirable. For example, if the local police are trying to identify and arrest a child molester, the police will use classifications to reduce the number of possible offenders. First, they will eliminate females, then eliminate certain age groups, and next use other factors to further reduce the list of possible suspects. This is a form of discrimination.

The term "*discrimination*" is often used to indicate an unjust or unfavorable treatment of an identifiable group. Most types of classifications are a form of discrimination. Some forms of classification are necessary. As responsible citizens, we want to be able to discriminate between capable and incapable, safe and dangerous, polite and rude, even perhaps good and evil. But classifications that are based on arbitrary or illegal factors are not necessary. But such simplifications may be intellectually lazy, and often they sometimes result in gross injustice.

Classification of people is not only necessary, but is also a useful and acceptable procedure. When the police chief is deciding who to promote to lieutenant, she may discriminate against those officers who have demonstrated a lack of management skills as well as those officers who tend to be overly aggressive in dealing with suspects. This is a form of discrimination. Accordingly, when we discuss the evils of discrimination, what we are generally referring to are those discriminations that are either illegal or unethical.

137

## Speaking of Race

According to a study by Siri Carpenter (2009), people who avoid mentioning race appear more prejudiced than people who mention it. Carpenter contended that white people often avoid mentioning race because they fear that even noticing skin color might somehow make them appear racist. She cited two new studies by psychologists at Tufts and Harvard universities that indicate that such blindness may actually work in the opposite way.

In one test described by Carpenter, white participants studied a batch of photographs, then tried to deduce, as quickly as possible, which one of the pictures a black partner was holding by asking questions about each one in succession. Asking whether the person in the picture was black or white would have sped up the selection process, yet that question was rarely asked. Black observers who observed the test perceived the whites who avoided asking about skin color as more prejudiced than the few who asked about skin color. Other black observers who watched only silent video clips of the interactions even rated the whites who avoided mentioning race as having more unfriendly nonverbal behavior.

# Overview of Federal Laws on Discrimination

## The Major Federal Laws Prohibiting Job Discrimination

- Title VII of the Civil Rights Act of 1964 (Title VII), which prohibits employment discrimination based on race, color, religion, sex, or national origin;
- the Equal Pay Act of 1963 (EPA), which protects men and women who perform substantially equal work in the same establishment from sex-based wage discrimination;
- the Age Discrimination in Employment Act of 1967 (ADEA), which protects individuals who are 40 years of age or older;
- Title I and Title V of the Americans with Disabilities Act of 1990 (ADA), which prohibit employment discrimination against qualified individuals with disabilities in the private sector and in state and local governments;
- Sections 501 and 505 of the Rehabilitation Act of 1973, which prohibit discrimination against qualified individuals with disabilities who work in the federal government; and
- the Civil Rights Act of 1991, which, among other things, provides monetary damages in cases of intentional employment discrimination.

Under Title VII of the Civil Rights Act of 1964, the Americans with Disabilities Act (ADA), and the Age Discrimination in Employment

Act (ADEA), it is illegal to discriminate in any aspect of employment, including

- hiring and firing;
- compensation, assignment, or classification of employees;
- transfer, promotion, layoff, or recall;
- job advertisements;
- recruitment;
- testing;
- use of company facilities;
- training and apprenticeship programs;
- fringe benefits;
- pay, retirement plans, and disability leave; and
- other terms and conditions of employment.

Illegal discriminatory practices under these laws also include

- harassment on the basis of race, color, religion, sex, national origin, disability, or age;
- retaliation against an individual for filing a charge of discrimination, participating in an investigation, or opposing discriminatory practices;
- employment decisions based on stereotypes or assumptions about the abilities, traits, or performance of individuals of a certain sex, race, age, religion, or ethnic group or individuals with disabilities; and
- denying employment opportunities to a person because of marriage to, or association with, an individual of a particular race, religion, national origin, or an individual with a disability. Title VII also prohibits discrimination because of participation in schools or places of worship associated with a particular racial, ethnic, or religious group.

## Other Discriminatory Practices under Federal Equal Employment Opportunity (EEO) Laws

Title VII prohibits not only intentional discrimination but also practices that have the effect of discriminating against individuals because of their race, color, national origin, religion, or sex.

## Age Discrimination in Employment Act (ADEA)

The ADEA's broad ban against age discrimination also specifically prohibits the following:

- Statements or specifications in job notices or advertisements of age preference and limitations. An age limit may only be specified in the rare circumstance when age has been proved to be a bona fide occupational qualification (BFOQ).
- Discrimination on the basis of age by apprenticeship programs, including joint labor-management apprenticeship programs.
- Denial of benefits to older employees. An employer may reduce benefits based on age only if the cost of providing the reduced benefits to older workers is the same as the cost of providing benefits to younger workers.

## Equal Pay Act (EPA)

The Equal Pay Act (EPA) prohibits discrimination on the basis of sex in the payment of wages or benefits, where men and women perform work of similar skill, effort, and responsibility for the same employer under similar working conditions. Note the following:

- Employers may not reduce wages of either sex to equalize pay between men and women.
- A violation of the EPA may occur when a different wage is paid to a person who worked in the same job before or after an employee of the opposite sex.
- A violation may also occur when a labor union causes the employer to violate the law.

## The Civil Rights Act of 1991

The Civil Rights Act of 1991 made major changes in the federal laws against employment discrimination enforced by the Equal Employment Opportunity Commission (EEOC). Enacted in part to reverse several Supreme Court decisions that limited the rights of persons protected by these laws, the act also provides additional protections. The act authorizes compensatory and punitive damages in cases of intentional discrimination and provides for obtaining attorneys' fees and the possibility of jury trials. It also directs the EEOC to expand its technical assistance and outreach activities.

## Illegal Discrimination

Title VII of the Civil Rights Act of 1964, as amended, prohibits employment discrimination based on race, color, religion, sex, and national origin. Prior to 1972, the act applied only to private employers. The Equal Employment

Opportunity Act of 1972, however, amended Title VII to expand its coverage to employees of state and local governments as well as to employees of the federal government. Accordingly, since 1972, the act prohibits employment discrimination by law enforcement agencies.

## Scope of the Act

Title VII makes it an unlawful practice for an employer, including a police department, to fail or refuse to hire or to discharge a person or to discriminate against any individual with respect to the terms of employment including compensation, conditions of employment, or privileges of employment because of such person's race, color, religion, sex, or national origin (protected classes). It is also an unlawful practice to limit, segregate, or classify an employee or applicant because of those factors.

In 1978, the act was amended to make it clear that basis of sex includes discrimination on the basis of pregnancy or childbirth. Basis of sex, however, refers to gender, not sexual activity. Sexual activity is controlled under other statutes.

As noted earlier, it is not unlawful to distinguish between employees based on a bona fide seniority or merit system. In addition, employees can be paid differently based on measures of quality or quantity of production, professionally developed tests, or because the employees work in different locations, if the differences are not caused by intent to discriminate against a protected class. For example, it is permissible to provide officers who work in one section of the community higher pay than other officers if there is a logical reason, e.g., degree of danger involved. It would be an unlawful employment practice, however, to provide pay incentives to those officers assigned to a SWAT team, and then not allow females the opportunity to be assigned to the team.

## Title VII Suits

Suits against a law enforcement agency for unlawful employment practices may be brought in either state or federal court in the court district where the unlawful practice occurred, where the officer or employee would have worked except for the unlawful act, where the administrative records of the agency are kept, or, if no other place, within the court district of the agency's headquarters.

Only a person who has been the object of discrimination may bring a Title VII suit. In cases involving nonpublic employees, the EEOC may bring suit on behalf of an individual or as a representative of a class. The EEOC cannot sue a state government or political subdivision thereof. In the latter cases, only the individual aggrieved or the attorney general of the United States may bring suit under Title VII. Note that in many states, the state attorney general may also bring an employment discrimination suit under a state act.

## Table 8.1.  Poster on equal employment opportunities that is required to be posted at places of employment.

### Equal Employment Opportunity Is THE LAW

**Employers Holding Federal Contracts or Subcontracts**

Applicants to and employees of companies with a Federal government contract or subcontract are protected under the following Federal authorities:

**Race, Color, Religion, Sex, National Origin**

Executive Order 11246, as amended, prohibits job discrimination on the basis of race, color, religion, sex, or national origin and requires affirmative action to ensure equality of opportunity in all aspects of employment.

**Individuals with Disabilities**

Section 503 of the Rehabilitation Act of 1973, as amended, prohibits job discrimination because of disability and requires affirmative action to employ and advance in employment-qualified individuals with disabilities who, with reasonable accommodation, can perform the essential functions of a job.

**Vietnam Era, Special Disabled, Recently Separated, and Other Protected Veterans**

The Vietnam Era Veterans' Readjustment Assistance Act of 1974, as amended, 38 U.S.C. 4212, prohibits job discrimination and requires affirmative action to employ and advance in employment qualified Vietnam era veterans, qualified special disabled veterans, recently separated veterans, and other protected veterans. A recently separated veteran is any veteran during the three-year period beginning on the date of such veteran's discharge or release from active duty in the U.S. military, ground, naval, or air service.

**Retaliation**

Retaliation is prohibited against a person who files a charge of discrimination, participates in a discrimination proceeding, or otherwise opposes discrimination under these Federal laws.

Any person who believes a contractor has violated its nondiscrimination or affirmative action obligations under the authorities above should contact immediately:

The Office of Federal Contract Compliance Programs (OFCCP), Employment Standards Administration, U.S. Department of Labor, 200 Constitution Avenue, N.W., Washington, DC 20210, (202) 693-0101 or call an OFCCP regional or district office listed in most telephone directories under U.S. Government, Department of Labor. For individuals with hearing impairment, OFCCP's TTY number is (202) 693-1337.

**Private Employment, State and Local Governments, Educational Institutions, Employment Agencies, and Labor Organizations**

Applicants to and employees of most private employers, state and local governments, educational institutions, employment agencies, and labor organizations are protected under the following Federal laws:

**Race, Color, Religion, Sex, National Origin**

Title VII of the Civil Rights Act of 1964, as amended, prohibits discrimination in hiring, promotion, discharge, pay, fringe benefits, job training, classification, referral, and other aspects of employment on the basis of race, color, religion, sex (including pregnancy and sexual harassment), or national origin. Religious discrimination includes failing to reasonably accommodate an employee's religious practices where the accommodation does not impose undue hardship.

**Disability**

Title I and Title V of the Americans with Disabilities Act of 1990 (ADA), as amended, protect qualified applicants and employees with disabilities from discrimination in hiring, promotion, discharge, pay, job training, fringe benefits, classification, referral, and other aspects of employment on the basis of disability.

The law also requires that covered entities provide qualified applicants and employees with disabilities with reasonable accommodations, unless such accommodations would impose an undue hardship on the employer.

**Age**

The Age Discrimination in Employment Act of 1967, as amended, protects applicants and employees forty years of age or older from discrimination on the basis of age in hiring, promotion, discharge, compensation, terms, conditions, or privileges of employment.

**Sex (Wages)**

In addition to sex discrimination prohibited by Title VII of the Civil Rights Act of 1964, as amended, the Equal Pay Act of 1963, as amended, prohibits sex discrimination in payment of wages to women and men performing substantially equal work in jobs that require equal skill, effort, and responsibility under similar working conditions in the same establishment.

**Retaliation**

Retaliation is prohibited against a person who files a charge of discrimination, participates in an OFCCP proceeding, or otherwise opposes discrimination under these Federal laws.

If you believe that you have been discriminated against under any of the above laws, and to ensure that you meet strict procedural timelines to preserve the ability of EEOC to investigate your complaint and to protect your right to file a private lawsuit, you should immediately contact:

The U.S. Equal Employment Opportunity Commission (EEOC), Washington, DC 20507 or an EEOC field office by calling toll free 1-800-669-4000. For individuals with hearing impairments, EEOC's toll free TTY number is 1-800-669-6820.

**Programs or Activities Receiving Federal Financial Assistance**

Race, Color, Sex, National Origin

In addition to the protection of Title VII of the Civil Rights Act of 1964, as amended, Title VI of the Civil Rights Act prohibits discrimination on the basis of race, color, or national origin in programs or activities receiving Federal financial assistance. Employment discrimination is covered by Title VI if the primary objective of the financial assistance is provision of employment or where employment discrimination causes or may cause discrimination in providing services under such programs.

Title IX of the Education Amendments of 1972 prohibits employment discrimination on the basis of sex in educational programs or activities that receive Federal assistance.

**Individuals with Disabilities**

Section, 504 of the Rehabilitation Act of 1973, as amended, prohibits employment discrimination on the basis of disability in any program or activity that receives Federal financial assistance in the federal government, public or private agency. Discrimination is prohibited in all aspects of employment against persons with disabilities who, with or without reasonable accommodation, can perform the essential functions of a job.

If you believe you have been discriminated against in a program of any institution that receives Federal assistance, you should contact immediately the Federal agency providing such assistance.

*Note. Poster courtesy of the Equal Employment Opportunity Commission (EEOC). Publication OFCCP 1420. Revised August 2008.*

## Types of Violations under Title VII

Prohibited practices under Title VII generally fall into one of three classes: disparate treatment, retaliation, and disparate impact. Each of these is discussed more in detail in this chapter. In addition, religious discrimination and affirmative action's programs are also addressed.

## Disparate Treatment

A disparate violation occurs when the employee is treated less favorably than his or her peers because of race, sex, and so on. For example, there would be illegal disparate treatment if during a layoff of police personnel, the criteria used to select the officers to be laid off were based on race or another protected classification. Disparate treatment requires intent to discriminate. Intent has been inferred, however, in cases involving subconscious sex stereotyping. For example, disparate treatment was found in one case where a female was not promoted because she did not dress "like a woman should."

One form of disparate treatment is the "pattern and practice" form. This is the case when a department has systematically engaged in disparate treatment of a specific race, sex, and so forth. In these situations, the disparate treatment is a standard operating practice.

## Retaliation

Retaliation, like disparate treatment situations, is based on intentional discrimination. In this case, the complaining individual alleges that he or she engaged in a statutorily protected activity and as the result suffered an adverse employment action. The adverse employment action must be made with a retaliatory motive. The retaliatory motive, however, does not need to be the sole cause of the adverse employment action. For example, if a marginal police officer was fired because the officer attempted to organize a police union within the department, the officer is the victim of an unlawful retaliation. Note: one court allowed a former police officer to sue a police department because he was given an adverse employment reference. The court found that the adverse reference was primarily based on the fact that the officer was actively involved in union activities while a member of the police department.

## Constructive Discharge

In constructive discharge cases, the individuals claim that their employers intentionally made their working conditions so intolerable that they were forced to quit or resign. Several cases have held that to constitute a constructive discharge, there must be a denial of an individual's reasonable expectation for working conditions, benefits, or future promotions.

## Disparate Impact

Disparate impact claims are those that involve a facially neutral test, requirement, or practice that affects a protected group more than others and cannot be justified by business necessity. Note the discrimination in these situations may be unintentional. For example, if a police department required all cadet applicants to be capable of lifting 250 pounds, the lifting requirement may unfairly eliminate more females than males. Accordingly, the lifting requirement would be subject to disparate impact claims unless the department can establish that it is a bona fide job requirement.

## Religious Discrimination

Title VII in prohibiting religious discrimination defined *religion* as:

> The term "religion" includes all aspects of religious observance and practice, as well as belief, unless an employer demonstrates that he is unable to reasonably accommodate to an employee's or prospective employee's religious observance or practice without undue hardship on the conduct of the employer's business.

The movie *"Chariots of Fire"* concerned a track star who refused to compete in a race on a Sunday because of his religious beliefs. Accommodations were made for this athlete. If a police officer has religious problems regarding working on Wednesdays, is the police department required to make accommodations for him or her? Would it matter if the police officer were a ten-year veteran or only an applicant for employment?

The U.S. Supreme Court has held that Title VII requires an employer to make only those accommodations to an employee's religious belief or practices that do not impose more than a *de minimis* cost to the employer.

## Affirmative Action Programs

Affirmative action programs are programs that are designed to give minorities a preference based on the concept that affirmative action is needed to remedy the continuing effects of past discriminatory practices. There are possible legal problems with affirmative action programs that discriminate in favor of minorities. Any time that one protected class is given preference over another, a police department is taking a chance. The present trend by police departments is to obtain court approval before establishing affirmative action programs.

In order to establish a prima facie case of illegal employment discrimination, a plaintiff must prove that he or she suffered an adverse employment action. An employee faced with a threatened employment action does not suffer a cognizable injury from an action that does not occur. Threats do not rise to the level of an adverse employment action because they result in no materially adverse consequences or objectively tangible harm.

## Title VII Prelitigation Requirement

Before filing a lawsuit under Title VII of the Civil Rights Act of 1964, a plaintiff must exhaust their administrative remedies. The first step that a federal employee must take to exhaust their administrative remedies is to initiate a timely contact with an equal employment opportunity counselor to arrange for informal counseling regarding the matter or matters alleged to be discriminatory.

# Racial Discrimination

I say to you quite frankly that the time for racial discrimination is over. (Former President Jimmy Carter, 2005, as reported by Brinkley, 2005, p. 78)

42 U.S. Code § 1982 provides property rights of citizens:

All citizens of the United States shall have the same right, in every State and Territory, as is enjoyed by white citizens thereof to inherit, purchase, lease, sell, hold, and convey real and personal property.

42 U.S.C. § 1981 protects employees from racial discrimination both in entering into an employment contract, and in enjoying the benefits, privileges, terms, and conditions of employment. To establish a Section 1981 claim, a plaintiff must show that: (1) he or she is a member of a racial minority; (2) the defendant had intent to discriminate on the basis of race; (3) the discrimination interfered with a protected activity as defined in Section 1981, i.e., the making or enforcing of a contract.

## Definition of Race

The definition of race under § 1982 was an issue in *Trujillo v. Bd. of Educ.* (2006). According to the court, one of the first issues that must be decided in racial discrimination cases is whether the plaintiff (individual claiming to be a victim of discrimination) falls within a racial or ethnic group the U.S. Congress intended to protect when it enacted 42 U.S. Code § 1981. The U.S. Supreme Court has noted that, although a variety of ethnic groups, including Arabs, are now considered to be within the Caucasian race, conceptions of race were plainly different during the mid-nineteenth century, at the time § 1981 became law. Looking to dictionaries from the middle years of the nineteenth century, the Court found that Arabs, Hebrews (or Hebrews of the Semitic race), Jews, blacks, Gypsies, Basques, and Chinese were all popularly considered distinct races, as were Englishmen, Anglo-Saxons, Germans, Scandinavians, Swedes, Norwegians, Finns, Greeks, Latins, Italians, Spanish, Mexicans, Hungarians, Russians, and Mongolians. The Supreme Court has affirmed a broad, rather than a restrictive or technical, meaning of race and held that § 1981 was intended to protect from discrimination identifiable classes of persons who are subjected to intentional discrimination solely because of their ancestry or ethnic characteristics. Accordingly, when a plaintiff can show discrimination based on race, including ethnicity or ancestry, a § 1981 cause of action will lie. If a plaintiff can show discrimination based only on national origin, a § 1981 cause of action will not lie, but the Civil Rights Act may apply. The court noted that a claim of discrimination "based on Mexican American ancestry" would fall "within § 1981's protection against racial discrimination," but concluded that § 1981 "does not protect individuals from discrimination based on national origin" (*Trujillo v. Bd. of Educ.*, 2006).

## Sexual and/or Gender Discrimination

*Sexual harassment* is the unwanted sexual attention, advances, and/or requests for sexual favors, whether verbal or physical, that affect an employee's job conditions or creates a hostile working environment. Sexual harassment includes practices ranging from direct requests for sexual favors to workplace conditions that create a hostile environment for persons of either gender, including same-sex harassment. (The "hostile environment" standard also applies to harassment on the bases of race, color, national origin, religion, age, and disability.)

*Pregnancy-based discrimination* is discrimination against pregnancy, childbirth, and related medical conditions, and must be treated in the same way as other temporary illnesses or conditions.

Despite the fact that women have increasingly occupied managerial positions in recent years, most researchers have concluded that women managers continue to face a number of challenges in their managerial roles. For example, there are negative beliefs and judgments from coworkers about their levels of commitment (Lane & Piercy, 2003). Women managers are promoted or advanced slower than expected promotion or advancement as compared to equally qualified or educated men (Stroh, Brett, & Reilly, 1992).

Sexual harassment includes some tortious conduct, such as unwelcome sexual advances and some forms of verbal or physical conduct of a sexual nature. Sexual harassment also includes some conduct that may be considered criminal in nature. The bottom line in determining whether conduct constitutes sexual harassment is that the gravamen depends on the nature of the alleged conduct, and not upon any technical format of the complaint or procedural aspects of a case.

Sexual harassment is a form of sex discrimination that violates Title VII of the Civil Rights Act of 1964. Sexual harassment can occur in a variety of circumstances. Listed below are some of the key points that the EEOC lists regarding sexual harassment:

- The victim as well as the harasser may be a woman or a man. The victim does not have to be of the opposite sex.
- The harasser can be the victim's supervisor, an agent of the employer, a supervisor in another area, a coworker, or a nonemployee.
- The victim does not have to be the person harassed but could be anyone affected by the offensive conduct.
- Unlawful sexual harassment may occur without economic injury to or discharge of the victim.
- To be harassment, the harasser's conduct must be unwelcomed.

In one case, the U.S. Court of Appeals for the 9th Circuit held that in order to evaluate whether a female employee has been sexually harassed, the proper legal standard to use is that of the "reasonable woman." Accordingly, the courts should view the challenged conduct through the eyes of a "reasonable woman." The court stated that using the gender-neutral standard of a "reasonable person" tends to be male biased and tends to systematically ignore the experiences of women. The court also ruled that in order to avoid liability, employers must take strong and effective steps to remedy sexual harassment in the workplace, even if that involves permanently removing the harasser (*Ellison v. Brady*, 1991).

Sexual harassment has been a constant area of concern for employers. The late newspaper columnist Art Buchwald in one of his sarcastic columns advised job applicants to specify whether or not they wanted to be sexually harassed on the job and by whom. This is not a joking matter, since studies indicate that about 50 percent of all female employees have at one time or another been sexually harassed on the job. The courts often hold employers liable for allowing or permitting sexual harassment.

In cases of sexual harassment by management or supervisory personnel, the employer is normally accountable under the theory that the employer has placed the supervisor or manager in the position of authority. The employer should have a standing policy putting employees on notice that sexual harassment will not be tolerated by any employee.

In one case, a female employee failed to get promoted because the employee who was promoted was willing to have a sexual affair with the supervisor. A Delaware federal court judge held this to be a form of unlawful sex bias and, indirectly, sexual harassment. This case points out that the sexual harassment guidelines are broadly interpreted by the courts.

The employer should establish procedures whereby employees who feel that they are being sexually harassed by managerial employees may report the matter to a manager at a higher level without fear of reprisal.

Sandra Bundy was employed by the District of Columbia Department of Corrections. She contended that she received and rejected sexual propositions from a fellow employee who later became her supervisor. In addition, she claimed that she received sexual propositions from other supervisors. When she was not recommended for promotion, she complained to the EEOC and later filed her claim in court. The court of appeals held that:

- Sexual harassment includes psychological work conditions as well as physical abuse.
- The employer is accountable for the acts of managers and supervisors.
- The employer should have established specific procedures to help prevent sexual harassment (Bundy v. Jackson, 1981).

To establish a case for gender discrimination, the complaining individual must show that (1) she or he belongs to a protected class; (2) she or he was qualified for the position; (3) she or he suffered an adverse employment action; and (4) she or he was replaced by someone outside her or his protected class, or that similarly situated employees outside her or his protected class were treated more favorably under circumstances nearly identical to hers or his (*Manning v. Chevron Chemical Co., LLC*, 2003).

By amendment, Congress clarified the terms "because of sex" or "on the basis of sex" to include discrimination on the basis of pregnancy (42 U.S.C.S. § 2000e(k)). A court will analyze claims brought pursuant to the Pregnancy Discrimination Act (42 U.S.C.S. § 2000e) in the same way as other Title VII claims of disparate treatment. A plaintiff alleging pregnancy discrimination must show, through either direct or indirect evidence, that the discrimination complained of was intentional.

## Hostile Work Environment

There are five elements necessary to establish a hostile work environment claim: (1) the plaintiff suffered intentional discrimination because of his or her membership in the protected class, (2) the discrimination was pervasive and regular, (3) the discrimination detrimentally affected the plaintiff,

(4) the discrimination would have detrimentally affected a reasonable person of the same protected class in that position, and (5) the failure of the employer to take appropriate action to prevent the problem (*Andrews v. City of Philadelphia*, 1990).

## Age Discrimination

The Age Discrimination in Employment Act 29 U.S.C.S. § 621 et seq.), (ADEA) prohibits an employer from discriminating against any individual in hiring or discharge, or with respect to his compensation, terms, conditions, or privileges of employment, on the basis of age. In order to establish a claim of age discrimination, a plaintiff must show (1) that he or she is a member of the protected group, that is, at least 40 years of age; (2) that he or she was performing the job adequately; (3) that he or she was discharged; and (4) that he or she was replaced by a younger person. Before filing an ADEA or Title VII of the Civil Rights Act of 1964 complaint, an employee must first file a charge of discrimination with the EEOC within 300 days of the alleged unlawful employment practice.

As a general rule, a plaintiff may only raise claims in his or her judicial complaint that were previously included in an EEOC charge of discrimination. This rule serves to put the employer on notice of the alleged discrimination and to give the EEOC and the employer an opportunity to settle the dispute.

A claim of age discrimination can exist only when the plaintiff has presented sufficient evidence to show there is a genuine issue of material fact pertaining to whether the plaintiff's age actually motivated the allegedly discriminatory conduct. In determining whether the circumstantial evidence presented by the plaintiff in a given case is sufficient to establish a genuine issue of material fact, the United States Supreme Court has directed the application of the burden-shifting framework established in *McDonnell Douglas Corp. v. Green* (1973). The *McDonnell Douglas* framework comprises three burden-shifting steps. Initially, the burden rests with the plaintiff to establish a prima facie case of discrimination. If the plaintiff has established a prima facie case, the burden then shifts to the defendant to articulate some legitimate, nondiscriminatory reason for its employment action. Finally, if the defendant articulates a nondiscriminatory reason, then the burden shifts to the plaintiff to show that the proffered reason is merely a pretext for discrimination.

## Title IX Issues

Title IX of the Education Amendments of 1972 (20 U.S.C.S. § 1681) prohibits sex discrimination by recipients of federal education funding. 20 U.S.C.S. §

1681(a) provides that no person in the United States shall, on the basis of sex, be excluded from participation in, be denied the benefits of, or be subjected to discrimination under any education program or activity receiving federal financial assistance. The United States Supreme Court has held that: Title IX implies a private right of action to enforce its prohibition on intentional sex discrimination; Title IX authorizes private parties to seek monetary damages for intentional violations of Title IX; and the private right of action encompasses intentional sex discrimination in the form of a recipient's deliberate indifference to a teacher's sexual harassment of a student or to sexual harassment of a student by another student.

## 1983 CLAIMS

42 U.S.C.S. § 1983 is designed to provide a comprehensive remedy for the deprivation of federal constitutional and statutory rights. The relief available under § 1983 for violations includes equitable remedies, with the overarching goal to make victims of illegal discrimination whole. To that end, the make-whole standard of relief should be the touchstone of relief fashioned by the courts.

## Americans with Disabilities Act (ADA)

> The purpose of the ADA was to provide clear and comprehensive national standards to eliminate discrimination against individuals with disabilities. As a result, individuals with disabilities are now able to live in their homes and have access to new careers. (Jim Ramstad, 2008)

### Titles I and V of the ADA

The ADA prohibits discrimination on the basis of disability in all employment practices. It is necessary to understand several important ADA definitions to know whom the law protects and what constitutes illegal discrimination.

### Individual with a Disability

Under the ADA, an individual with a disability is a person who has a physical or mental impairment that substantially limits one or more major life activities, has a record of such an impairment, or is regarded as having such an impairment. Major life activities are activities that an average person can perform with little or no difficulty such as walking, breathing, seeing, hearing, speaking, learning, and working.

## Qualified Individual with a Disability

A qualified employee or applicant with a disability is someone who satisfies skill, experience, education, and other job-related requirements of the position held or desired and who, with or without reasonable accommodation, can perform the essential functions of that position.

## Reasonable Accommodation

Reasonable accommodation may include, but is not limited to, making existing facilities used by employees readily accessible to and usable by persons with disabilities; job restructuring; modification of work schedules; providing additional unpaid leave; reassignment to a vacant position; acquiring or modifying equipment or devices; adjusting or modifying examinations, training materials, or policies; and providing qualified readers or interpreters. Reasonable accommodation may be necessary to apply for a job, to perform job functions, or to enjoy the benefits and privileges of employment that are enjoyed by people without disabilities. An employer is not required to lower production standards to make an accommodation. An employer generally is not obligated to provide personal-use items such as eyeglasses or hearing aids.

## Undue Hardship

An employer is required to make a reasonable accommodation to a qualified individual with a disability unless doing so would impose an undue hardship on the operation of the employer's business. Undue hardship means an action that requires significant difficulty or expense when considered in relation to factors such as a business' size, financial resources, and the nature and structure of its operation.

## Prohibited Inquiries and Examinations

Before making an offer of employment, an employer may not ask job applicants about the existence, nature, or severity of a disability. Applicants may be asked about their ability to perform job functions. A job offer may be conditioned on the results of a medical examination, but only if the examination is required for all entering employees in the same job category. Medical examinations of employees must be job related and consistent with business necessity.

## Drug and Alcohol Use

Employees and applicants currently engaging in the illegal use of drugs are not protected by the ADA when an employer acts on the basis of such use. Tests for illegal use of drugs are not considered medical examinations and, therefore, are not subject to the ADA's restrictions on medical examinations. Employers may hold individuals who are illegally using drugs and individuals with alcoholism to the same standards of performance as other employees.

## Exhaustion of Administrative Remedies

Title I of the ADA (42 U.S.C.S. § 12101 et seq.) requires a plaintiff to exhaust his or her administrative remedies before filing suit. The first step to exhaustion is the filing of a charge of discrimination with the EEOC. In filing an EEOC charge, a plaintiff should set forth particular information generally describing the action or practices complained of. The next step in determining whether a plaintiff has exhausted her administrative remedies is to the determine the scope of allegations raised in the EEOC charge, because a plaintiff's claim in federal court is generally limited by the scope of the administrative investigation that can reasonably be expected to follow the charge of discrimination submitted to the EEOC. While a court construes the text of the EEOC charge liberally when determining whether a basis lies for an ADA claim, plaintiff may seek judicial relief for discrimination not described in an EEOC charge if the discrimination is reasonably related to the allegations in the EEOC charge.

## State Statutes

In addition to the federal statutes prohibiting discrimination, each state has similar statues. To discuss each state's discrimination protections in this chapter is impossible. The following provisions from the Iowa and Montana codes are submitted to provide a favor as to the extent of state regulations in the area of prejudice and illegal discrimination.

Under the Iowa Civil Rights Act, discrimination in education occurs when any educational institution discriminates on the basis of race, color, or national origin in any program or activity (Iowa Code § 216.9(1)). Iowa Code § 216.9(1)(a) states discriminatory practices include, but are not limited to, exclusion of a person or persons from participation in, denial of the benefits of, or subjection to discrimination in any academic, extracurricular, research, occupational training, or other program or activity.

Under the Iowa Code, discrimination in public accommodation occurs when any owner, agent, or employee of a "public accommodation," which may include public schools, refuses or denies to any person because of race, color, or national origin the accommodations, advantages, facilities, services, or privileges thereof or when any owner, agent, or employee of a public accommodation discriminates against a person on the basis of race, color, or national origin in the furnishing of such accommodations, advantages, facilities, services, or privileges. (Iowa Code § 216.7.)

Title 49 of the Montana Code, which is known as the Montana Human Rights Act (MHRA), declares that the right to be free from discrimination on the basis of one's gender or mental disability, among other attributes including race, age, and religion, is recognized as and declared to be a civil right (Mont. Code Ann. § 49-1-102(1) (2001)). Pursuant to this declaration, the MHRA prohibits particular types of discrimination in various settings such as employment, education, and public accommodations, among others (Mont. Code Ann. §§ 49-2-303 to 49-2-309 [2001]).

With respect to the employment setting, the MHRA defines "unlawful discrimination" with general terms and also by listing specific prohibited acts. In general terms, unlawful discrimination in employment is statutorily defined as the practice of making distinctions in a term, condition, or privilege of employment based on attributes such as age, gender, or mental disability, when the reasonable demands of the position do not require such distinction Mont. Code Ann. § 49-2-303(1)(a) [2001]). The MHRA also designates particular conduct in employment as unlawfully discriminatory, such as differentiating in employees' compensation based on race, refusing to employ an individual based on his or her religious beliefs, and utilizing an employment application that expresses a limitation as to age when the limitation is not based on a bona fide occupational qualification (BFOQ): A job qualification that is reasonably necessary to perform the job. (Mont. Code Ann. § 49-2-303(1)(a) and (c) [2001]).

## Disparate Impact Claims

Disparate impact claims under Title VII of the Civil Rights Act of 1964 challenge employment practices that are facially neutral in their treatment of different groups but that in fact fall more harshly on one group than another and cannot be justified by business necessity. The classic example of a subtle discrimination qualification is contained in the U.S. Supreme Court case *Griggs v. Duke Power Co.* (1971). The employer, Duke Power Co., required a high school diploma as a criterion for employment. Griggs, an African American, applied for a janitorial position with the company but was denied employment because he lacked a high school diploma. The Supreme Court held that since in the local employment area more whites than minorities had high school diplomas, that requiring a diploma had a disparate impact against minorities, even though it appeared to be racially neutral on its face.

The Court noted in *Griggs* that the Civil Rights Act does not require that less-qualified applicants be favored over better-qualified applicants simply because of minority origins. The Court stated that an employer was free to hire the best-qualified person for a position. But if a preemployment qualification has an adverse impact on a protected class (i.e., if it operates to exclude members of a protected class), then an employer has a burden of establishing that the preemployment qualification is reasonably necessary and related to job performance. For example, in the *Griggs* case, data revealed that in the local area, only 12% of the black males had completed high school, compared to 34% of the white males. Accordingly, the high school diploma eliminated 88% of the black male applicants compared to only 66% of the white male applicants.

The *Griggs* case established the BFOQ requirement, which means that if a preemployment qualification has an adverse impact on a protected group, the BFOQ must be reasonably necessary for the job. For example, as in the *Griggs* case, there is no valid employment reason to require that a janitor be a high school graduate.

In *Stewart v. City of St. Louis* (2007), the Firefighter's Institute for Racial Equality and four individual African American firefighters filed a court action against the city of St. Louis under Title VII of the Civil Rights Act of 1964 and 42 U.S.C. §§ 1981 and 1981a. The firefighters claimed that the promotion tests for the city of St. Louis Fire Department in 2000 and 2004 for fire captain and battalion chief had an adverse impact on African Americans, and they sought injunctive relief and damages. The court held that in order to prove business necessity, an employer must show that its selection criteria bear a manifest relationship to the employment in question. The employer must also demonstrate that the employment practice significantly serves legitimate employment goals.

## Disparate Impact Issues

Does the employer use a particular employment practice that has a disparate impact on the basis of race, color, religion, sex, or national origin? For example, if an employer requires that all applicants pass a physical agility test, does the test disproportionately screen out women? Determining whether a test or other selection procedure has a disparate impact on a particular group ordinarily requires a statistical analysis.

If the selection procedure has a disparate impact based on race, color, religion, sex, or national origin, can the employer show that the selection procedure is job related and consistent with business necessity? An employer can meet this standard by showing that it is necessary to the safe and efficient performance of the job. The challenged policy or practice should therefore be associated with the skills needed to perform the job successfully. In contrast to a general measurement of applicants' or employees' skills, the challenged policy or practice must evaluate an individual's skills as related to the particular job in question.

If the employer shows that the selection procedure is job related and consistent with business necessity, can the person challenging the selection procedure demonstrate that there is a less discriminatory alternative available? For example, is another test available that would be equally effective in predicting job performance but would not disproportionately exclude the protected group (Hirsch, 2003).

## National Origin Discrimination

It is illegal to discriminate against an individual because of birthplace, ancestry, culture, or linguistic characteristics common to a specific ethnic group.

A rule requiring that employees speak only English on the job may violate Title VII unless an employer shows that the requirement is necessary for conducting business. If the employer believes such a rule is necessary, employees must be informed when English is required and of the consequences for violating the rule.

The Immigration Reform and Control Act (IRCA) of 1986 requires employers to ensure that employees hired are legally authorized to work in the United States. An employer who requests employment verification only for individuals of a particular national origin or individuals who appear to be or sound foreign, however, may violate both Title VII and the IRCA; verification must be obtained from all applicants and employees. Employers who impose citizenship requirements or give preferences to U.S. citizens in hiring or employment opportunities also may violate the IRCA.

Additional information about the IRCA may be obtained from the Office of Special Counsel for Immigration-Related Unfair Employment Practices at 1-800-255-7688 (voice), 1-800-237-2515 (TTY for employees and applicants), or 1-800-362-2735 (TTY for employers) or at http://www.usdoj.gov/crt/osc.

## Religious Accommodation

An employer is required to reasonably accommodate the religious belief of an employee or prospective employee, unless doing so would impose an undue hardship.

## Retaliation

The elements of a retaliation claim under both Title VII of the Civil Rights Act of 1964, 42 U.S.C.S. § 2000e et seq., and 42 U.S.C.S. § 1981 are identical. To establish a case of retaliation under either statute, a plaintiff in a civil action must demonstrate that: (1) he or she engaged in protected opposition to discrimination, (2) that a reasonable employee would have found the allegedly retaliatory action materially adverse, and (3) that a causal connection existed between the protected activity and the materially adverse action. In a civil court action, the plaintiff (aggrieved employee) has the burden of establishing the aforementioned elements. After a plaintiff has established a case of retaliation, the burden shifts to the defendant (employer) to show a legitimate, non-retaliatory reason for adverse employment action. When a defendant meets this burden, the burden shifts back to the plaintiff to demonstrate that defendant's reasons are not valid.

The U.S. Supreme Court noted in *Gomez-Perez v. Potter* (2008) that a claim of retaliation against a person because that person has complained of sex discrimination is a form of intentional sex discrimination. Retaliation is, by definition, an intentional act. It is a form of discrimination because the complainant is being subjected to differential treatment. Moreover, retaliation is discrimination on the basis of sex because it is an intentional response to the nature of the complaint: an allegation of sex discrimination.

## Ethics in Practice

### *Robinson v. County of Los Angeles* (2009)

Plaintiff Richard Robinson ("Robinson"), a sergeant with the Los Angeles County Office of Public Safety ("OPS"), filed a civil rights complaint under 42 U.S.C. § 1983 against the County of Los Angeles ("Los Angeles") and several OPS officers ("defendants") alleging that he was denied promotion in violation of his First and Fourteenth Amendment rights because he made reports of misconduct within his department.

### Court's Judgment

A First Amendment claim against a public employer must establish: (1) engagement in constitutionally protected speech, (2) an adverse employment action, and (3) the employee's speech was a "substantial or motivating" factor in the adverse action.

When evaluating whether an employee's speech is constitutionally protected, courts must determine first whether the expressions in question were made by the speaker upon matters of public concern, second whether the state lacked adequate justification for treating the employee differently from any other member of the general public, and third whether the plaintiff spoke as a private citizen rather than a public employee.

To be protected under the First Amendment, an employee's speech must address a matter of legitimate public concern. The competency of the police force is surely a matter of great public concern. Only speech that deals with individual personnel disputes and grievances and that would be of no relevance to the public's evaluation of the performance of governmental agencies is generally not of public concern.

Robinson alleged he was retaliated against for, among other things, testifying in a class action lawsuit that the county had engaged in systematic discrimination and harassment against OPS officers, reporting numerous instances of possible corruption, discrimination, or misconduct by fellow OPS officers, and following up on those complaints. With the exception of the three incidents identified by the district court as individual personnel disputes, each of these is clearly a matter of public concern.

The defendants conceded that some of Robinson's internal reports of certain alleged misconduct involved matters of public concern but contended that others did not. They argued that Robinson's follow-up communications pressing his reports of misconduct are not matters of public concern.

The defendants suggested that Robinson's reports — regarding an officer suspected of working for an outside employer while on the clock and alleged discrimination against another officer — both addressed individual personnel disputes, not matters of public concern. Reports pertaining to others, even if they concern personnel matters including discriminatory conduct, can still be "protected under the public concern test." Robinson's testimony in a class action against the county is also of public concern, regardless of whether it had an impact on the result of that litigation. A public employee's testimony addresses a matter of public concern if it contributes in some way to the resolution of a judicial or administrative proceeding in which discrimination or other significant government misconduct is at issue — even if the speech itself would not amount to discrimination in isolation.

Courts must also seek to balance the interests of the employee, in commenting upon matters of public concern and the interest of the state, as an employer, in promoting the efficiency of the public services it performs through its employees. For us to find that the government's interest as an employer in a smoothly running office outweighs an employee's First Amendment rights, defendants must demonstrate actual, material, and substantial disruption, or reasonable predictions of disruption. The workplace disruption hurdle for government employers is higher in cases, like this one, where the speech involved unlawful activities rather than policy differences.

The defendants argued an exception to this clearly established law exists, citing *Sanchez v. City of Santa Ana*, 936 F.2d 1027, 1039 (9th Cir. 1990), which stated that there is "no constitutional violation in requiring officers to communicate 'through channels' before enlisting public opinion to their cause." *Sanchez* limited its holding, however, to cases where the "channels" policy "is reasonable and not arbitrary." "Even in a police department, the complained-of disruption must be 'real, and not imagined' " and the "disruption exception cannot 'serve as a pretext for stifling legitimate speech or penalizing public employees for expressing unpopular views.' " *Allen v. Scribner* 812 F.2d 426, 432 (9th Cir. 1987) "command policy designed to protect [a police department's] interest[s] will always take precedence over the interest of a public employee in open communication" and "must look to the particular circumstances of each case to determine the importance of enforcing the chain of command against an employee whose speech breaches that policy."

The Pickering balancing test can favor protected speech even where the speech violates the employer's written policy requiring speech to occur through specified "channels." (*Anderson v. Central Point School Dist.*, 746 F.2d 505, 506 (9th Cir. 1984); see also *Connick*, 461 U.S. at 153 n.14 (violation of a rule governing the circumstances when speech is permitted would strengthen a claimant's position in the Pickering balance but alone would not be dispositive).

The defendants correctly noted that we have sometimes found a police department's interests in discipline and esprit de corps to outweigh First Amendment interests, but even in these cases, the Pickering balancing was not conducted while genuine issues of material fact (including the extent of the workplace disruption) remained. See, for example, *Cochran*, 222 F.3d at 1196 (finding the city's interest in the proper functioning of its police department outweighed plaintiffs' expressive interests, but only after a detailed discussion of the facts as found at trial); *Kannisto v. San Francisco*, 541 F.2d 841, 843-44 (9th Cir. 1976; noting that "the facts in this case sharply contrast with those in Pickering").

Therefore, although the existence of a written "chain of command" policy may be relevant to evaluating workplace disruption, it is not dispositive, particularly given the allegations suggesting that Robinson's superiors may have been more concerned with the frequency with which Robinson reported misconduct than the persons to whom he directed those reports. When the Pickering test must be applied and "there are underlying factual issues regarding the extent of office disruption," it is proper to deny a motion for summary judgment (*Roth*, 856 F.2d at 1408).

Defendants also argue that Robinson's reports were made in conjunction with his official job duties and therefore were not protected by the First Amendment under *Garcetti v. Ceballos*, 547 U.S. 410, 126 S. Ct. 1951, 164 L. Ed. 2d 689 (2006). The district court found that whether the scope of

Robinson's duties included reporting police misconduct was contested and presented a "genuine issue of material fact for trial," a holding we lack jurisdiction to review (see *Johnson*, 515 U.S. at 319–20). In so concluding, the district court noted that the message that Robinson should make fewer misconduct reports, which he claimed he repeatedly received from his supervisors, "tends to undermine the assertion by Defendants that the reports Robinson made were within the scope of his duties unless one is to believe that certain duties must not be performed if one wants to advance in the organization."

Although OPS policy states that an OPS member "shall promptly report to his immediate supervisor any information or incident coming to his attention that might indicate the need for Office of Public Safety actions," formal job requirements are not dispositive. *Garcetti* rejected "the suggestion that employers can restrict employees' rights by creating excessively broad job descriptions," holding that formal job descriptions are "neither necessary nor sufficient to demonstrate that conducting [a] task is within the scope of the employee's professional duties" (*Garcetti*, 547 U.S. at 424–25). *Garcetti* therefore demands a "practical" inquiry (id.).

The appellate court held that the petitioner Robinson's complaint was sufficient to state a civil action against the County of Los Angeles.

## *Webb v. City of Philadelphia* (2009)

### Opinion by Chief Judge Scirica

Kimberlie Webb, Philadelphia police officer, claimed she has a constitutional right to wear religious garb with her police uniform. Does she?

In this employment discrimination case, the issue on appeal is whether a police officer's request to wear religious garb with her uniform could be reasonably accommodated without imposing an undue burden on the city of Philadelphia. On the facts presented, the district court held it could not. We agree.

Webb is a practicing Muslim, employed by the city of Philadelphia as a police officer since 1995. On February 11, 2003, Webb requested permission from her commanding officer to wear a headscarf while in uniform and on duty. The headscarf (a khimar or hijaab) is a traditional head covering worn by Muslim women. Webb's headscarf would cover neither her face nor her ears but would cover her head and the back of her neck. Her request was denied in view of Philadelphia Police Department Directive 78, the authoritative memorandum that prescribes the approved Philadelphia police uniforms and equipment. Nothing in Directive 78 authorizes the wearing of religious symbols or garb as part of the uniform.

On February 28, 2003, Webb filed a complaint of religious discrimination under Title VII of the 1964 Civil Rights Act (42 U.S.C. § 2000e-2(a)(1)) with the Equal Employment Opportunity Commission (EEOC) and the Pennsylvania Human Relations Commission. On August 12, 2003, while the matter was pending before the EEOC, Webb arrived at work wearing her headscarf. She refused to remove it when requested and was sent home for failing to comply with Directive 78. The next two days' events were indistinguishable: Webb arrived at work in her uniform and her headscarf, which she refused to remove, and was then sent home. On August 14, Webb was informed her conduct could lead to disciplinary action. Thereafter, she reported to work without a headscarf. Disciplinary charges of insubordination were subsequently brought against Webb, resulting in a temporary thirteen-day suspension.

On October 5, 2005, Webb brought suit against the city of Philadelphia, asserting three causes of action under Title VII—religious discrimination, retaliation/hostile work environment, and sex discrimination—and one cause of action under the Pennsylvania Religious Freedom Protection Act (RFPA), (71 Pa. Stat. Ann. § 2401). The district court found that Directive 78 and its detailed standards with no accommodation for religious symbols and attire not only promote the need for uniformity but also enhance cohesiveness, cooperation, and the esprit de corps of the police force. The district court held the city would suffer an undue hardship if forced to permit Webb and other officers to wear religious clothing or ornamentation with their uniforms.

Title VII of the 1964 Civil Rights Act prohibits employers from discharging or disciplining an employee based on his or her religion (42 U.S.C. § 2000e-2(a)(1)). "*Religion* is defined as "all aspects of religious observance and practice, as well as belief, unless an employer demonstrates that he is unable to reasonably accommodate to an employee's … religious observance or practice without undue hardship on the conduct of the employer's business" (42 U.S.C. § 2000e(j)). To establish a prima facie case of religious discrimination, the employee must show (1) she holds a sincere religious belief that conflicts with a job requirement, (2) she informed her employer of the conflict, and (3) she was disciplined for failing to comply with the conflicting requirement. Once all factors are established, the burden shifts to the employer to show either it made a good-faith effort to reasonably accommodate the religious belief or such an accommodation would work an undue hardship on the employer and its business.

Title VII religious discrimination claims often revolve around the question of whether the employer can show that reasonable accommodation would work an undue hardship. An accommodation constitutes an undue hardship if it would impose more than a de minimis cost on the employer. Both economic and non-economic costs can pose an undue hardship upon employers; the latter category includes, for example, violations of the seniority provision of a collective bargaining agreement and the threat of possible criminal sanctions.

Our most recent decision in this area is *Fraternal Order of Police Newark Lodge No. 12 v. City of Newark*, 170 F.3d 359 (3d Cir. 1999). In *Fraternal Order of Police*, we held the government cannot discriminate between conduct that is secularly motivated and similar conduct that is religiously motivated. The Newark Police Department forbade police officers from growing beards but granted medical exceptions for beards as required by the Americans with Disabilities Act (42 U.S.C. § 12112). Two Muslim police officers, whose religion required they grow beards, filed suit contending their First Amendment rights were infringed upon by the no-beards policy. We agreed, holding that the police department must create a religious exemption to its no-beards policy to parallel its secular one, unless it could make a substantial showing as to the hypothetical negative effects of a religious exemption.

In a similar case, a sister court of appeals determined a police department cannot be forced to let individual officers add religious symbols to their official uniforms. In *Daniels v. City of Arlington*, a police officer refused to remove a gold cross pin on his uniform, in non-compliance with a no-pins official policy. Because the Supreme Court has upheld appropriate restrictions on the First Amendment rights of government employees, specifically including both military and police uniform standards, the court of appeals for the fifth circuit determined the city's uniform standards were proper, and the city was unable to reasonably accommodate the officer's religious needs without undue hardship. Other courts have recognized the interests of a governmental entity in maintaining the appearance of neutrality. The importance of public confidence in the neutrality of its protectors is so great that a police department or a fire department should be able to plead undue hardship. It is not only important that the government and its employees in fact avoid practicing political justice, but it is also critical that they appear to the public to be avoiding it, if confidence in the system of representative government is not to be eroded to a disastrous extent.

The district court held Webb established a prima facie case of religious discrimination. We agree. Webb's religious beliefs are sincere, her employer understood the conflict between her beliefs and her employment requirements, and she was disciplined for failing to comply with a conflicting official requirement. Thus, the burden shifts, and the city must establish that to reasonably accommodate Webb (i.e., allow her to wear a headscarf with her uniform) would constitute an undue hardship. The city offered no accommodation, contending any accommodation would impose an undue hardship.

In the city's view, at stake is the police department's impartiality or, more precisely, the perception of its impartiality by citizens of all races and religions whom the police are charged to serve and protect. If not for the strict enforcement of Directive 78, the city contends, the essential values of impartiality, religious neutrality, uniformity, and the subordination of personal preference would be severely damaged to the detriment of the proper functioning of the police department. In the words of Police Commissioner Sylvester Johnson, uniformity "encourages the subordination of personal preferences in favor of the overall policing mission" and conveys "a sense of authority and competence to other officers inside the Department, as well as to the general public."

Commissioner Johnson identified and articulated the police department's religious neutrality (or the appearance of neutrality) as vital in both dealing with the public and working together cooperatively. "In sum, in my professional judgment and experience, it is critically important to promote the image of a disciplined, identifiable, and impartial police force by maintaining the Philadelphia Police Department uniform as a symbol of neutral government authority, free from expressions of personal religion, bent, or bias." Commissioner Johnson's testimony was not contradicted or challenged by Webb at any stage in the proceedings.

As a paramilitary entity, the Philadelphia Police Department requires a disciplined rank and file for efficient conduct of its affairs. A paramilitary law enforcement unit, such as the police, has many of the same interests as the military in regulating its employees' uniforms. Commissioner Johnson's thorough and uncontradicted reasons for refusing accommodations are sufficient to meet the more than de minimis cost of an undue burden.

Despite Webb's assertions, *Fraternal Order of Police* is distinguishable from this case. The focus of *Fraternal Order of Police* is the lack of neutrality in applying the no-beards regulation. As we explained, the department's decision to provide medical exemptions while refusing religious exemptions is sufficiently suggestive of discriminatory intent. The Philadelphia Police Department's Directive 78, by contrast, contains no exceptions, nor is there evidence the city allows other officers to deviate from it. In other ways, our decision in *Fraternal Order of Police* buttressed the district court's opinion. We recognized that "safety is undoubtedly an interest of the greatest importance" to the police department and that uniform requirements are crucial to the safety of officers (so that the public will be able to identify officers as genuine based on their uniform appearance), morale and esprit de corps, and public confidence in the police.

The district court correctly concluded the city would suffer undue hardship under Title VII if required to grant Webb's requested religious accommodation. We affirm the judgment of the district court.

## Questions in Review

1. How would you define "illegal discrimination"?
2. What is meant by the term "protected class"?

3. Why is there a problem with telling sexual-related jokes in the office?
4. What are the differences between national origin discrimination and a racial discrimination complaint?
5. What steps can be taken to eliminate illegal discrimination?

# Ethics and the Present Criminal Justice System

# 9

## Introduction

The purpose of this chapter is to introduce readers to the present state of ethics within the criminal justice system. The information in this chapter is important because it provides the foundation for several of the chapters that follow. In essence, we discuss two major conflicts. The first conflict is between the social order and the moral model. The social order describes the process of all citizens giving up certain liberties to receive certain benefits. The moral order is a concept that describes such principles as humanity, fairness, equality, and equitableness (Wuthnow, 1989).

The second conflict occurs between what is called the ideal model of justice and the serviceable model of justice. Similar to the social model and the moral model, the essence is to highlight the vast difference between the type of justice that would be carried out in a perfect world and the type of justice that is carried out in the real world (Wuthnow, 1989).

In examining the conflicts, we should consider three different concepts: money, politics, and liability. There are other salient concepts relevant to this information, but those concepts carry the lion's share of the load regarding major conflicts between what should be done in criminal justice and what is actually done in criminal justice agencies. Money, politics, and liability drive many of the happenings in all components of criminal justice. Each of these components is directly affected by these three factors. The question is, is it possible to deliver pure justice if money, politics, and liability are the major factors driving decision making and actions within the criminal justice system?

All students of criminal justice should become intimately familiar with what is being depicted by the scale of justice found in textbooks and most media outlets addressing the discipline of criminal justice. Each arm of the scale represents a different goal. On one side of the scale is freedom, individual liberties, personal rights, and privileges. On the other side is protection of society. The use of a scale in representing these conflicting interests is clever, and it ultimately depicts what should be a balance of protecting the greatest amount of citizens with the least amount of intrusion on freedoms and personal rights. In a perfect world, the scale would remain steady at perfect balance. Unfortunately, however, this is rarely the case.

Consider the individual stopped by a police officer for running a stop sign. Using this example, and before going any further, let's identify how each side of the scale is being represented:

1. *Protection of society:* The officer's objective in this stop is to first identify whether the driver is considered legal to operate a motor vehicle. In addition, the officer needs to ascertain whether the driver is of sufficient physical and mental health to operate a motor vehicle as well as if he or she is impaired in some way. The officer is also likely to ensure that the vehicle is safe to operate. For example, are the brakes functioning properly? Are the lights and equipment functioning properly? The goal is to protect society. How is this accomplished? By making sure this driver and vehicle are safely able to operate so that innocent citizens are not injured or killed.

2. *Individual rights and civil liberties:* How is the objective of this perspective fulfilled? By doing only what is minimally necessary to ensure the driver and vehicle are safe to travel. In essence, how can the officer obtain the necessary information with the least amount of intrusion on the individual's freedom to travel from one location to another? In this example, if the officer fails to stop the driver for running the stop sign, the community may be placed in danger. If the officer abuses his or her authority and power and unnecessarily restricts the driver's freedom, then obviously the driver's personal liberties have been violated.

The scale of justice depicts a profound moral and ethical philosophy of justice. It provides us with guidelines that should be used as guiding beacons that must represent the foundation of ethical thought and practice. When we are confronted with a decision point involving some aspect of criminal justice, the question that should immediately resonate is, how can we protect society with the least amount of intrusion? When the answer to this question is informed and guided by the concept of ethics, the scale will appear in a state of perfect balance.

## Social Order

Another way to depict the essence of the scale of justice is by describing the concepts of social order and moral order. Social order is similar to the idea of giving up certain rights in order to receive certain benefits. Man figured out long ago that in order to achieve a stable existence, we would find it most beneficial that certain norms be followed. In addition, we concluded that there needed to be laws in place to sanction those who did not follow the social order. Ultimately, what we are describing is the social contract constructed by our early ancestors as an attempt to protect themselves from rogue barons in order to enhance their chance of survival.

## Moral Order

Moral order on the scale of justice is analogous to the idea of rights and liberties. Moral order is concerned with humanity, dignity, and respect. Moral order is also about civility. Without humanity, dignity, and respect within in a society, there can be no civility. Without civility there is chaos. Oftentimes these types of discussions are pushed to the side, as there is a sense that mankind has evolved beyond the state of being uncivil even in the absence of a system of laws (Wuthnow, 1989). We do not have to look far, however, to discover examples that provide direct and clear contradictions. Consider the example of Hurricane Katrina.

Hurricane Katrina arrived in southeastern Louisiana in August of 2005. This was a massive storm that produced a violent and sustained storm surge that was able to reverse the flow of water in one the mightiest rivers on the North American continent, the Mississippi River. As a result of the storm surge, the levees protecting the city of New Orleans were breached. Large portions of the city were flooded as people desperately tried to survive, often by retreating into the attic of their home and in some cases cutting holes in the roof in order to escape the rising water. As a result of the flooding, the city was unable to maintain basic operations. Everyone was simply fighting to survive. The police department and emergency services were inoperable. For a period of time following the onslaught of flood waters, there were no assets available to maintain the social contract's responsibility of providing and maintaining order. The consequences of this breakdown were clear and extremely troubling. Without police presence, the city was reduced to a zone of chaos demonstrated through widespread looting, violence, and destruction. People were shown breaking into buildings, filling their arms and hands with all they could carry, and then fleeing. Most troubling is the fact that even police officers from other jurisdictions sent to New Orleans to assist were later convicted of various acts of criminality, including theft.

The point behind this example is that we can never become complacent. In today's modern world, squarely in the center of the technological era, the need for a social contract is as paramount as it was for our ancestors. And, just as was the case then, the contract must be balanced through a guiding and moral theory of ethics. We must continue to strive for a balance between social order and moral order.

## Ideal Model

A final analogy is useful in further illuminating the constant struggle in maintaining balance between the need for law and order and the need for protecting the rights and liberties of individual citizens. Remember without balance, the scale of justice leans heavily to one side, and the basics of humanity, dignity, and respect suffer greatly. The two concepts used in this analogy consist of the ideal model of justice and the serviceable model of justice. The two concepts represent a clear conflict because the basic guidelines of each are not congruous.

The ideal model of justice, as the name denotes, represents the type of justice that is considered pure. In this model, justice is free of the toxins that serve to make its distribution dangerous to consumers. In the medical field, toxins may include bacteria that cause infection, cancers that shut down vital organs, and excesses of foods high in fat and cholesterol. In the criminal justice system, the concept of toxins can be used to describe bias, prejudice, egoism, abuse, and brutality. Therefore, the ideal model of justice is used to describe a perfect state of balance between protecting individuals and protecting society, without unduly hindering the freedoms and liberties we all cherish in America's bureaucratic system of governance.

## Serviceable Model

The serviceable model is a concept used to describe what is often referred to as "what happens in the real world of criminal justice." The serviceable model basically stands for the idea of "this is not a perfect world, and the ideal model of justice is not realistic." One of the best phrases used to depict the essence of the serviceable model is one that most, if not all, recruits hear as they transition from the police academy or an employment orientation program to the field-training unit: "Forget what they taught you in the academy, that will get you killed out here. I am going to show you how to survive. It may not always be pretty, and it may not always be legal, but remember it is how you write the report. What is important is not HOW you get things done but that you get things done and are able to go home after each tour." The degree and extent to which the essence of this message is portrayed varies by department and training staff. It is, however, for all practical purposes a universal message that each new criminal justice employee should be ready to receive in some manner. Some elements of the message may be beneficial. In most occupations, there is no substitute for actual experience. And in some cases, individuals may learn methods that are more efficient for them in carrying out certain tasks that are different from what was demonstrated in the academy or classroom training. The concept of ethics, however, does not lend itself well to this particular context. The methods in which we treat people with respect and dignity should not be open or available for alteration. For example, criminal justice officials should treat everyone with respect and dignity, not just those who extend respect first. The idea of criminal justice personnel adopting the philosophy of "I will treat you with respect if you treat me with respect" is an attitude well represented by the serviceable model. In the serviceable model, respect and dignity are based on a contract: if you give it, I will give it. Again, ethics should not be a component of criminal justice that is relegated to the serviceable model, because to do so disrupts the scale of justice. To not treat someone ethically diminishes or even destroys the ideas of humanity and righteousness.

There are three very important concepts that are embedded within each component of criminal justice: money, politics, and liability. These three concepts have a herculean impact on how justice is meted out and also directly affect the idea of justice.

First, it should be noted that money, politics, and liability are all necessary to keep the wheels of justice moving. The danger, however, is that each is often used in the wrong capacity, and when this occurs, serious damage to the image of criminal justice results. Let's examine each concept individually and note the role it is meant to serve and the contradictory role in which it often serves.

## Money

Obviously, the criminal justice system must have money to operate. Money is necessary to pay salaries, buy equipment, and provide buildings and structures for offices, vehicles for police officers, surveillance cameras for corrections, and many other vital assets needed by all criminal justice employees. In relation to these types of assets, the system of criminal justice is not removed from capitalism. In essence, the products and services used in the system designed to carry out justice cost money.

The concept of money within criminal justice becomes extremely troubling is when money is able to alter the type of justice that is delivered. Consider the example of a police officer not arresting a wealthy individual for the commission of a particular crime but arrests another person for the same crime based on that person's lower economic status. Consider the defendant charged by a prosecutor for a criminal act. Ask yourself, within the court process, who is more likely to receive quality legal representation. It will probably be someone who has money to hire the best-qualified attorney. This is meant to be an indictment of the countless dedicated lawyers who work for public defender's offices. The fact of the matter, however, is that these officers are overwhelmed, and employees often have no choice but to engage in what is described as assembly-line justice (Schmalleger, 2008).

## Politics

Many criminal justice leaders come to their positions as a result of the political process. Sheriffs, district attorneys, and many chiefs of police are elected to serve by the people. This is often a useful process because the representation of these officials is decided by popular vote. The people of the jurisdiction have the ability to select someone they feel is most qualified to represent their interests. The problematic nature of this process, however, lies in the fact that often the political process is used to affect how justice is served. Politics and money are intimately related. Who is ultimately elected to some position? Usually the answer is whoever had the most access to the most amount of money. Therefore, consider the elected sheriff or district attorney who orders an employee to not take action or to drop legitimate charges because the individual in question is related to someone who happened to provide a substantial monetary contribution to the last campaign.

## Liability

Liability is a concept that is much more difficult to accurately articulate in this context. Obviously, liability is central to the system of justice. It is the concept through which employees found to be violating the law or their authority and power are held accountable. Officers who use excessive force can be liable for any damage that may result. Attorneys who do not properly represent their client can also be held liable and forced to repair any damage that may have resulted.

Similar to politics, money is also at the heart of liability. Usually when someone is found liable, the individual and/or organization is ordered restore one to his or her original state by paying out money for the reparations. In this sense, liability is central to the system of justice. Not many wardens, chiefs of police, judges, or attorneys will maintain their employment for any substantial period of time if their actions result in the agency's continuously having to pay out large sums of money due to their wrongdoing.

What, then, is the problem with liability in criminal justice organizations? The problem lies in the fact that due to liability issues and fears, officials engage in actions that are meant to insulate the agency from having to pay out money as opposed to doing what is best for an individual or group and also what is ethical. This is the domain in which the lines become blurred. The question becomes, "Are we doing what is right, or are we doing what is most likely to keep us from having to pay out money?"

The scale of justice is central to all of criminal justice. Regardless of how the arms of the scale are described, the moral order, the social order, the ideal model, or the serviceability model, the central tenet remains. The goal of criminal justice is to provide protection, support, service, and quality of life for all citizens via respect and dignity without unnecessarily infringing on each individual's personal liberties and freedoms. Here are some issues to consider when examining the remaining chapters: can the scale of justice be balanced? If so, how?

## Ethics in Practice

### Does a Police Officer Have Freedom of Speech?

### *Nixon v. City of Houston (2007)*

On January 27, 2006, Thomas Nixon, a patrol officer with the Houston Police Department (HPD) in Texas, filed a § 1983 suit against the city of Houston and Chief of Police Harold Appellees for employment retaliation in violation of his First Amendment right to free speech. Specifically, Nixon claimed that his fifteen-day temporary suspension and his later indefinite suspension ("termination") from the HPD for making various statements during media interviews and in publications he authored violated his First Amendment rights.

Between May 2004 and January 2006, Nixon wrote a monthly column titled "The Insider" in *002 Magazine*, a local Houston periodical. In such articles, Nixon identified himself as a police officer, discussed his police-related activities, commented on his duties as an officer and on HPD policies, and—according to the HPD—made "caustic, offensive, and disrespectful" statements regarding certain groups of citizens, including minorities, women, and the homeless.

On January 18, 2005, there was a highly publicized high-speed police pursuit involving state and local law enforcement officers, including HPD officers, and a fleeing suspect. After the fleeing suspect had been identified, HPD supervisors ordered all HPD officers to discontinue the pursuit but permitted them to follow at a distance. Nonetheless, the fleeing suspect eventually collided with an innocent motorist. Although Nixon was not involved in the pursuit, he knew about it from local television reports he saw while he was off duty, at home, and preparing for his shift.

As soon as his shift started, Nixon proceeded to the scene of the accident—even though he was never instructed to do so. Upon arriving, Nixon asked a supervisor if anyone was going to make a statement to the media and suggested that he (Nixon) do so. After the supervisor failed to respond (other than by laughing), Nixon proceeded to speak to the media. Nixon, however, was not designated as an HPD spokesperson and was not authorized to make statements to the media at the scene. In his statement, Nixon criticized the HPD's decision to disengage the pursuit and stated he was "embarrassed to be a police officer" because the department did not stop fleeing suspects.

The HPD eventually received a citizen complaint about Nixon's articles. Thereafter, on or about September 28, 2005, the HPD initiated an Internal Affairs investigation to determine if Nixon and his articles violated any HPD policies. The investigation determined that Nixon's activities related to authoring and publishing the articles violated numerous HPD policies and undermined the efficiency of the services provided by the HPD. Consequently, the HPD temporarily suspended Nixon for fifteen days without pay beginning on February 1, 2006.

**Court's Opinion**

It is clear that Nixon's January 18, 2005, media statement at the scene of the accident is not protected by the First Amendment because it was made pursuant to his official duties and during the course of performing his job. Nixon spoke to the media while on duty, while in uniform, and while working at the scene of the accident. Before he made the statement, he made an attempt to get the approval of a supervisor to do so. His statement was intended to inform the public of the circumstances of the high-speed chase, the subsequent accident, and the HPD's high-speed chase policy. Quite simply, there is no relevant analogue to speech by citizens. The fact that Nixon's statement was unauthorized by the HPD and that speaking to the press was not part of his regular job duties is not dispositive—Nixon's statement was made while he was performing his job, and the fact that Nixon performed his job incorrectly, in an unauthorized manner, or in contravention of the wishes of his superiors does not convert his statement at the accident scene into protected citizen speech. Furthermore, speaking with the media is arguably one of an officer's job responsibilities, as HPD's Media Relations Policy directs: "In emergency or scene related situations, officers will provide the media with information regarding the scene or event in a timely manner."

Nixon's interest in commenting upon matters of public concern—although significant—is outweighed by the government's substantial interests in the efficient provision of government services. Nixon's 2006 media statements undermined the HPD's interests in maintaining discipline and order among employees and in promoting and maintaining public confidence in the HPD. Nixon posed as an official HPD spokesperson at the scene of an accident and criticized the HPD's handling of the high-speed pursuit at issue.

The court dismissed his complaint.

## Police in Transition

*"Police in Transition," by Jeremy Travis**

### The Principles of Democratic Policing

The first question, then, is, what does democratic policing look like? To shed light on that question, I wish to commend to you a document that was developed two years ago in the crucible of the conflict in Bosnia and Herzegovina.[1] In the context of the Youngstown accord, the warring factions came together to articulate a set of principles to guide the development of a new police force in their country. I believe that the seven principles set forth in this historic document—and the operational standards that were defined as necessary to their implementation—have widespread application, to stable democracies and emerging democracies alike. Allow me to summarize them.

First, the police must operate in accord with the principles of democracy. This means, in operational context, that the police should be trained in the law, should understand international standards of human rights, and should act in accordance with the criminal code. Police operations themselves should be governed by written policies that are available to the public. In other words, the management, execution, and articulation of all police activity should reflect commitment to the rule of law.

Second, the police, as recipients of public trust, should be considered as professionals whose conduct must be governed by a code of professional conduct. More than a mere collection of rules, this code should reflect the highest ethical values and should provide the basis upon which allegations of misconduct can be judged and disciplinary action taken.

Third, the police must have as their highest priority the protection of life. This principle has particular applications for the police use of force—namely, that the use of deadly force is appropriate only to save a life. The signatories also agreed that instances of the use of force should be investigated to determine whether they met these standards.

Fourth, the police must serve the community and consider themselves accountable to the community. To implement this principle, the signatories agreed to provide transparency to their operations—to publicly disseminate reports on crime and police operations, to establish mechanisms for the public to request police service, to create forums for open discus-

* Plenary address at the Fourth Biennial Conference: International Perspectives on Crime, Justice, and Public Order in Budapest, Hungary, June 21, 1998), by Jeremy Travis, director, National Institute of Justice, is reprinted with permission from the *FBI Law Enforcement Bulletin*, March 2009.

sion of crime problems, and to establish external review of allegations of police misconduct.

Fifth, the police must recognize that protection of life and property is the primary function of police operations. The agreement also states that, notwithstanding the importance of criminal investigations, the primary concern of police operations must be the prevention of crime.

Sixth, the police must conduct their activities with respect for human dignity and basic human rights. Specifically, the agreement stated that torture or other cruel or degrading treatment could not be practiced nor countenanced and that officers should be expected to report all instances of alleged human rights violations.

Finally, the police are expected to discharge their duties in a nondiscriminatory manner. The agreement specifically states that "discrimination on the basis of race, sex, religion, or ethnicity in the delivery of police services is incompatible with policing in a democratic state."

I submit that these seven principles provide a solid foundation for a sustained discussion on the attributes of democratic policing. They apply equally forcefully to policing in the United States and policing in Bosnia-Herzegovina. They articulate accountability to the rule of law, transparency in the conduct of police activities, fidelity to principles of equality, commitment to the value of human life and human dignity, and recognition that effective policing requires partnership with the communities being served.

## Effective Leadership*

### Organizational Ethics through Effective Leadership

Captain Brandon Zuidema is a staff officer and Major H. Wayne Duff is the deputy chief of police with the police department in Lynchburg, Virginia.

Is the criminal justice policy, procedure, or law meant to enhance or preserve human dignity or righteousness, or is it meant to ensure that as long as it is followed, the employees and organizations will not be forced to pay out money?

Members of the law enforcement profession find it disheartening when officers make unethical decisions. And studies pertaining to police corruption and dishonest behavior have not resulted in a consensus concerning why the issue exists or how best to address it. However, an organization's prevalence of corruption can correlate with the quality of

* Reprinted with permission from Zuidema, B. V. and Duff, Jr., W. H., Organizational ethics through effective leadership. FBI Law Enforcement Bulletin, pp. 4–9, March, 2009.

its leaders. To this end, agencies should strive to develop strong, ethical leadership to deter this problem in their ranks.

## Facilitating an Ethical Workforce

To help discourage corruption among law enforcement personnel, departments must incorporate an organization-wide emphasis on ethical behavior, beginning with leaders. However, this does not entail a "do this or else" approach but, rather, an understanding of what constitutes ethical decision making and why it is critical to policing. Through repetition, this emphasis can become as much a part of day-to-day functioning as the agency's policies and procedures.

Law enforcement leaders can encourage ethical behavior among personnel in several ways. First, they should incorporate these ideals into the mission and values of the organization. The stated values of the Lynchburg Police Department (LPD) in Virginia consist of leadership (includes the desire to do the right thing), professionalism (part of which is lawful and ethical behavior), and dedication. And employees easily can recall these terms because they coincide with the agency's initials. The LPD prominently displays these values for community members and officers to see daily on the department's police cars, brochures, and Web site.[1]

Second, leaders can make the focus on ethical behavior part of organizational functions, such as formal events and internal training sessions. For instance, at every public ceremony it holds, the LPD invites all sworn law enforcement officers to recite the International Association of Chiefs of Police (IACP) Oath of Honor. Public and private reminders of the importance of values, such as ethical behavior, lend them long-term credence.

Third, departments can emphasize ethical behavior in their organizational philosophy. The LPD has remained committed to community policing and its focus on empowering officers to make decisions and solve problems individually and jointly with citizens. In this approach, leaders accept officers' errors, or bad decisions, as part of the learning process. Agencies must recognize that if their personnel do not make mistakes, they are not doing anything. When people take risks, failures will occur. To encourage ethical behavior amidst both right and wrong decisions, leaders must differentiate between "mistakes of the head" (honest errors resulting from a lack of training or experience) and "mistakes of the heart" (based on unethical decisions) and deal with each appropriately.[2]

Finally, and perhaps most important, agencies should not tolerate unethical behavior or decision making. That may seem to oversimplify the issue, but, in reality, it does not. One instance of unethical conduct not dealt with appropriately can overturn all efforts at instilling the importance of ethical behavior. Organizational policy and procedure must clearly dictate that unethical conduct will not be tolerated, and leaders must deal with such behavior consistently.

## Developing and Maintaining Ethical Leadership

Agencies must focus their attention on both developing new leaders and maintaining the effectiveness of existing ones. Leadership can be defined as "an individual's ability to influence, motivate, and enable others to contribute toward an organization's success."[3] Effective leaders care about fellow employees, the department, and the community. They must be ethical and possess the desire and ability to do the right thing no matter how hard it is.[4]

In terms of developing new leaders, a virtual explosion of leadership training has occurred in law enforcement over the past five years. Organizations such as the IACP; the Virginia Association of Chiefs of Police (VACP), through its training arm, the Virginia Police Chief's Foundation; and numerous local law enforcement agencies and criminal justice academies have implemented training aimed at developing new leaders, not just supervisors. Recognizing the need to enhance leadership development efforts, agencies must nurture and mentor up-and-coming individuals who eventually will lead the organization. This supports effective succession planning.

Constant improvement of leaders, the agency, and the community are critical. Therefore, leadership training and development must remain at the forefront of a department's strategic planning efforts. The majority of programs now found in law enforcement include classroom sessions on leadership philosophy and traits, ethical behavior, and decision making and employee development and discipline. Many initiatives also focus on issues more closely tied to supervision, such as critical incident management, supervisory liability, and media relations, thereby encouraging more effective leadership among emerging supervisors.

While developing such a program may seem achievable only by large organizations with vast training budgets, this is not the case. In 2002, the LPD recognized its pressing need to introduce new and developing leaders to many of the concepts previously provided only through informal mentoring or advanced training of police command staff. While informal mentoring can prove successful, agencies cannot afford to rely on it to ensure the development of their leaders. At the same time, most departments cannot or do not commit to the creation and support of a formal mentoring program for leaders. This results in a tremendous void in a critical component of agency success.

With the cooperation of the Central Virginia Criminal Justice Academy, the LPD moved forward with developing and implementing a program aimed at providing meaningful training for new law enforcement leaders. The agency identified a twenty-four-hour combination of leadership, ethics, and supervisory training components for developing leaders in the sixty-two departments represented in its regional academy. The LPD used existing relationships with a number of law enforcement and academic professionals to identify instructors and make the program a reality. Sessions cover many areas of leadership and supervision.

"Laws of leadership" and traits of successful leaders include the following:

- Effective communication
- Team building
- Goals and objectives
- Ethics and ethical decision making
- Employee development and dealing with problem personnel
- Generational issues for leaders and employees
- Stress management
- Media relations
- Legal issues and supervisory liability
- Critical incident management

The LPD also enhanced the program for its own personnel by developing an additional 16 hours of training aimed at better preparing them for agency-specific leadership and supervisory responsibilities. This portion comprises several sessions: department mission and values; Lynchburg city government, Special Operations Division; employee evaluation system, significant incident (Internal Affairs) investigations; accreditation; and unit overviews, including call-out procedures for canine, communications, criminal investigations, and vice/narcotics.

Because of interest in the training, the LPD continues to prepare for new sessions. The authors also developed a two-day leadership course for the Virginia Center for Policing Innovation, further evidence that organizations want to adopt a proactive approach to leadership development. From a budgetary standpoint, outside of time spent arranging for instructors and appropriate lesson plans, the LPD has committed no organizational or outside fiscal resources.

The LPD has found that the officers who complete the training gain not only practical knowledge but also increased confidence in their ability to lead and supervise. They have a better recognition of their responsibility and the need to study leadership and ethics to be effective law enforcement leaders. The seemingly endless "revolving door" of personnel (along with knowledge and experience) that agencies face highlights the importance of opportunities, such as this leadership training program.

## Encouraging Ethical Behavior

Agencies must do more than develop effective leaders. Leadership instructors and mentors throughout academia have recognized the need to remain flexible in how they lead, aware of new and unique approaches to leadership, and committed to ethical behavior no matter what challenges they face. Experts have made such suggestions as adapting leadership methods to employee behavior and "sharpening the saw" by routinely reevaluating if leadership efforts accomplish what agencies intend.[5] One law enforcement authority pointed out the criticality of understanding the changes in tactics, techniques, technology, and people.[6] Leaders must understand these trends and adjust to them, as they are both significant and inevitable. As they deal with multiple generations of employees with unique needs and expectations, leaders cannot assume that what proved effective yesterday will work tomorrow or even today in terms of providing leadership and instilling ethical standards for the workforce.

## Law Enforcement Oath of Honor

On my honor, I will never betray my badge, my integrity, my character, or the public trust. I will always have the courage to hold myself and others accountable for our actions. I will always uphold the Constitution, my community, and the agency I serve.

During the keynote presentation at the 2007 VACP annual conference, the speaker emphasized the need for leaders to practice self-examination and to make changes when necessary.[7] This message was powerful and timely as people continue to hear of misconduct and corruption in law enforcement organizations. As most agencies pursue some form of community policing, the ability to establish strong partnerships and working relationships with citizens based on trust becomes more difficult each time police officers make unethical decisions. Strong, effective leadership requires constantly stressing, among other things, ethical behavior and living by the Oath of Honor. To achieve this, agencies must continually expose leaders to organizational and professional expectations of ethics and integrity to allow them to set high standards for their own behavior and that of their subordinates. The LPD does this through training during annual supervisors' meetings, repeated emphasis on department values in goals and planning documents, and due diligence in investigating and addressing all incidents of unethical behavior.

## Conclusion

While law enforcement agencies cannot completely eliminate corruption or mistakes of the heart in the profession, leaders must concentrate on strengthening their leadership skills and abilities to create an environment in which such unacceptable behavior will occur less frequently and, when it does, will not be tolerated. They must avoid getting caught up in the day-to-day tasks required of law enforcement administrators that, while critical, can adversely affect their leadership efforts. Leaders must acknowledge their mistakes and those of subordinates and learn from them. They also must be willing to ask themselves if they are leading in a manner consistent with their values and ethics, as well as those of their organization and profession.

## Questions in Review

1. What is meant by "scale of justice"?
2. Compare and contrast social order and moral order.
3. Compare and contrast idealism and serviceability.
4. Identify the connections between ethics, the criminal justice system, and money, politics, and liability.

## Notes

1. http://www.lynchburgpolice.org
2. Samuel Feemster, "Spirituality: The DNA of Law Enforcement Practice," *FBI Law Enforcement Bulletin*, November 2007, 8–17.
3. The authors base this definition on their work and research in the area.
4. Feemster, 8–17.
5. Stephen Covey, *The 7 Habits of Highly Effective People* (New York: Free Press, 2004); and Kenneth Blanchard and Spencer Johnson, *The One Minute Manager* (New York: William Morrow, 1982).
6. Ronald Ruecker, "Working Together in the Year Ahead," *The Police Chief*, November 2007.
7. Stephen Gower, lecture given at the 2007 VACP annual conference in Williamsburg, VA.

# Ethics and Criminal Prosecutions

# 10

## Introduction

> It has been observed that a Grand Jury can indict anyone or anything—even a ham sandwich. Now, under the majority's holding, apparently anyone can present the People's case to the Grand Jury—even an unadmitted layperson masquerading as an attorney. Because this position makes a mockery of both the rules prohibiting legal practice by laypersons and the Grand Jury system itself. (Vito J. Titone, Jr., in dissent in *People v. Carter*, 77 N.Y.2d 95 (1990)

In *People v. Carter* (1990), quoted above, the defendant had appealed his conviction of possession and sale of a controlled substance. It was later discovered that the assistant district attorney who presented the case before the grand jury was not admitted to the New York bar, a requirement to practice law in New York. The appellate court held that the fact that the assistant district attorney was not a lawyer did not result in a deprivation of the defendant's constitutional due process rights. The majority of the justices in this case apparently ignored the fact that as a member of the bar, the prosecutor has certain ethical duties imposed upon him or her.

Before any considerations regarding the ethical obligations of a prosecutor or police officer, we must keep in mind that the primary responsibility of a prosecutor is not to prosecute, but to promote justice. The duty of a defense counsel, however, is not to promote justice but to represent the client zealously within the bounds of the law. In a criminal trial, the defense's duty is to his or her client within the bounds of the law. Our system of justice functions on the adversary system wherein the prosecutor represents the people and the defense represents the accused, with the judge acting as the referee. As noted by R. R. Kidston (1958, p. 148), former senior crown prosecutor of New South Wales

> A prosecutor is a "minister of justice." The prosecutor's principal role is to assist the court to arrive at the truth and to do justice between the community and the accused according to law and the dictates of fairness.
>
> A prosecutor is not entitled to act as if representing private interests in litigation. A prosecutor represents the community and not any individual or sectional interest. A prosecutor acts independently, yet in the general public interest. The "public interest" is to be understood in that context as an

historical continuum: acknowledging debts to previous generations and obligations to future generations.

A similar statement by a Colorado appellate court in *People v. Marin* (1983, p. 1353) noted,

A prosecutor's duty is to seek justice. A prosecutor has the responsibility of a minister of justice and not simply that of an advocate. This responsibility carries with it specific obligations to see that the defendant is accorded procedural justice and that guilt is decided upon the basis of sufficient evidence.

## Police Investigative Misconduct

A law enforcement official using his or her authority provided under the "color of law" is allowed to stop individuals and even to search them if necessary and retain their property under certain circumstances. If the officer abuses that discretionary power, he or she is violating a person's civil rights might occur. An unlawful detention and/or an illegal confiscation of property are also examples of such an abuse of power.

An officer violates both ethics and the law by fabricating evidence against or conducting a false arrest of an individual. The Fourteenth Amendment secures the right to due process, and the Eighth Amendment also prohibits the use of cruel and unusual punishment. In an arrest or detention context, these rights make the unnecessary use of force illegal because it amounts to summary punishment. Under our system of law, a person accused of a crime is to be allowed the opportunity to have a trial and not be subjected to punishment without having been afforded the opportunity of the legal process.

Title 42, U.S.C. § 14141, makes it unlawful for state or local law enforcement agencies to allow officers to engage in a pattern or practice of conduct that deprives persons of rights protected by the Constitution or laws of the United States. The law is commonly referred to as the Police Misconduct Statute. The U.S. code gives the U.S. Attorney General's Office the authority to seek civil remedies, in addition to criminal sanctions, in cases where it is determined that law enforcement agencies have policies or practices that foster a pattern of misconduct by law enforcement or correctional officers. Most of the FBI's color of law investigations would fall into five broad areas: excessive force; sexual assaults; false arrest/fabrication of evidence, deprivation of property, and failure to keep from harm.

## Prosecutor Misconduct

In *Berger v. United States* (1935), the Supreme Court held that the prosecutor had overstepped the bounds of the propriety and fairness that should characterize the conduct of such an officer in the prosecution of a criminal offense is clearly shown by the record. He was guilty of misstating the facts in his cross-examination of witnesses; of putting into the mouths of such witnesses things that they had not said; of suggesting by his questions that statements had been made to him personally out of court, in respect of which no proof was offered; of pretending to understand that a witness had said something that he had not said and persistently cross-examining the witness upon that basis; of assuming prejudicial facts not in evidence; of bullying and arguing with witnesses; and, in general, of conducting himself in a thoroughly indecorous and improper manner. The U.S. attorney's argument to the jury was undignified and intemperate, containing improper insinuations and assertions calculated to mislead the jury.

The Court noted that it is impossible, however, without reading the testimony at some length and thereby obtaining knowledge of the setting in which the objectionable matter occurred, to appreciate fully the extent of the misconduct. The Court noted that the trial judge sustained objections to some of the questions, insinuations, and misstatements and instructed the jury to disregard them. But, according to the Court, the situation was one that called for stern rebuke and repressive measures and, perhaps, if these were not successful, for the granting of a mistrial. The Court held that it was impossible to say that the evil influence upon the jury of these acts of misconduct was removed by such mild judicial action as was taken.

The Court stated that the United States attorney is the representative not of an ordinary party to a controversy but of a sovereignty whose obligation to govern impartially is as compelling as its obligation to govern at all and whose interest, therefore, in a criminal prosecution is not that it shall win a case but that justice shall be done. As such, he is in a peculiar and very definite sense the servant of the law, the twofold aim of which is that guiltty shall not escape or innocencent suffer. He may prosecute with earnestness and vigor—indeed, he should do so. But, while he may strike hard blows, he is not at liberty to strike foul ones. It is as much his duty to refrain from improper methods calculated to produce a wrongful conviction as it is to use every legitimate means to bring about a just one.

## Personal Attacks on Opposing Counsel

In *People v. Woods* (2006), a California appellate court held that it was improper for a prosecutor to resort to personal attacks on the integrity of opposing counsel. In her closing argument, the prosecutor stated, "Do you know what's interesting about the defense witnesses in this case? They were conjured up in the last week and a half." Defense counsel objected, but the court overruled the objection. The prosecutor continued, saying, "It was over the weekend that Mr. Timmons was conjured up, and he is going to come in and help his friend."

## Animosity between Counsel

In *State v. Noriega* (1984), the defendant was charged in an Arizona state court with burglary in the first degree and with aggravated assault. The Superior Court of Pima County (Arizona) convicted the defendant as charged and sentenced her to two consecutive life terms without the possibility of parole for 25 years. In court, the prosecutor approached defense counsel. He informed the defense attorney that he would seek the maximum sentence of mandatory life imprisonment against his client and that no plea bargain would be offered in the case. At this point, both attorneys exchanged insults, including obscenities. Three days later, on October 25, 1982, the prosecutor wrote a letter to defense counsel. In that letter, the prosecutor blamed defense counsel for sparking their altercation.

He wrote thereafter,

> When I approached your table after the matter was continued, I wanted to let you know that the case was not negotiable due to the seriousness of your client's conduct.
>
> The name-calling by you which followed—including calling me "a slime"—may have made you fell [sic] better but certainly accomplished nothing in terms of dealing with this particular case.
>
> I am not particularly proud of my response to your outburst, but, on the other hand, it seemed the least objectionable to me, from a professional standpoint, considering the other alternatives which crossed my mind.
>
> I have no intention of fueling the flames of personal motivation [sic] which seem about to engulf your professional well-being, therefore I shall not communicate with you on a personal basis.
>
> Moreover, since you "don't give a s…t in this case and seem to have slipped to the point of allowing your personal feelings to cloud your professional judgment, I would suggest that you ask that the case be reassigned to another attorney within your office."
>
> Perhaps the new attorney would care, at least enough to point out reasons, if any exist, why I'm wrong and should negotiate.
>
> Certainly, you would agree with me that personal feelings should not enter into the negotiation and disposition of criminal cases.
>
> Should you wish to apologize you may reach me at …
>
> All future communications in this case must be in writing.

The defense counsel characterized the prosecutor's suggestion that he might be willing to negotiate with a different defense attorney as a veiled threat to foreclose plea negotiations as long as defense counsel remained on the case. On appeal, the government contended that the prosecutor refused to negotiate because of the seriousness of the accused's crimes and background and that defense counsel had simply suggested no persuasive reason why he should negotiate.

On October 27, 1982, the defense counsel wrote a letter to the prosecutor insisting that the prosecutor had been overcome by prosecutorial vindictiveness and demanding that he withdraw from the case. No plea negotiations preceded this dispute, nor were plea negotiations conducted thereafter. In January 1983, the prosecutor announced on the record that no plea agreement would be offered to the appellant. Plea agreements were offered to the codefendants, who were represented by different attorneys, though neither appeared as culpable as the defendant. On February 22, 1982, defense counsel moved to dismiss the prosecutor, alleging prosecutorial vindictiveness. The trial court denied the motion without finding whether or not the alleged threat was actually made. The trial court did so because, after the making of the alleged threat, the decision to seek a life sentence against the appellant was reviewed and subsequently affirmed by a panel of three prosecuting attorneys that included the prosecutor in question.

The court noted that given defense counsel's apparent personal animosity for him, the prosecutor recommended that the case be reassigned to another defense attorney, though he did not foreclose other ways of resolving the problem. Because their altercation occurred 20 days after the appellant was charged, reassignment of another attorney was still a practical option. The prosecutor also properly remarked that he was not proud of his conduct and that personal feelings should not enter into the disposition of criminal cases. The court stated that it did not approve of the hostile tone of the prosecutor's letter. The court also noted that a prosecuting attorney is held to a higher standard of conduct than an ordinary attorney. The court stated,

> The prosecutor is not the representative of an ordinary litigant; he is the representative of a government whose obligation to govern fairly is as important as its obligation to govern at all. The prosecutor's interest in a criminal prosecution is not that it shall win a case but that justice shall be done. Thus, while he may strike hard blows, he is not at liberty to strike foul ones. It is the prosecutor's duty to refrain from improper methods calculated to produce a wrongful conviction just as it is his duty to use all proper methods calculated to bring about a just conviction.

## Ethical Duty to Disclose Information

A few years ago, the U.S Attorney's Office in San Diego, California, was prosecuting a known drug dealer for bringing controlled substances into the United States. The defense had made several offers to enter into a plea agreement that were refused by the assistant U.S. attorney. The day before the trial, the prosecutor discovered that her main witness was confined in a Mexico jail and would not be able to testify. The trial judge had previously indicated that he would allow no more delays in the case. The day of the trial, the prosecutor approached the defense counsel and indicated that the government had changed its position and would consider a plea agreement. An agreement was reached, and the defendant pleaded guilty. After the defendant was sent to prison, the defense counsel discovered that the prosecutor knew that the main witness was unavailable and that she probably could not have proved the case against the defendant.

*Did the prosecutor have an affirmative duty to notify the defense that the major witness in the case was unavailable at trial?*

The bar association held that while the prosecutor had an affirmative duty to disclose any evidence favorable to the defense, she had no duty to inform the defense as to the status of her witnesses.

In *Kyles v. Whitley* (U.S. 1995), the U.S. Supreme Court noted that the prosecution has an affirmative duty to disclose evidence favorable to a defendant. The suppression by the prosecution of evidence favorable to an accused upon request violates due process when the evidence is material either to guilt or to punishment, irrespective of the good faith or bad faith of the prosecution. The prosecutor in a criminal case shall make timely disclosure to the defense of all evidence or information known to the prosecutor that tends to negate the guilt of the accused or mitigates the offense.

The leading case on the prosecutor's duty to disclose is *Brady v. Maryland* (1963). After Brady had been convicted in a Maryland state court on a charge of murder in the first degree (committed in the course of a robbery) and had been sentenced to death, he learned of an extrajudicial confession of his accomplice, tried separately, admitting the actual homicide. This confession had been suppressed by the prosecution notwithstanding a request by Brady's counsel to allow him to examine the accomplice's extrajudicial statements. Upon appeal from the trial court's dismissal of his petition for postconviction relief, the Maryland Court of Appeals held that suppression of the evidence by the prosecution denied Brady due process of law, and remanded the case for a retrial.

The U.S. Supreme Court affirmed. Justice Byron White stated, "We now hold that the suppression by the prosecution of evidence favorable to an accused upon request violates due process where the evidence is material either to guilt or to punishment, irrespective of the good faith or bad faith of the prosecution."

In *United States v. Keogh* (1968), the U.S. Court of Appeals for the Second Circuit noted that the law as to prosecutorial suppression of evidence could be classified into three types:

- deliberate bad faith suppression by the prosecutor for the very purpose of obstructing the defense, or the prosecutor's intentional failure to disclose evidence whose high probative value to the defense could not have escaped the prosecutor's attention;

- deliberate refusal by a prosecutor to honor a request for evidence when the evidence is material to guilt or punishment, irrespective of the prosecutor's good faith or bad faith in refusing the request; and
- where suppression was not deliberate and no request for evidence was made but where hindsight discloses that it was so material that the defense could have put the evidence to "not insignificant use."

The court in Keogh ruled that the standard of materiality in suppression cases varies with the type of suppression. The court stated that to warrant relief in cases where suppression was not deliberate and no request was made but hindsight discloses the usefulness of the evidence to the defense, the standard of materiality must be considerably higher than in the other categories. By "standard of materiality," the court was referring to how critical the information was to the results of the case.

## Presentation of Inadmissible Evidence by the Prosecutor

In *Williams v. State* (1987), the principal issue on appeal was whether prosecutorial misconduct necessitates reversal of an appellant's conviction. The court noted that the prosecutor's conduct was far from ideal.

In his closing argument, the prosecutor stated that:

She [murder victim] didn't meet him for dinner, did she? That's because Mr. Williams had something else in mind. What he had in mind was not a date for dinner. It was a date for death. Happy Valentine's Day from Oscar to Toy with malice. Cupid uses arrows. Mr. Williams used bullets on February the 12th, 1982.

The appellate court stated that it was quite clear that "holiday" arguments are inappropriate and had no purpose other than to arouse the jurors' emotions. The prosecutor also improperly placed the jury in the position of the victim by stating the following:

Something caused her to turn back around to where she is shot and discovered in the position where she is found. Perhaps her name or a voice she recognized. In any event, she turned around. Can you imagine what she must have felt when she saw that it was the defendant and he had a gun?

The court also held that the prosecutor also used testimony, twice ruled inadmissible, that of a policeman who thought the appellant's chief alibi witness was lying, and he contended that the appellant purchased the alibi testimony, although there was no evidence from which to draw such an inference. The court noted that a prosecutor may not argue facts or inferences not supported by the evidence. Nor may he disparage legitimate defense tactics, but in this case the prosecutor derided impeachment of a defense witness as a poor reward for a public-spirited citizen. Also the court noted that the prosecutor was in violation of a direct admonition from the bench (as well as a rule of professional conduct), made statements to media representatives concerning intended witnesses and proof.

The court held that though there was clear and repeated misconduct on the part of a prosecutor, the defendant's conviction for the murder of his wife was affirmed because the evidence of his guilt was so overwhelming as to cause the misconduct to be harmless.

## Decision to Prosecute

In the American system of justice, the decision to prosecute or not to prosecute is generally made by the prosecutor with only limited oversight. In this section, we will examine the ethical issues that should be considered when prosecutors are making the decision to prosecute. Consider the following scenario: two criminals brutally rape and murder a twelve-year-old child. The prosecutor wants to send both individuals to prison for life, but she has problems with the evidence. The only possibility of successfully prosecuting either individual is based on making a deal with one of the murderers for his testimony. Which is more ethical, making a deal with a murderer and rapist to punish one of the offenders or refusing to deal with a murderer and rapist and allowing both defendants to go unpunished?

As noted by the court in *United States v. Al Jibori* (1996):

> While the nation's prosecutors retain "broad discretion" to enforce our criminal laws, this discretion is bound by constitutional constraints such as the Due Process Clause of the Fifth Amendment, which prohibits a decision to prosecute from being based on an unjustifiable standard such as race, religion, or other arbitrary classification.

In *United States v. Gist* (2008), the defendant claimed that the government decided to prosecute him because he exercised his Fifth Amendment right to remain silent. The court noted that a defendant bears the initial burden of proof in a vindictive prosecution claim and is required to establish at least the appearance of vindictiveness. The court noted that prosecutorial vindictiveness might occur when the government penalizes a defendant for invoking legally protected rights. However, the court noted that there was no prosecutorial vindictiveness when the prosecutor's decision to prosecute was based on the usual determinative factors.

In order to show that the decision to prosecute by a prosecutor was not based on the "usual determinative factors" and to simply obtain an evidentiary hearing, a defendant must make a substantial threshold showing of an improper motivation on the prosecutor's part. Prosecutorial vindictiveness is not established simply because a defendant exercised a legal right and was subsequently indicted for an additional offense. In support of a motion to dismiss, a defendant must show that the prosecution was "motivated by actual vindictiveness." A defendant must also "present evidence that absent this motive, the defendant would not have been prosecuted" (*United States v. Gist*, 2008).

In *United States v. Mariani* (2000), the defendant, Mariani, was charged with mail fraud in connection with the waste disposal industry. The United States attorney prosecuting the case, David Barasch, was previously employed as an assistant to Governor Robert Casey. During this time he played a role in attempting to regulate the waste management industry. Mariani alleged that because of this, the prosecutor took a hands-on approach to acquiring an indictment from the grand jury and had an improper motive for prosecution. The court ruled there was no "substantial threshold showing of either specific animus or ill will on the part of U.S. Attorney or that, absent such factors, they [the defendants] would not have been prosecuted."

In Government of *Virgin Islands v. Bryan* (1990), the defendant Bryan filed a motion to dismiss the criminal information against him, claiming selective prosecution. He was being prosecuted for shoplifting. The defendant claimed that because of his dissident political views and his frequent vocal criticism of various branches and agencies of the government—both local and federal—he had been singled out for prosecution. Bryan claimed that the government's decision to prosecute him, but not others, for allegedly taking merchandise without permission amounted to selective prosecution and was a violation of his First Amendment right to free speech. The government opposed the motion, claiming that its decision to prosecute the defendant in no way singled out defendant nor was it made on a basis such as race, religion, or some other arbitrary factor or that the defendant's prosecution was intended to prevent his exercise of a fundamental right or was instituted in retaliation for his exercising such a right. Rather, the government claimed the decision to prosecute the defendant was based simply on the right of the government to exercise its broad discretion in determining which cases to prosecute. The court held that because the defendant failed to demonstrate a colorable claim in support of his motion to dismiss for selective prosecution, his motion was denied.

While in the vast majority of cases the defense of selective prosecution has been unsuccessful, there are several exceptions. In *United States v. Correa-Gomez* (2001), the government charged the defendant with encouraging and inducing seven illegal aliens to enter the United States and harboring them during their tenure as employees at his restaurants. The defendant moved to dismiss the indictment for selective prosecution. The evidence indicated that between 1996 and 2000, the Immigration and Naturalization Service (INS) conducted 17 raids against businesses owned by non-Hispanics within the Eastern District of Kentucky. The raids resulted in the apprehension of 218 illegal aliens—199 of whom presented false cards when they were hired—and zero criminal prosecutions. Other than the fact that the defendant was prosecuted, his case was factually unremarkable when compared to those similarly situated to him. When the INS raided his restaurant, they apprehended 14 illegal aliens, nine of whom gave false cards to the defendant when they were hired. The court held that these facts indicated the defendant was similarly situated to the other non-Hispanic business owners who were not charged with criminal wrongdoing.

The court noted that an illegal alien's presentation of paperwork that appeared genuine was an affirmative defense to prosecution. The court concluded that the government applied this rebuttable presumption to every business owner prior to the defendant but not to the defendant. The court held that the government's decision not to give him the same benefit of the doubt it extended to other similarly situated non-Hispanic business owners confirmed that the defendant had been singled out for prosecution.

## Law Enforcement's Decision to Prosecute

Often the prosecutor decides to prosecute based on the recommendations of the police, the decision to prosecute is the prosecutor's discretion. For example, in *Eubanks v. Gerwen* (1994), the plaintiff filed a civil suit against the defendant police officers, alleging malicious prosecution under 42 U.S.C.S. § 1983 and a state law malicious prosecution claim. The plaintiff had filed the suit after a confidential informant led the police to arrest the plaintiff for possession of cocaine, for which he was ultimately acquitted. The plaintiff alleged that a confidential informant had set him up to get a better sentence for himself on a pending criminal charge. On appeal, the appellate court ordered the dismissal of the suit against the defendant police officers because the prosecutor, not the defendants, made the ultimate decision as to whether to prosecute the plaintiff criminally.

## Judicial Misconduct

A *Los Angeles Times* article reported that two Pennsylvania judges were charged with taking kickbacks of more than $2 million to send young offenders to a privately run, for-profit detention center. The judges pleaded guilty in a federal court in Scranton to "honest services fraud" and tax fraud. The plea agreements call for more than seven years in prison for the judges. (Los Angeles Times, 2009, p. A13, February 13.)

In *Matter of LaBombard* (2008), Dennis LaBombard, justice of the Ellenburg Town Court, New York, sought review of a determination by the Commission on Judicial Conduct finding that he had engaged in serious judicial misconduct and that recommended that he be removed from office. The court agreed with the commission's recommendation that LaBombard be removed from his office as town justice. The following paragraphs were taken from the court's decision.

LaBombard had been a town justice since 1996. In September 2006, he was served with a complaint containing seven charges of misconduct, four of which were sustained by the commission after a hearing before a referee. Charge I arose from the petitioner's decision to preside over a case involving members of his family. His step-grandson and step-granddaughter were charged with criminal trespass in the third degree, a class B misdemeanor, as a result of an incident that occurred in the Town of Clinton. The charges were lodged in the petitioner's court, rather than Clinton Town Court, because one of the defendants was related to a town justice in Clinton. The prosecuting assistant district attorney—who was not aware of the petitioner's relationship to two of the defendants—offered to dispose of the charges by adjournment in contemplation of dismissal on the condition that each defendant agree to perform twenty-five hours of community service. Justice LaBombard adjourned the cases in contemplation of dismissal but, without the knowledge of the prosecutor, did not impose the community service requirement.

Charge II also involved his step-grandson, who had been charged with a class E felony in a case pending in another town court. Justice LaBombard contacted the town justice assigned the case and identified himself, knowing that the other judge was aware that he was a fellow jurist. After inquiring about the date of the next court appearance, he advised the court that his step-grandson was a "good kid," and made additional remarks about other individuals involved in the case, giving the impression that the co-defendants were more culpable than his step-grandson.

The next charge stemmed from Justice LaBombard's decision to preside over an arraignment and bail proceeding involving the son of a former co-worker with whom he had worked in the same department for several years. Based on his own statements to commission staff, he apparently recognized that his familiarity with this individual could warrant recusal; he stated that if the offense had not been a felony and had been before him for disposition, he would have disqualified himself. Instead, he arraigned the defendant and, based on the recommendation of the district attorney's office, set bail at

$5,000 cash or $10,000 bond. Unable to make bail, the defendant was taken into custody. The next day he received an ex parte telephone call from defendant's mother, his former co-worker, who indicated that the defendant would lose his job if he remained in jail. Following this conversation, he authorized defendant's release on his own recognizance.

The final charge concerned Justice LaBombard's conduct after he was involved in a minor motor vehicle accident with another motorist. The collision did not result in property damage or personal injury but a verbal altercation ensued when both drivers exited their vehicles. He repeatedly and gratuitously told the other motorist that he was a judge, suggesting that because of his judicial status, she must have been in the wrong and had caused the accident. When the motorist entered a nearby barbershop to call the police, he followed her into the shop and continued referring to his judicial status.

As the commission determined, Justice LaBombard's conduct violated several of the rules governing judicial conduct. As a judge, he was under a duty to conduct himself in such a manner as to inspire public confidence in the integrity, fair-mindedness, and impartiality of the judiciary. Few principles are more fundamental to the integrity, fair-mindedness, and impartiality of the judiciary than the requirement that judges not preside over or otherwise intervene in judicial matters involving relatives.

The handling by a judge of a case to which a family member is a party creates an appearance of impropriety as well as a very obvious potential for abuse and threatens to undermine the public's confidence in the impartiality of the judiciary. Any involvement by a judge in such cases or any similar suggestion of favoritism to family members has been and will continue to be viewed by this court as serious misconduct.

The same is true of intervention by a judge in proceedings involving family members pending in another court, particularly when that intervention takes the form of ex parte contact with the judge presiding over the relative's case. And we have noted that the absence of a specific request for favorable treatment or special consideration is irrelevant. In this case, he engaged in serious misconduct when he sat on a criminal matter involving his two step-grandchildren and intervened in a case against his step-grandson pending in another court.

## New York Rules of Judicial Conduct Cited by the Court

- *22 NYCRR 100.2[C]:* A judge shall not lend the prestige of judicial office to advance the private interests of the judge or others, nor shall a judge convey or permit others to convey the impression that they are in a special position to influence the judge.
- *22 NYCRR 100.3[B][6]:* A judge shall not initiate, permit, or consider ex parte communications or consider other communications

made to the judge outside the presence of the parties or their lawyers concerning a pending or impending proceeding.

- *22 NYCRR 100.3[E][1]:* A judge shall disqualify himself or herself
  in a proceeding in which the judge's impartiality might reasonably be questioned.
- *22 NYCRR 100.3 [E][1]:* The finding of misconduct does not depend
  on whether the children of the spouse of a judge's child are relatives
  within the sixth degree of consanguinity or affinity under Judiciary
  Law § 14. The petitioner did not dispute that he had a familial relationship with his step-grandchildren. As such, his decision to sit on
  the case clearly presented a situation in which the judge's impartiality might reasonably be questioned, thereby warranting recusal.

## Sexual Harassment by a Federal Judge

*When a judge is accused of a serious crime such as sexual assault, should the
judge be allowed to continue to function in the federal district court?*

In 2009, U.S. District Court Judge Samuel Kent pleaded guilty to lying
to a committee of the U.S. Court of Appeals, Ninth Circuit. He also admitted he engaged in repeated "non-consensual sexual contact" with two female
court employees and lied to cover it up (Bazelon, 2009, p. E1). The allegations
against Kent were first made in spring 2007 when his case manager filed a
misconduct complaint with the 5th Circuit Judicial Council accusing Kent of
pushing up her shirt and bra, putting his mouth on her exposed breast, and
pushing her head toward his crotch. After the incident in 2007 became public, other complaints were received regarding Kent. Finally in late 2007, the
U.S. Department of Justice started a criminal investigation of Kent.

Four months after the case manager's complaint was filed, the chief
judge, Edith Jones, reprimanded Kent and suspended him with pay for four
months. Kent returned to his judicial duties in January 2008 and was allowed
to function as a federal trial judge until January 2009, when he pleaded guilty
and resigned from the bench. Lara Bazelon stated, "The 5th Circuit's years of
inaction in the Kent case and the near-total secrecy that blanketed its handling of the matter called into question the legitimacy of the process and the
outcome" (Bazelon, 2009, p. E1).

## Ethical Responsibilities of an Appellate Justice

Most ethical examinations of judicial behavior look at the ethical duties of a
trial judge. How the conduct of an appellate justice can become the focus of

an inquiry depends in many cases on the duties and responsibilities of appellate justices.

Sharon Keller, the presiding judge of the Texas Court of Criminal
Appeals, the court of last resort for criminal matters in Texas state courts,
provided a source of discussion in those regards. Justice Keller wrote an
opinion in which she rejected Roy Criner's request for a new trial. Criner, a
mentally retarded individual, had been convicted of rape and murder. DNA
tests conducted after trial established that the semen in the victim did not
belong to Criner. Justice Keller stated, "We can't give new trials to everyone
who establishes, after conviction, that they may be innocent." She stated
on a television news program, "We would have no finality in the criminal
justice system, and finality is important." Justice Keller appeared to consider
finality more important than correcting a trial mistake that sent an innocent person to prison. Criner was eventually pardoned by the state governor
(Kovach, 2009, p. A26).

Michael Richard was scheduled to be executed in Huntsville, Texas, on
September 25, 2007. Earlier that day, the U.S. Supreme Court announced that
it would hear arguments considering the constitutionality of lethal injections.
As a result of the Supreme Court's announcement, which placed a temporary
stay on executions, Richard's counsel, a non-profit defender service, began
preparing an emergency appeal to halt the execution. The service experienced
computer problems and called Justice Keller's court and asked for a few extra
minutes to file its request to stop the execution. According to the reports,
Justice Keller had gone home earlier that day to meet with a repairman. She
was called by court personnel and asked if they could keep the clerk's office
open. It was reported that Justice Keller stated: "We close at 5." Richard was
executed at 8:20 p.m. that evening. Later the Supreme Court upheld lethal
injection as constitutional ("Locking Justice's Door," Houston Chronicle,
2009). After an investigation, in February 2009, the Texas State Commission
on Judicial Conduct charged Justice Keller with incompetence, violating her
duties, and casting public discredit on the judiciary (State Commission on
Judicial Conduct, 2009).

## Practicum: Justice for Sale

In 2009, the U.S. Supreme Court considered the right to a fair hearing before
an impartial justice system. The facts of the case were taken from *Hugh M.
Caperton, Harman Dev. Corp. v. A. T. Massey Coal Co.* (2009). U.S. S. Ct.
Briefs LEXIS 111. In the case, a West Virginia jury decided that the coal company Massey Energy, had fraudulently forced a competitor, Harman Mining,
into bankruptcy. Massey's chief executive made the decision to appeal the
case. Prior to the case being heard by the West Virginia Supreme Court,

the chief executive spent almost 3 million dollars to help elect Justice Brent Benjamin to the court. As noted in the briefs presented to the U.S. Supreme Court, "CEO and president of A. T. Massey Coal Co. spent $3 million supporting Justice Benjamin's campaign for a seat on the West Virginia Supreme Court of Appeals. The chief executive spent this money in support of Justice Benjamin while Massey was preparing to appeal a $50 million fraud verdict to the West Virginia Supreme Court of Appeals."

When the case was heard before the state supreme court, Justice Benjamin declined to recuse himself. Justice Benjamin stated, "No objective information is advanced to show that this justice has a bias for or against any litigant." Justice Benjamin later provided the deciding vote to set aside the jury verdict.

The appellants contended that they were denied due process rights because the case was not heard by a fair and impartial state supreme court. The appellants contended that judicial elections have created a crisis of public confidence and cited national surveys from 2001 and 2004 that found that over 70% of Americans believe that campaign contributions have at least some influence on judges' decisions in the courtroom.

As stated in the brief:

For the Court not to recognize a due process violation under these circumstances would send a message that concerns about judicial elections are not so serious as to pose a threat to the independent judicial system our Constitution requires. Such a ruling would constitute a significant setback for the state judicial selection reform movement, which is premised on the idea that judicial elections and campaign contributions can, in some cases, threaten the appearance or reality of impartial justice. A ruling by the Court that the facts of even this case do not present a constitutionally significant threat to equal justice would significantly undermine this premise, and weaken state reform efforts.

The counsel for Massey contended,

The American Bar Association's Model Code of Judicial Conduct provides that "a judge shall disqualify himself or herself in any proceeding in which the judge's impartiality might reasonably be questioned." ABA Model Code of Judicial Conduct Rule 2.11(A) (2007). That rule "has been adopted in some form in virtually every state." ABA Br. 14. "Reasonableness," of course, will depend on all manner of facts and circumstances particular to the adopting State. But this bedrock protection against even apparent judicial bias, which goes well beyond common law requirements (Resp. Br. 15-19), is now firmly rooted in state law and practice.

States have an overriding interest in ensuring the fairness of their courts and the impartiality of their judges. Historically, States have been free to police judicial bias—both real and apparent—through statutes, rules, and bar codes. The Due Process Clause has not required recusal except in the most extreme cases—namely, where a judge either has a pecuniary "interest in the outcome of" a case or is "actually biased" against one of the parties. *Bracy v. Gramley*, 520 U.S. 899, 904 (1997). Petitioners' position here—which would require recusal as a matter of federal constitutional law whenever a judge might feel a "debt of gratitude" to an interested party that suggests a "probability of bias"—would carry the Court well beyond existing due-process doctrine and make virtually every state-court recusal dispute a "federal case." Because petitioners' proposed extension is neither necessary nor wise, the Court should reject it.

The facts presented to the court in the briefs included the following:

- Eight states utilize partisan elections.
- Thirteen states utilize nonpartisan elections.
- One state holds partisan primaries but nonpartisan general elections.
- In thirteen states, the governor appoints from among nominees selected through a judicial nominating commission (JNC) or its equivalent.
- In two states, the governor appoints, but the nominee is subject to confirmation by the JNC or similar board.
- In one state, the governor nominates from among JNC recommendations, and the legislature then formally makes the appointment.
- In two states, the governor appoints, subject to senate confirmation.
- In seven states, the governor appoints from among JNC nominees, subject to confirmation by the senate (or, in one state, the house and senate).
- In one state, the governor nominates from JNC recommendations, and an "executive council" — a body separately elected every two years through partisan elections — then formally makes the appointment.
- In two states, the legislature itself makes the selections.

*If you were sitting as a justice on the U.S. Supreme Court, how would you rule?* To find out how the Supreme Court ruled, research the decision of *Hugh M. Caperton, Harman Dev. Corp. v. A. T. Massey Coal Co.* (pending).
*How should judges be selected to ensure fair and impartial hearings?*

## Defense Counsel Ethics

The defense counsel is considered as an officer of the court. As an officer of the court, what duties does a defense counsel have to correct mistakes made by the court? In a jury trial, it is quite common for a defense counsel to explain in the defense's opening statement to the jury that he or she is the sole spokesperson for the defendant, that the state has the vast resources of the police and district attorney's office to further the interests of the state, and that "I am the only person working for the defendant. My resources are limited, whereas the police and prosecutors resources are vastly superior."

Under our adversary system of prosecution, there are in theory two opposing sides, the prosecution and the defense, and the judge or jury acts as the referee or fact-finder. In actual practice, in the vast majority of cases the defense has only limited resources and cannot match the investigative resources of the state. Note: the defense generally refers to the prosecution as either the "prosecution" or the "state," whereas the prosecution refers to his or her side as the "people" of the state. Both sides are looking to gain a psychological edge with the jury.

Frequently non-lawyers will state that they would never defend a guilty person. Co-author Cliff Roberson, an attorney, contended that he would prefer to defend a guilty person than an innocent person. This is based on the personal feeling that if the attorney loses the case and the guilty person goes to prison or is otherwise sanctioned, the defendant deserved it. But when you are defending a person who you believe is innocent, you worry that your mistakes will result in an innocent person going to prison.

## What Are the Duties of a Defense Counsel?

The right to be heard would be, in many cases, of little avail if it did not comprehend the right to be heard by counsel. (Justice George Sutherland, *Powell v. Alabama*, 1932, p. 53)

Consider the statement by Alan Dershowitz in a newspaper report:

I am not interested in my client's innocence or guilt; I am not interested in seeing that justice is done when I'm the defense attorney. I am interested in seeing them acquitted. It's not the defense attorney's job to do justice. His job is to defend vigorously his client. ... It's not a happy experience to get people off who are guilty. I don't expect any prizes or plaudits for it. ... What we do is a necessary evil—a very necessary evil. ("Alan Dershowitz Interview," Los Angeles Herald-Examiner, 1982, p. 7)

Compare Dershowitz's statement with that of noted attorney Jay Goldberg:

I am a mercenary. A person who is accused of something comes into my office and he wants me to be his sword, he wants me to protect his rights. I must, if I accept his case, close my eyes to the needs of society and I do what I can to protect him within legal ethics, without any regard to society's needs or anyone else's needs. The fact is that society gains the most of all by seeing to it that the rule of law applies to all. It is not tested with the law-abiding middle class, but with the people who need it the most. (*New York Times*, 1969, p. 14)

The American Bar Association (ABA) has established standards for both defense and prosecution of criminal cases. Selected standards are set forth below on what the ABA considers as the duties of a defense counsel.

## *ABA Standard 4-1.2: The Function of Defense Counsel*

(b) The basic duty defense counsel owes to the administration of justice and as an officer of the court is to serve as the accused's counselor and advocate with courage and devotion and to render effective, quality representation ...

(f) Defense counsel should not intentionally misrepresent matters of fact or law to the court ...

(h) It is the duty of defense counsel to know and be guided by the standards of professional conduct as defined in codes and canons of the legal profession applicable in defense counsel's jurisdiction. Once representation has been undertaken, the functions and duties of defense counsel are the same whether defense counsel is assigned, privately retained, or serving in a legal aid or defender program.

## *ABA Standard 4-3.6: Prompt Action to Protect the Accused*

Many important rights of the accused can be protected and preserved only by prompt legal action. Defense counsel should inform the accused of his or her rights at the earliest opportunity and take all necessary action to vindicate such rights. Defense counsel should consider all procedural steps which in good faith may be taken, including, for example, motions seeking pretrial release of the accused, obtaining psychiatric examination of the accused when a need appears, moving for change of venue or continuance, moving to suppress illegally obtained evidence, moving for severance from jointly charged defendants, and seeking dismissal of the charges.

## How Does a Prosecutor's Duty Compare with Those of a Defense Counsel?

The prosecutor must argue the State's case forcefully, but while the prosecutor may strike hard blows, he may not strike foul ones, for the prosecutor's primary duty is to seek justice, not to attain convictions. (*Durmer v. Rogers*, 2006, p. 74612)

Because the prosecutor represents the government and people of the State, it is reasonable to say that jurors have confidence that he will fairly fulfill his duty to see that justice is done whether by conviction of the guilty or acquittal of the innocent. His comments during opening and closing carry the full authority of the State. Hence, we cannot sit idly by and condone prosecutorial excesses. (*State v. Goode*, 1994, p. 94)

As noted by the preceding excerpts, the duties of a defense counsel are to serve as the accused's representative and to, within legal limits, defend the accused to the best of his or her ability, whereas the duty of a prosecutor is not to prosecute but to promote justice.

## Ethics in Practice

### United States v. Theodore F. Stevens (2009)

The following is a statement made by Attorney General Eric Holder regarding *United States v. Theodore F. Stevens* on April 1, 2009:

In connection with the post-trial litigation in *United States v. Theodore F. Stevens*, the Department of Justice has conducted a review of the case, including an examination of the extent of the disclosures provided to the defendant. After careful review, I have concluded that certain information should have been provided to the defense for use at trial. In light of this conclusion, and in consideration of the totality of the circumstances of this particular case, I have determined that it is in the interest of justice to dismiss the indictment and not proceed with a new trial.

The Department's Office of Professional Responsibility will conduct a thorough review of the prosecution of this matter. This does not mean or imply that any determination has been made about the conduct of those attorneys who handled the investigation and trial of this case.

The Department of Justice must always ensure that any case in which it is involved is handled fairly and consistent with its commitment to justice. Under oftentimes trying conditions, the attorneys who serve in this Department live up to those principles on a daily basis. I am proud of them and of the work they do for the American people.

### Excerpts from *United States v. Theodore F. Stevens*, 593 F. Supp. 2d 177, 182-183 (D.D.C. 2009)

U.S. District Court Judge Emmet G. Sullivan:

It is for these reasons, and because this incident is not the first one in this case where the government represents to the Court that it made a "mistake" and that there was no "bad faith" or intent to "mislead" the Court or defense counsel in the face of serious allegations of government misconduct, that the

Court has directed that a declaration be provided by the Attorney General. As the defendant points out in his objection to the motion for reconsideration, the pattern is unmistakable. Over and over again the government has been caught in false representations and otherwise failing to perform its duties under the Constitution and the Rules. And over and over again, when caught, the government has claimed that it has simply made good faith mistakes. When the government failed to produce Rocky Williams's exculpatory grand jury testimony, the government claimed that this testimony was immaterial. When the government sent Mr. Williams back to Alaska without advising the defense or the Court, the government asserted that it was acting in "good faith." When the government affirmatively redacted exculpatory statements from FBI Form 302s, it claimed that "it was just a mistake." When government counsel told the Court that Allen had not been re-interviewed the day before a hearing on its *Brady* disclosures, this was a "mistaken understanding." When the government failed to turn over exculpatory statements from Dave Anderson, it claimed that they were immaterial. When the government failed to turn over a critical grand jury transcript containing exculpatory information, it claimed that it was "inadvertent." When the government used "business records" that the government undeniably knew were false, it said that it was unintentional. When the government failed to produce the bank records of Bill Allen and then sprang them on the defense, it claimed this check was immaterial to the defense.

This case, and this most recent incident, involves numerous attorneys and offices throughout the Department of Justice. Those attorneys have not been able to provide a cohesive or credible answer to this Court's questions regarding the determination of whistle-blower status. Therefore, the Court believes it appropriate and necessary to get an answer from someone with direct oversight over all of the various offices, individuals, and divisions involved. Nevertheless, the Court is sensitive to the many demands placed on the Attorney General at this time and, therefore, the Court will modify its January 14, 2009 Order to require that the Attorney General or his designee(s) provide the required declaration(s) and supporting documentation.

On April 9, 2009, the federal judge set aside former senator Ted Stevens's conviction. The judge also appointed an independent, nongovernment attorney to investigate possible misconduct by the government lawyers who prosecuted the eighty-five-year-old former senator from Alaska. The judge stated, "In nearly 25 years on the bench, I've never seen anything approaching the mishandling and misconduct that I've seen in this case."

In October 2008, Stevens was found guilty of seven counts of lying on Senate ethics forms. He lost his bid for re-election in November 2008. The election was very close, and the criminal trial probably caused Stevens to lose his reelection bid. Apparently, in December 2008, an unnamed FBI whistle-blower accused prosecutors of withholding evidence from the defense. The whistle-blower reported that someone with the government had an inappropriate relationship with an oil industry executive who was the government's key witness.

A dismissal motion, which resulted in the criminal case being dismissed, was filed by the U.S. Justice Department. The Justice Department acknowledged that Stevens was not given access to the notes taken by prosecutors during an April 2008 interview with a witness. The notes showed that responses by the witness were inconsistent with testimony he gave against Stevens and that information from the interview could have benefited Stevens at trial, according to the motion.

Stevens had maintained his innocence throughout a government investigation that led to an indictment and conviction for failing to disclose hundreds of thousands of dollars of "freebies" from an oil-field services company on Senate ethics forms. In a statement by Stevens that was read to the court, Stevens said that his faith in the justice system had been restored. He stated:

> Until recently, my faith in the criminal justice system was unwavering. But what some members of this prosecution team did nearly destroyed my faith. Their conduct has consequences they must know can never be reversed. But I now have new hope that others may be spared from similar miscarriages of justice. (http://www.cnn.com, 2009)

Stevens added that he would "encourage the enactment of legislation to reform laws relating to the responsibilities and duties of those entrusted with the solemn task of enforcing federal criminal laws" (http://www.cnn.com, April 21, 2009).

Paul O'Brien, one of the new government attorneys assigned to the case, made no attempt to justify the conduct of the previous prosecution team. "We deeply regret this occurred," he said. "We apologize to the court." In issuing his ruling, Judge Sullivan noted the Justice Department's investigation into potential misconduct by government prosecutors had gone on for six months with no result. "The silence is deafening," Judge Sullivan said. The judge previously had excoriated prosecutors during the trial and held the prosecution in contempt at one point.

## Practicum

Is it ethical for the police to violate the law in order to win convictions?

Spotsylvania County, Virginia, is located about 60 miles south of Washington, D.C. In 2007, the county sheriff allowed his detectives to receive sexual services from massage parlors as part of a campaign by the sheriff's office to stamp out prostitution in the county. During several visits to a certain parlor, detectives allowed women to perform sexual acts on them on four occasions and once left $350 according to papers filed in the local courts. The sheriff acknowledged the practice and said that it was not new and that only unmarried detectives are assigned to such cases. According to Sheriff Howard Smith, most prostitutes are careful not to say anything incriminating, so sexual contact is necessary to get a conviction. Smith stated that if he thought he could get a conviction without that, "we would not allow it" (Jackman, 2006, p. A8).

Criminal law professor Jon Gould of George Mason University is reported to have stated: "I've never heard of that anywhere else in any police department. You don't have to go through with the act to prove solicitation." Professor Gould also stated that practice was an improper use of taxpayer money (Jackman, 2006, p. A8).

If you were a citizen of Spotsylvania County, would you support the program? Justify your opinions.

## Questions in Review

1. What should be the limits on the use of deception to obtain a conviction?
2. Are there any circumstances where a police officer is allowed to mislead a court?
3. How do the primary duties of defense counsels and prosecutors differ?
4. What should a prosecutor consider when making the decision to prosecute a criminal offender?
5. Under what circumstances should a judge be removed from the bench?

# Ethics and the Police  $\Huge 11$

## Introduction

In this chapter, we examine several facets of policing that are critical to understand, especially as they relate to the concept of ethics. Keep in mind the ultimate objective of police departments should be to serve the community in which they work. The manner in which this service is provided is the paramount consideration and precisely what this chapter is aimed at examining. For a community to be healthy from a criminal justice point of view, it must be serviced by an ethical police force that is committed to providing just service all of the time, not just when it is convenient or when an officer happens to be in a good mood. Quality and equitable services must resonate and trump any contradictory alternative.

The chapter first explores a paradox. Anytime an entity is charged with delivering a service or product that is paradoxical in nature, the challenges are immediately heightened. Policing is certainly a discipline that operates squarely within a paradox of which the parameters are central to our existence and well-being. The parameters of this paradox are freedom on one side and protection on the other. As noted in Chapter 9, these parameters represent each arm of the scale of justice.

To achieve some objective, one must take action. The action taken by police officers, or the lack thereof, is where the concept of ethics is engaged. Of course, the thought processes and the foundations from which officers decide to act are informed by ethical theory, but the action taken in relation to some circumstance is what is ultimately going to be scrutinized as ethical. The thought process used to decide the type of action is secondary to the action itself within the context of evaluating ethical behavior. It is the action of officers that is examined and ultimately judged as right or wrong. In relation to an officer's action, three important factors should be explored: the individual officer, the community in which the officer serves, and the organization with whom the officer is employed. In Chapter 5, each of these factors were discussed when we examined the foundation from which corruption may be explained or better understood. They are relevant once again to the discussion of ethical behavior. These factors are central determinants that serve to provide the foundation on which decisions are made.

**Figure 11.1** Policeman accepting illegal beer during Prohibition.

Integrity and professionalism, as noted in Chapter 5, are central to any discussion concerning ethical behavior of police officers. Figure 11.1 showing the policeman receiving a mug of beer from an illegal bar during Prohibition is an example of the type of unethical conduct that will reflect on the integrity and professionalism of a police department. If these constructs are absent within some action taken by a police officer, it is unlikely that the action will survive a strict test that scrutinizes the action concerning ethics. In addition, the ultimate concept related to ethical conduct, discretion, was examined.

The concept of discretion is the most delicate and crucial aspect of police work. What an officer decides to do or not do in relation to some incident is precisely related to the employment of discretion. For some incidents, the idea of discretion is null. Consider, for example, the officer who arrives at a residence where a murder occurred. A man just shot his wife after learning of her extramarital affair. The man freely confesses and even shows officers where he placed the murder weapon. In such a circumstance, there is not much to ponder. The man will be arrested and charged with the appropriate derivative of willfully and unlawfully killing another person. Fortunately, however, these incidents are rare. Generally the officer's time will be spent responding to and handling calls for service that are much less serious and allow the officer to use discretion in determining how to resolve some conflict. These are the incidents that this discussion is aimed at exploring: where an officer has a range of decisions that are legal and their relevant possibilities. These are the decision points that impact how individuals and communities judge the quality of service provided by their respective law enforcement agencies.

The chapter concludes with the question: "Is there a way to ensure ethical behavior among police officers?" This is a difficult question to ponder but one that is extremely important.

## Paradox of Policing

In order to properly frame an informed discussion on police ethics it is critical to first understand the context in which American policing takes place. The United States of America was founded on democratic principles. The American government is based on the concept of democracy, which is a concept that describes the process of governing based on the will of the people. Central to American democracy is our ability to vote. We elect our government representatives whom we believe are most capable of truly reflecting our ideals and philosophy through the enactment of policies and laws aimed at protecting our interests. Democracy also denotes the very powerful concept of freedom. Of course we are not completely free; we all have to live and abide by rules, policies, regulations, and laws. However, if one takes a minute to reflect on the daily happenings of our lives it becomes clear that we are mostly free. For example, no one makes you attend college or live in a certain place or drive a certain vehicle. Sure we have economic parameters that govern the size of our home or the type of vehicle we choose to drive, but within those parameters we are free to make our own choices. We are free to engage in the religion of our choice, free to communicate and voice our concerns, and free to gather in groups. In essence, we are mostly free to govern our lives according to our own wishes, desires, and ideologies. So what does freedom have to do with policing, and how does it represent one of the constructs in a profound paradox?

Consider the role of the police. In essence, the police provide a service aimed at protecting life and liberties as well as maintaining order. How do the police often accomplish these tasks? In many cases they attempt to restore order and security via the process of placing someone under arrest. What is the ultimate consequence of being arrested? The offender is stripped of freedom. Once in custody, everything is decided for the offender: when to eat, what to wear, what to eat, and so on. This is the ultimate paradox. Policing is a discipline charged with, in many cases, removing our most cherished right that many of our ancestors fought so bravely to preserve: freedom. This is precisely why the concept of ethics and its relation to policing is so important.

Police officers possess awesome authority and power that result in their ability to profoundly impact the lives of citizens throughout the United States of America. Consider the following quotes by G. T. Marx (2001, p. 148):

> Democratic societies experience a continual tension between the desire for order and the desire for liberty. Both are essential. While as the case of the police state suggests, one can have the former without the latter, it is not possible to have a society with liberty which does not also have a minimum degree of order. The balance between these will vary depending on the context and time period. Democratic policing seeks to avoid the extremes of either anarchy or repression.

In essence, Marx is arguing that there must be a balance. If we were totally free with no rules, regulations, or order we would experience chaos, as noted in Chapter 9 through the example of Hurricane Katrina. On the other hand, if police over-step their bounds and abuse their authority and power, all our freedoms are stripped away, and the result is a repressed society that will either cower and not reach its fullest potential or will rise up in opposition.

Consider a second quote by Marx that further illuminates this critical role of the police:

> In an open democratic society which respects the dignity of the individual and values voluntary and consensual behavior and the non-violent resolution of conflicts, police, with their secrecy and use of violence, are an anomaly. They are charged with using undemocratic means to obtain democratic ends.

Police offer an ethical and moral paradox that will forever make democratic citizens uncomfortable.

This quote precisely captures the gravity of the issue at hand. In essence, we empower police to use tactics that are contradictory to democratic principles in order to achieve order, stability, and safety. This paradox is extremely sensitive and must be respected. We must constantly strive to maintain balance within this paradigm. If we give too much power to police, the balance becomes disrupted, and the scale of justice tilts too heavily to one side. If the police abuse their authority and power, we experience the same result. Ethics, therefore, is the vehicle through which we work to inform our police and citizens on the manner in which actions should be carried out.

## Objective of Policing in America

In order to fully appreciate the role of ethics in policing we must understand the exact mission of the police. The reason it is important to understand the mission is because it is based on the mission that police action is carried out. In other words, the actions of police officers, while operating in their official capacity, should be in relation to performing some task that contributes to the realization of an objective. In order to capture the objective of American policing and the manner in which it should be carried out, we have borrowed the Law Enforcement Code of Ethics adopted by the International Association of Chiefs of Police (IACP). The Law Enforcement Code of Ethics was adopted by the Executive Committee of the IACP on October 17, 1989, during its 96th annual conference in Louisville, Kentucky, to replace the 1957 Code of Ethics adopted at the 64th annual IACP conference. (To retrieve a copy of the code, visit the following website: http:// ethics.iit.edu/codes/coe/int.assoc.chiefs.police.law.enforcement.coe.1989. html) This code is meant to serve as an umbrella of ethical considerations that should be considered by all law enforcement agencies. Of course, specific law enforcement agencies throughout the United States may alter the wording in order to develop their own unique codes, but the essence remains consistent.

Every section of this code is critical in order to maintain the delicate balance in the ever-present paradox of policing in a democracy. Ethics is related to all matters contained within the code, but it may be argued that it is most relevant concerning "...*and ensuring the rights of all to liberty, equality and justice.*" This is among the most central tenets of the objective of American policing organizations. When we think of the role of police, we often migrate intellectually to protection and security within our communities. And rightly so; our ability to live freely without fear depends on this vital task. But just as important is the objective of preserving rights and carrying out duties in a manner that enhances perceptions of equality and justice. Remember that the foundation of justice is fairness. Therefore, it must be the case that in all circumstances, the objectives of the police include fairness and equality regardless of the persons involved.

## Police Action

As noted in the introduction, the actions of police officers are what will ultimately be reviewed and scrutinized and ultimately judged as right or wrong. Consider, once again, the beating that Rodney King endured at the hands of several Los Angeles police officers. At the time, this incident was broadcast nationwide on every news channel. Consider the focus of each person viewing the clip. Do you think most people were pondering the theory of ethics while they were watching the clip? As most people watched, they probably felt a deep-seated emotion of either fear or anger followed by a sense of shock and awe. In essence, the attention was solely on the actions of the officers involved.

Action is the point at which power is mobilized. It is precisely the point at which some overt movement or verbalization is employed by a police officer aimed at achieving some objective. For example, when an officer determines that probable cause exists to place someone under arrest, the action consists of the employment of the officer's power to handcuff the suspect: the physical movements necessary to place the offender's hands behind his back followed by the placement of handcuffs on his wrists. Action can also consist of verbal messages. In fact verbal messages are often just as powerful as physical actions in affecting the well-being of another. Consider the officer who tells a possible suspect, "Shut up. I don't care what you have to say. Not only am I about to arrest you, but I am then going to arrest everyone else, including your family." There should be no question that this is a form of action that is central to the idea of ethics. In the same circumstance, another officer might choose a much more ethical form of verbal action and state something like, "Sir, I know you are scared and confused. However, I need you to remain quiet so that I can better understand what has transpired."

Why are the actions of police officers so important within the context of ethical thought? Simply stated, the actions of police officers are critical because for every action there is a consequence. As noted by Williams and Arrigo (2008), each consequence produces further effects that also have consequences. In essence, the single action of a police officer may ultimately produce consequences that resonate far beyond the participants and witnesses of the original action. This is the primary reason why all police action is important. Some incidents may appear to be routine or trivial, but if they require the use of an officer's power to engage in some action, they will be consequential and will impact people down the line who are not even present at the time of the action.

Directly stated, police action must be that which is directly related to accomplishing a lawful objective in a manner that serves to balance the scale of justice as opposed to disrupting its balance. Whenever possible, the actions of officers should be such that they are able to stand alone and not need to be defended or justified. Consider an incident that took place in Birmingham, Alabama, in 2008. A white male suspect driving a white minivan fled from police after they attempted to stop him. While fleeing from officers, the driver, attempting to avoid spikes in the roadway, swerved and actually ran over the officer attempting to set up the spikes. The pursuit continued until the driver eventually lost control of the van and crashed. During the crash, the van flipped over several times, ejecting the driver. During the course of being ejected, the driver was knocked unconscious and came to rest a few feet from the final location of the van. As officers approached the suspect, who was still unconscious, they began striking him with their batons and fists. The incident was captured on a dash camera in one of the responding officer's police cruiser. What are your reactions to the actions taken in this incident?

Ultimately, five police officers were fired. Why were they fired? After all, this suspect ran over one of their brother officers. The answer is because of their *actions*. As a police officer, how do you defend the action of repeatedly striking a suspect who is unconscious? Is the suspect being combative? Is the suspect resisting? Is the suspect attempting to disarm one of the officers? No. The suspect was not moving and was simply lying unconscious. An important note to always remember is that the use of force is governed by the actions of a suspect. No literature governing an officer's use of force makes reference to an incident where someone can be struck based on what they have done even though they are not actively resisting.

This suspect actually ran over a police officer, which is certainly considered by most to be a very heinous act. And some may argue that the officers were experiencing an uncontrollable surge of powerful emotion related to the severity of this driver attempting, either directly or indirectly, to kill an officer in order to affect an escape. Is the idea of these officers experiencing powerful emotion a plausible argument on their behalf for their actions? It may be plausible, and it is certainly understandable, but it is not acceptable or legal. We cannot have double standards for police and criminals. Do we understand or dismiss the actions of a man who murders his wife? Do the circumstances matter? Not if the man's actions constitute murder. Action therefore trumps emotion or reason when judged under the ethical microscope.

## Factors That Determine Action

Based on this premise, some may argue that if action is paramount within an ethical context, why bother with trying to understand the reasoning or factors that guide the action? After all, the reasoning is irrelevant. We would argue, however, the exact opposite. It is critical to understand the factors that produce and drive action. Will such an inquiry do anything to help the officers in Birmingham get their jobs back? No, but it may help current and future officers better understand the foundations of their action on which they too may someday be judged. In essence, we must constantly strive to improve the actions of police officers in every circumstance or encounter with public citizens, even those who have run over a police officer and are now unconscious.

There are three central, albeit broad, factors that should be considered when attempting to understand the motives of action. In essence, the factors are the individual, the community, and the organization. As noted above these factors were discussed previously in Chapter 5. We now discuss a fourth component, which was not discussed in Chapter 5 but is arguably the most robust factor related to the action of a police officer: the police subculture (Carter & Radelet, 1999). Discussions regarding the police subculture are legion. It is likely one of the most researched concepts within the discipline of criminal justice. And rightly so, it is a powerful and influential mechanism that contains norms, values, and attitudes of how police officers should act (engage in action) and is forcefully reinforced through peer pressure and informal mores that ultimately govern whether an officer will be accepted and therefore be a successful member of the organization.

Subculture is a concept that describes the "meanings, values, and behavior patterns that are unique to a particular group in society" (Carter & Radelet, 1999, p. 179). Schmalleger (2008) defined the police subculture as "The set of informal values that characterize the police force as a distinct community with a common identity." In Chapter 9, we used the example of the training officer telling the recruit to forget what was learned in the academy because he was going to really learn how to police while in the street and through observing the actions of veteran officers. This message depicts the essence of a subculture and precisely when it begins to be implemented.

What a recruit learns in the academy is a sanitized version of law enforcement. This is the common message articulated by veteran officers who have succumbed fully to the values and norms of the police subculture. And, as noted by Schmalleger (2010), the police subculture is much more powerful and robust than the lessons learned in the academy.

Therefore, the police subculture must be considered central to a discussion of ethics. In essence, the actions of individual officers will be as ethical as the subculture in which they operate. Consider, for example, the unwritten rule of "If a suspect runs from us (the police) he 'catches' a beating when caught. Maybe after the beating, if it is severe enough, he won't run next time." This unwritten rule is an example of a value that is placed within the larger concept of the police subculture. It would be accurate, therefore, to consider the rule analogous to the subculture. It is a rule among other rules that serve to create the intellectual concept of the police subculture.

It is within the context of a police subculture that we also find the phrase "us versus them." In essence, the police come to see the world as two distinct groups: police officers in one group and all non-sworn police officers in the other group. This is a very isolating framework from which to operate. To better understand the foundation from which this framework is constructed, consider the challenges of police. They are only called when people feel they have no other choice to resolve some conflict. Has there ever been an incident when someone called the police and had an officer dispatched in order to tell him what a wonderful job he is doing? The police are called when humanity is at its worst. This constant state of being exposed to the worst of society's ills profoundly contributes to the existence of the police subculture.

It becomes very difficult for police officers to interact with non-police officers. Consider an example of an officer who just completed a tour, and his last call of the day involved a seventeen-year-old girl who hung herself because she did not want to tell her parents she was pregnant. After such an emotionally charged experience, some officers may find it difficult to engage others in conversations where their main concern is the fact that it is expected to rain next week and they will likely not be able to engage in their weekly round of golf.

In the subculture of policing is where many police officers learn how they are supposed to act while on duty. In the example in Birmingham where the officers repeatedly struck the unconscious driver, did their police subculture and the rules within inform their behavior? It is likely that it did, because one of the most central tenets of a police subculture is to "protect their own." Within the context of the subculture, it is unacceptable for a fellow officer to be harmed, let alone run over, without exacting severe and swift retaliatory actions. The reasoning behind this is very clear to the police. It can be summated with "If we don't take care of our own, no one else will. And if we let people get away with hurting us, they will further take advantage of this perceived weakness." The worst crime that a driver can commit in the eyes of the police is "contempt of cop."

At this stage of the discussion, a couple of points should be articulated in regards to the police subculture:

1. Informal rules are dangerous because in essence the police are deciding to act in a manner that is beyond their authority.
2. The police do not have the authority to teach people lessons, with punishment, who disobey the law or who endanger or injure a fellow officer.
3. Punishing individuals is not the responsibility of police officers; it is the responsibility of the court system.
4. The rules or customs within the police subculture demand officers to engage in actions that may not be ethical and in many cases not legal. It is unethical for any officer to physically beat a suspect who is not actively resisting.

Where do we go from here? How do we combat the idea of a police subculture that is incredibly powerful, deeply ingrained, and fiercely guarded? This is not an easy question to answer. And this is precisely when veteran officers often espouse, "That stuff sounds good in books, but it doesn't apply to the real world." It may be easier to formulate responses in written form than to actually carry them out, because when formulating written responses, you are not under the pressure of powerful emotions that accompanies circumstances that call ethics into question. This realization does nothing, however, to reduce the importance of engaging in actions that are ethical. The remaining portions of this chapter discuss the factors related to actions that can be judged ethical regardless of the circumstance.

## Integrity and Professionalism

Integrity is a concept that describes action that is honest and decent. Action that is composed of integrity forwards the ideas of humanity and righteousness. In order for police action to be ethical, the action must be carried out by officers who have a basic sense of integrity. These are officers who are interested in doing what is right for humanity as opposed to doing what is right by the police subculture.

Professionalism generally describes competence, ability, and being skillful and masterful when carrying out some objective or service. We combine integrity and professionalism because of the following line of reason. Action that is ethical is action that is righteous. Action that is righteous in a policing context is action that is NOT governed by negative emotion. To be able to remove negative emotions from one's process of reasoning, or deciding on a particular action, one must be professional. That is, a person must be competent in their ability to reason and honest in their choice to act ethically. Both integrity and professionalism are central to ethical action.

To further highlight the salience of integrity and professionalism, we have included two mission statements. The mission statements are those of the Houston, Texas Police Department and the Lafayette, Louisiana Police Department. Both statements were retrieved from the official Web sites of each respective department. Notice how both statements directly address the issues of integrity and professionalism.

## Houston, Texas Police Department Mission Statement

Mission statement: The mission of the Houston Police Department is to enhance the quality of life in the city of Houston by working cooperatively with the public and within the framework of the U.S. Constitution to enforce the laws, preserve the peace, reduce fear, and provide for a safe environment.

1. *Preserve and Advance Democratic Values*
   We shall uphold this country's democratic values as embodied in the Constitution and shall dedicate ourselves to the preservation of liberty and justice for all.
2. *Improve the Quality of Community Life*
   We shall strive to improve the quality of community life through the provision of quality and equitable services.
3. *Improve the Quality of Work Life*
   We shall strive to improve the working environment for the department's employees by engaging in open and honest communication and demonstrating a genuine concern for one another.
4. *Demonstrate Professionalism*
   We shall always engage in behavior that is beyond ethical reproach and reflects the integrity of police professionals.
5. *Principles*
   Life and individual freedoms are sacred.
   All persons should be treated fairly and equitably.
   The role of the police is to resolve problems through the enforcement of laws, not through the imposition of judgment or punishment.
   The neighborhood is the basic segment of the community.
   Because law enforcement and public safety reflect community-wide concern, the police must actively seek the involvement of citizens in all aspects of policing.
   The fundamental responsibility of the police is provision of quality services.
   The department's employees are its most valuable asset.
   Employee involvement in departmental activities is essential for maintaining a productive working environment.

Employees should be treated fairly and equitably in recognition of basic human dignity and as a means of enriching their work life.

## Lafayette, Louisiana Police Department Mission Statement

*Mission statement*: The mission of the Lafayette Police Department is to serve the community with a sense of courage, dedication, compassion, and integrity. We will strive to earn the community's respect through the delivery of professional police services in an efficient and effective manner. We will work hard to establish a climate of mutual respect and trust through positive interaction with the citizens of Lafayette. This will be accomplished through a broad-based combination of traditional and innovate police services while always protecting constitutional and basic human rights.

## 11.7 Discretion

Similar to integrity and professionalism, police officer discretion is critical to understand, especially as it relates to ethics. "Discretion is the authority to make decisions of policy and practice" (Delattre, 2002, p. 44). In other words, discretion is what officers use when deciding whether to take action. Why is discretion so critical, and why is it so important that it be used ethically? Delattre answered this question by stating, "Discretion is a special kind of liberty — the freedom to make decisions that affect the lives of others, which other citizens are not empowered to make" (2002, p. 44). The profundity of this statement lies primarily in the fact that citizens do not possess this power. As a result, citizens will always maintain vigilance in observing the manner in which officers use this power.

An analogy may help to further illuminate the importance of using discretion properly. Suppose you are the supervisor of an employee who comes in for work late one morning. You decide the employee does not have a reasonable explanation for being tardy and further decide that you are going to "write up" the employee and officially document the circumstance. The decision to write up the employee is a result of using discretion. As a supervisor you had several options: (1) you could have ignored the incident; (2) you could have inquired but engaged in no formal action; (3) you could have documented the incident in your own personal records but not officially; (4) you could officially document the incident and place the documentation in a personnel file.

In most circumstances, police officers have a wide range of options in deciding how to handle a particular incident. The reason police officers are granted discretion is because it would be impossible and unreasonable to enforce every law on the books to its letter. Humans are complex beings, and there is no way to exhaust all possible scenarios through which behavior should be governed. In addition, in many instances there will be particular circumstances within an incident that would make the enforcement of a particular law unreasonable.

In fact, most circumstances in which police are summoned are anything but clear. Consider the traffic accident where both drivers are adamant their light was green; or the fight between two brothers both of whom claim the other was the aggressor and both were merely defending themselves; or the convenience store that has a sign on the front door stating, "We do not accept bills over $20." A patron pulls in and fills his gas tank. He then attempts to pay the cashier with a $100 bill. The cashier refuses to accept the $100 bill, claiming his boss will fire him. The patron calmly states all he has is this $100 bill. The cashier then replies he is going to call the police and the patron cannot leave without paying. As the responding officer, how would you handle this situation?

From a legal standpoint, there is not much an officer can do. This is really a civil matter, and based on what we have provided, no laws have been violated. The manner, however, in which the responding officer brings this incident to a close is critical. Consequently, this is precisely when the concept of discretion is engaged. Let's dig deeper into this example with a little critical thinking.

*Question:* First, who is the officer there to serve?
*Answer:* Both the cashier and the patron.
*Question:* What is the concern of the cashier?
*Answer:* Two things. (1) He cannot have anything in the cash register larger than a $20 bill. (2) If the patron does not pay him, then the register will be short the cost of the gas.
*Question:* What is the concern of the patron?
*Answer:* To purchase the gas he pumped into his vehicle with the money he has in his possession and be on his way. The ultimate concern for the patron is to be able to leave in a reasonable amount of time. *Remember, he has broken no law.*

These questions and answers are a critical part of the process of deciding how to act. Informed discretion, therefore, considers the concerns and needs of all parties involved in an incident. Let's consider a few possibilities that the officer could choose in handling this incident. First, he could simply state, "I don't know why you called me. This is a civil matter, and I am leaving." This may serve the patron well but certainly not the cashier. What if the officer tells the patron he must go to another location and exchange the $100 bill for smaller bills then return to the store to pay the cashier? The officer does not have legal authority to employ this discretion, but who is going to question a police officer for fear of going to jail? In this case the cashier would be served well, but not the patron.

The goal of any good police officer is to exhaust every alternative in search of the best response for the people involved in an incident. This is not always easy. It takes time, and the police subculture does not look upon what some may consider "coddling" the public very favorably. What is not realized from within the subculture, however, is that to not make every attempt to serve all participants to the best of an officer's ability denotes a lack of integrity and professionalism, and is a poor display of discretion. So how then can both the cashier and the patron be served in a sufficient manner? Certainly there are many possibilities, and to some degree the officer would need some cooperation from the two parties. But what if the police officer explained to the cashier in a non-judgmental manner that legally there was nothing he can do in this incident, and if the cashier would consider taking the $100 bill on this one occasion, the officer would be willing to write a short supplemental report documenting the circumstances so that the cashier's supervisor would understand why he had accepted the large bill.

The point is that discretion is the foundation from which action resonates. Discretion is analogous to reasoning; it is the process an officer engages in to determine their next action. It cannot be overstated just how critical this process is in shaping the views and opinions citizens have of the police. How do you get the community engaged with the police? How is the philosophy of community policing realized? It is by officers first engaging in ethical actions that are formulated and guided by the wise and passionate use of discretion.

*Should police officers be evaluated on their attitudes, ability to adapt, and interactions with the public?*

The Chicago Police Department is looking at this question. The department began evaluating its officers in a new way in 2009, examining not only the officers' job performance but also their attitudes, ability to adapt, and interactions with the public. The department changed its evaluation rating system after complaints that it was too inconsistent and essentially a "popularity contest." Under the new system, officers will be judged on their accountability and dependability, problem solving and decision-making, adaptability and responsiveness, communication with others, and job knowledge and professional development.

The department issued a general order in May 2009 that gave detailed examples. For example, officers who fail to spot a suspect in a vehicle stop or deal angrily with the public can be tagged with "requires improvement" or "unacceptable" marks. Officers can also earn "exceeds expectations" marks for going out of their way to volunteer for extra assignments or for suggesting changes to improve current policies. Other examples mention officers' attitudes toward department bosses or change, a tenet sources say was included because of poor morale in the department. A deputy chief stated that though attitude can affect officers' performances, the department was really trying to focus on getting officers to maintain professionalism. The ratings could have a real impact on officers' careers, even leading to termination for incompetence for the poorest performers.

The general order does not mention officers having to make a certain number of arrests or issue a certain number of tickets, but officers could be judged for that too, if they're not addressing the needs in their districts. The general order provides the officers with guidelines on what is expected of them and how they're going to be evaluated. Mark Donahue, president of the Fraternal Order of Police, said the union objects to the evaluation system because it should be subject to collective bargaining.

## Is It Possible to Ensure Ethical Behavior among Police Officers?

Of course, the obvious answer to this question is no. Human beings are too complex to ensure anything. Is it possible to do a better job with ethics among police officers? Absolutely! There are three suggestions that may help achieve this objective:

1. Hire the right people.
2. Be more accurate with recruiting practices.
3. Continuously educate and train the people you hire.

The third suggestion has been covered in various locations throughout this book. The first two suggestions, however, are just as important and will therefore be the focus in this section. If the profession of policing is going to be respected and accepted among broad swaths of our society, the right people must be hired. Agencies must identify the necessary characteristics that increase the likelihood that an individual officer will be able to consistently maintain good judgment, use appropriate discretion, and treat people with respect, dignity, and compassion. The characteristics that are most important to look for include people who are psychologically and emotionally well adjusted. They are not people who are attracted to policing as a result of a lust for power and excitement. Of course some aspects of policing are exciting, but over the long term, the excitement is not what is going to maintain a healthy and well-balanced approach to this type of work. Their foundation must be a strong will and desire to help people via treating them with respect and taking actions that are informed, legal, and, above all else, ethical.

One of the ways to attract the "right people" to policing is to make the position descriptions more accurate. Often recruiters use catchy phrases that sound good but contain little truth. Consider the recruiter who began each engagement with the following: "If you are looking for constant excitement, adrenaline rushes like you have never experienced, and the ability to make a difference, this job is for you. It is a 24 hour war zone out there, and we need people who are capable, trustworthy, and reliable to be there when brother officers are in need." So what type of person is going to be attracted to this type of position? A person who seeks action and excitement and who probably has a high threshold for satisfying these needs. Do you think the call at the convenience store is going to fulfill this type of person's needs for adventure?

To further illuminate this point, consider the following example: "Searching for adventure and the opportunity to pounce on a suspect? Or do you want an officer who is able to calm himself in a manner sufficient to communicate reassurance, empathy, and compassion?"

The point to this example is that most situations encountered by police officers are those that require the officer to effectively communicate and restore peace and security to those who are troubled. We must accurately depict the true nature of police work to all who possess an interest in this type of occupation. This does not mean that some incidents do not consist of violent encounters with angry or deranged suspects. Certainly this does occur, and officers must be able to effectively traverse such encounters. But to advertise the position of police officer solely on the ability to deal with violent encounters is not realistic and, in the long run, provides a great dis-service to both the departments and the communities they serve. What ends up happening is neither the department nor the individual is satisfied with the employment arrangement. Individuals who come to the job looking for constant excitement and adventure quickly become dissatisfied based on the realistic observation that little of their time is spent in such circumstances.

Recruitment practices must be realistic. How is this related to the concept of ethics? We would argue that officers who are disgruntled based on the dissonance between the requirements of their actual duties and the requirements of what they perceived were going to be their duties contribute to a reduced quality of interaction with the citizens they are attempting to serve. These officers quickly develop a sense of apathy for citizens, and instead of looking forward to serving, they spend much of their time disappointed due to the lack of action they were looking for when they entered the profession of policing.

## Conclusion

A well-written and comprehensive code of ethics is critical for all police departments. The primary objective of a code of ethics is similar to that of a theory in a criminal investigation. It serves as a guiding principle used to inform appropriate action. It is also important that we focus on the primary duties of police officers and make sure the code of ethics is congruous with the various responsibilities. The primary duty of police officers is to enforce laws fairly and equitably. That is really the essence of what is expected of police officers.

It is critical to understand the immense impact of the police subculture on police action. The subculture of policing is one that is generally concerned with physical abilities and the trustworthiness of an officer to adequately back up fellow officers. The subculture of policing also makes several assumptions that can be very destructive to police–community relations. For example, in some cases the subculture calls for officers to mete out their own forms of justice and punishment. This type of action must be avoided in order to garner credibility from the community they serve.

Finally, consider the following points that may serve as a guide to assist one in traversing a career in law enforcement (Delattre, 1994):

1. It is always wrong for a police officer to accept money or other goods or services in exchange for favors of any kind. The only honest dollar is the officer's salary, and everything else can be compromising. It does not matter whether other police officers, mayors, judges, and lawmakers accept gifts of value and extort bribes; doing so is still always wrong.

2. It is always wrong to deliberately use more force than is necessary, whether to apprehend or subdue a suspect, quiet a situation, or for any other purpose. It is always wrong for police to beat people up in order to "punish" them, to rough up suspects in custody or in handcuffs, and to use the badge as an excuse to assault others.

3. It is always wrong to falsify or plant evidence against anyone, to file false reports, and to commit perjury. It does not matter whether the purpose of falsification is to protect police who have behaved wrongly or to secure conviction of suspects. Falsification, frame-ups, and perjury are always wrong.

4. It is always wrong to prejudge others because of color, gender, ethnic background, nationality, or any other fact of birth. People deserve to be treated as individuals, not as mere members of groups they happen to belong to by birth. It is always wrong to use denigrating words to refer to the gender, color, or origins of others. It is always wrong to enforce the law differently with people who differ only in color, gender, economic condition, and the like.

5. It is always wrong to give illegal substances or prescription drugs to informants (or anyone else). It is always wrong to skim money or drugs from drug busts, even with the intention of harming drug dealers.

6. It is always wrong to bring a hangover to work, to use alcohol on the job, and to consume illegal substances of any kind at any time.

7. It is always wrong to commit acts that put pressure on a partner or other police to lie or cover up wrongdoing. True friends never call upon one another to betray the badge and honorable service by lying or looking the other way because of a misguided sense of loyalty. A cop who expects another cop to lie for the sake of friendship or loyalty is always wrong.

8. It is always wrong to fail to back up a partner or other officers in a dangerous situation and to place another officer or member of the public in a needlessly dangerous situation.

## Questions in Review

1. Discuss the importance of a code of ethics.
2. How would you describe the primary duties of police officers?
3. Discuss the police subculture.
4. Discuss the concept of discretion.
5. Discuss the importance of honest and accurate recruitment practices.

# Ethics and Corrections $\quad$ 12

## Introduction

The basic ethical questions in corrections involve asking whether our society has the right to punish or correct individuals who commit crimes against the society and, if so, where the right comes from. We often answer these questions with the general assumption that the state has the power to control us for the greater good of society.

The social contract theory is often used to justify a state's right to punish an offender. Under the social contract theory, we give certain powers to the state in return for protection by the state. If we overstep the bounds of the retained rights, then the state has the right to punish us. Accordingly, there is a social contract between the individual and the state. As described by Thomas Hobbes in 1691 (1985), it is a voluntary agreement among people defining the relationship of individuals with one another and with government and by this process forming a distinct organized society.

Punishment power by the state is limited under the social contract theory. As noted by von Hirsch (1976), it is generally assumed to be limited by the following restrictive guidelines:

- Our liberties are to be protected as long as they are consistent with the liberties of others.
- The state is obligated to use the minimum punishment necessary to protect our liberties. Excessive punishment by the state is in itself a violation of the social contract.
- The state must be prepared to justify any intrusion into a citizen's liberty.
- The requirements of justice should constrain the pursuit of crime prevention.

Cesare Beccaria (1774), considered as the founder of the classical school of criminology, in his *On Crimes and Punishment* contended that the true measure of crimes is the harm they do to society. He stated that it is an error to believe that the true measure of crimes is to be found in the intention of the people who commit them. Sometimes men with the best intentions do the greatest injury to society, and at other times, intending the worst for it, they do the greatest good. At the time of his writing (January 1764), Beccaria was objecting to the existing practices in the Italian penal system. He especially disliked the capricious and purely personal justice that judges were dispensing. He also objected to the severe and barbaric punishments of that day. The judges exercised their power to add to any punishments prescribed by law and thus to promote their personal views as to the special circumstances involved (Roberson & Wallace, 1998).

In his writings about the concept of the contractual society and the need for punishment, Beccaria stated that laws are the conditions under which independent and isolated men unite to form a society, and that men weary of living in a continual state of war and enjoying a liberty rendered useless by the uncertainty of preserving it, sacrificed some of their liberty so that they might enjoy the rest of it in peace and safety. Tangible motives in the form of punishments are needed to protect society and to prevent it from plunging into its original chaos. Those who infract the law must be punished to protect society (Roberson & Wallace, 1998).

Beccaria contended that only laws can decree punishments for crimes, and the authority for making those laws resides only with the legislator who represents the entire society united by a social contract. A magistrate should not be allowed, under any pretext of zeal or concern for the public good, to augment the prescribed punishments.

## Subculture in Corrections

The American Correctional Association published a code of ethics for correctional personnel. The overriding theme of their code is that the correctional personnel will respect and protect the civil and legal rights of all individuals, including prisoners. In addition, members are cautioned against using their professional position to secure personal privileges or advantages. It is often said that, within the corrections system, a subculture exists in which the inmate is the enemy and the use of force and deception is acceptable. Even the occasional use of deceit to cover up wrongs is acceptable (Muraskin & Muraskin, 2001). In examining the ethical considerations of correctional personnel, Pollock (2006) divided them into two general groups: correctional officers and their supervisors and treatment professionals. She concluded that treatment professionals in the corrections system face a number of ethical issues that are similar to those faced by treatment professionals, such as medical doctors, in the outside world. We devote most of this chapter to discussing the issues facing correctional officers and the public issues involving punishment.

Kauffman (1988, pp. 85–92) concluded that the correctional officer subculture accepts the following norms:

- Always go to the aid of another officer.
- Don't lug drugs.
- Don't rat on fellow officers.
- Never make an officer look bad in front of inmates.
- Always support an officer in a dispute with an inmate.
- Don't be sympathetic toward inmates.
- Maintain officer solidarity against all outside groups.
- Be concerned about fellow officers.

## Sentencing

Judge Jack B. Weinstein, senior U.S. district judge for the Eastern District of New York, noted in the 58th annual Benjamin Cardozo Lecture at the Association of the Bar of the City of New York, November 28, 2007,

> A judge must remember whose government this is: it is the people's. This view controls the court's attitude towards those who come before it. The judges are the representatives of the litigants' government, there to serve and help them as well as the public at large. The attitude required of the people's servants plays out in a range of matters from sentencing of individuals by avoiding unnecessary harshness to devising effective techniques for satisfying valid claims of large masses of people injured in toxic tort or pharmaceutical cases.

### The Case against Socrates

In 399 BC, Socrates was charged with the offense of impiety (corrupting young minds and believing in new gods). He was tried before a jury of 500 members. The trial lasted only 1 day. He was found guilty by a margin of 30 jurors. The prosecution proposed the death penalty. Socrates had a right to propose an alternative penalty. He stated,

> Shall I [propose] imprisonment? And why should I spend my days in prison, and be the slave of the magistrates? Or shall the penalty be a fine and imprisonment until the fine is paid? There is the same objection. I should have to lie in prison, for money I have none, and cannot pay. And if I say exile, I must indeed be blinded by the love of life, if I am so irrational as to expect that when you, who are my own citizens, cannot endure my discourses and arguments, and have found them so grievous and odious that you will have no more of them, that others are likely to endure them.

The jury condemned him to death. He committed compulsory suicide by drinking poison, the Athenian method of execution (Roberson & Wallace, 1998, p. 284).

## Purposes of Punishment

The problem of punishment causes constant anguished reassessment, not only because we keep speculating on what the effective consequences of crime should be but also because there is a confusion of the ends and means. We are still far from answering the following ultimate questions: What is the right punishment? On what grounds do we punish others (Schafer, 1969)?

There is an old Chinese proverb that states, "It is better to hang the wrong fellow than no fellow." This proverb is based on the concept that when a crime is committed, there should be certainty that punishment will follow. Accordingly, if a crime has occurred, punish the person most likely to have committed it. While this practice would probably reduce crime, how does it conflict with our requirement of establishing the criminal's guilt beyond a reasonable doubt?

California Rules of Court Rule 410 provides that the general objectives of sentencing include the following:

1. Protecting society
2. Punishing the defendant
3. Encouraging the defendant to lead a law-abiding life in the future and deterring him from future offenses
4. Deterring others from criminal conduct by demonstrating its consequences
5. Preventing the defendant from committing new crimes by isolating him for the period of incarceration
6. Securing restitution for the victims of crime
7. Achieving uniformity in sentencing

## Retribution

Retribution generally means "getting even." Retribution is based on the ideology that the criminal is an enemy of society and deserves severe punishment for willfully breaking its rules. Retribution is often mistaken for revenge. There are, however, important differences between the two. Both retribution and revenge are primarily concerned with punishing the offender, and neither is overly concerned with the impact of the punishment on the offender's future behavior or behavior of others. Unlike revenge, however, retribution attempts to match the severity of the punishment to the seriousness of the crime. Revenge acts on passion, whereas retribution follows specific rules regarding the types and amounts of punishment that may be inflicted. The biblical response of an "eye for an eye" is a retributive response to punishment. While the eye-for-an-eye concept is often cited as an excuse to use harsh punishment, it is less harsh than revenge-based punishment, which does not rule out two-eyes-for-an-eye punishment. Sir James Stephen, an English judge, expressed the retributive view by stating, "The punishment of criminals was simply a desirable expression of the hatred and fear aroused in the community by criminal acts" (Packer, 1968, p. 37). This line of reasoning conveys the message that punishment is justifiable because it provides an orderly outlet for emotions that if denied may express themselves in socially less acceptable ways. Another justification under the retribution ideology is that only through suffering punishment can the criminal expiate his sin. In one manner, retribution treats all crimes as if they were financial transactions. If you got something or did something, then you must give equivalent value (suffering).

Retribution is also referred to as "just deserts." The just deserts movement reflects the retribution viewpoint and provides a justifiable rationale for support of the death penalty. This viewpoint has its roots in a societal need for retribution. It can be traced back to the individual need for retaliation and vengeance. The transfer of vengeance motive from the individual to the state has been justified based on theories involving theological, aesthetic, and expiatory views. According to the theological view, retaliation fulfills the religious need to punish the sinner. Under the aesthetic view, punishment helps reestablish a sense of harmony through requital and thus solves the social discord created by the crime. The expiatory view is that guilt must be washed away (cleansed) through suffering. There is even a utilitarian view that punishment is the means of achieving beneficial and social consequences through the application of a specific form and degree of punishment deemed most appropriate to the particular offender after careful individualized study of the offender (Johnson, 1974, p. 173).

## Deterrence

Deterrence is a punishment viewpoint that focuses on future outcomes rather than past misconduct. It is also based on the theory that creating a fear of future punishments will deter crime. It is based on the belief that punishments have a deterrent effect. There is substantial debate as to the validity of this concept. Specific deterrence deters specifically the offender, whereas general deterrence works generally on others who might consider similar acts. According to this viewpoint, the fear of future suffering motivates individuals to avoid involvement in criminal misconduct. This concept assumes that the criminal is a rational being who will weigh the consequences of his or her criminal actions before deciding to commit them.

One of the problems with deterrence is determining the appropriate magnitude and nature of punishment to be imposed to deter future criminal misconduct. For example, an individual who commits a serious crime and then feels bad about the act may need only slight punishment to achieve deterrent effects, whereas a professional shoplifter may need severe fear-producing punishments to prevent future shoplifting.

Increases in crime rates and high rates of recidivism are often used to cast doubt on the effectiveness of the deterrence approach. Recidivism may cause some doubt about the efficacy of specific deterrence, but it says nothing about the effect of general deterrence. In addition, unless we know what the crime rate or rates of recidivism would be if we did not attempt to deter criminal misconduct, the assertions are unfounded. Are we certain that the rates would not be higher had we not attempted to deter criminals?

## Incapacitation

At least while the prisoner is in confinement, he or she is unlikely to commit crimes against innocent persons outside of prison. To this extent, confinement clearly helps reduce criminal behavior. Under this viewpoint, there is no hope for the individual as far as rehabilitation is concerned. Therefore, the only solution is to incapacitate the offender.

There are two variations in the incapacitation viewpoint. Collective incapacitation refers to sanctions imposed on offenders without regard to their personal characteristics, such as all violent offenders. Selective incapacitation refers to incapacitation of certain groups of individuals who have been identified as high-risk offenders, such as robbers with a history of drug use. Under selective incapacitation, offenders with certain characteristics or history would receive longer prison terms than others convicted of the same crime. The purpose of incapacitation is to prevent future crimes, and the moral concerns associated with retribution are not as important as the reduction of future victimization. As Packer (1968, p. 55) stated, "Incapacitation is a mode of punishment that uses the fact that a person has committed a crime as a basis for predicting that he will commit future crimes." Packer also stated that the logic of the incapacitation position is that until the offender stops being a danger, we will continue to restrain him. Accordingly, Packer contended that the logical conclusion is that offenses that are regarded as relatively trivial may be punished by imprisonment for life.

## Rehabilitation

The rehabilitation approach is that punishment should be directed toward correcting the offender. This approach is also considered the treatment approach. This approach considers criminal misconduct as a manifestation of a pathology that can be handled by some form of therapeutic activity. While this viewpoint may consider the offender as "sick," it is not the same as the medical approach. Under the rehabilitation viewpoint, we need to teach offenders to recognize the undesirability of their criminal behavior and make significant efforts to rid themselves of that behavior. The main difference between the rehabilitation approach and the retribution approach is that under the rehabilitation approach, the offenders are assigned to programs designed to prepare them for readjustment or reintegration into the community, whereas the latter approach is more concerned with the punishment aspects of the sentence. Packer saw two major objections to making rehabilitation the primary justification for punishment. First, we do not know how to rehabilitate offenders. Second, we know little about who is likely to commit crimes and less about what makes them apt to do so. As long as we are ignorant in these matters, Packer contended, punishment in the name of rehabilitation is gratuitous cruelty.

## Death Penalty

Cesare Beccaria stated the following on the death penalty:

> Was there ever a man who could have wished to leave to others the choice of killing him? It is conceivable that the least sacrifice of each person's liberty should include sacrifice of the greatest of all goods, life? ... The punishment of death, therefore, is not a right, for I have demonstrated that it cannot be such; but it is the war of a nation against a citizen whose destruction it judges to be necessary or useful. If, then, I can show that death is neither useful nor necessary I shall have gained the cause of humanity.
>
> There are only two possible motives for believing that the death of a citizen is necessary. The first: when it is evident that even if deprived of liberty he still has connections and power such as to endanger the security of the nation—when, that is, his existence can produce a dangerous revolution in the established form of government. ... I see no necessity for destroying a citizen, except if his death were the only real way of restraining others from committing crimes; this is the second motive for believing that the death penalty may be just and necessary. (Roberson & Wallace, 1998, pp. 59–60)

### Should the Issue of Death Penalty Imposition Be Based on Economics?

Should a state abolish the death penalty not because of the state's concern for the morality of the death penalty but merely to save money? This is a question that has been debated recently in several states.

The question of whether costs should be considered by a juror in imposing the death penalty was discussed in *Bigby v. State* (2008, p. 716). The questioning of a potential juror by the defense counsel included the following questions and responses:

*Question*: It says we don't want to decide whether someone lives or dies based on a dollar-and-cents question. We don't want jurors doing that. We want them to answer these questions based on evidence and not factor in, well, if we go ahead and execute him, we don't have to pay all this money.

*Answer*: Right.

*Question*: Some people say, I'm not sure I could do that. I'd probably factor it in some. Do you feel that way?

*Answer*: Perhaps. I mean, you asked for honesty.

*Question*: No, and that's exactly what I want you to do. I think you held your hand up about an inch indicating —

*Answer*: It's like I said, I mean, you know, you have to make investments to mitigate risks every day. I mean, that's why some of us have alarms on our homes, and, you know, putting someone in prison for life, that would be an investment in mitigating risk for their future actions in society.

In the *Bigby* case, the potential juror was apparently of the opinion that it was cheaper to execute a person than to keep the individual confined for life. In considering the issue of whether the decision to use the death penalty should be based on dollars and cents, consider the following excerpts from Justice John Paul Stevens's concurring opinion in the *Baze v. Rees* decision (2008, p. 1542):

Death cases raise many more issues, and far more complex issues, than other criminal cases, and they are attacked with more gusto and reviewed with more vigor in the courts. This means there is a strong possibility that the conviction or sentence will be reconsidered—seriously reconsidered—five, ten, twenty years after the trial. ... One has to wonder and worry about the effect this has on the families of the victims, who have to live with the possibility—and often the reality—of retrials, evidentiary hearings, and last-minute stays of execution for decades after the crime. Thus, they conclude that "we are left in limbo, with machinery that is immensely expensive, that chokes our legal institutions so they are impeded from doing all the other things a society expects from its courts, and that visits repeated trauma on victims' families." ... Some argue that these costs are the consequence of judicial insistence on unnecessarily elaborate and lengthy appellate procedures. To the contrary, they result in large part from the States' failure to apply constitutionally sufficient procedures at the time of initial conviction or sentencing. They may also result from a general reluctance by States to put large numbers of defendants to death, even after a sentence of death is imposed. California condemns many murderers, but few are ever executed. ... [Note that] California death row inmates account for about 20% of the Nation's total death row population, but that the State accounts for only 1% of the Nation's executions. In any event, they are most certainly not the fault of judges who do nothing more than ensure compliance with constitutional guarantees prior to imposing the irrevocable punishment of death.

  We are left, then, with retribution as the primary rationale for imposing the death penalty. And indeed, it is the retribution rationale that animates much of the remaining enthusiasm for the death penalty. As Lord Justice Denning argued in 1950, "some crimes are so outrageous that society insists on adequate punishment, because the wrong-doer deserves it, irrespective of whether it is a deterrent or not." Our Eighth Amendment jurisprudence has narrowed the class of offenders eligible for the death penalty to include only those who have committed outrageous crimes defined by specific aggravating factors. It is the cruel treatment of victims that provides the most persuasive arguments for prosecutors seeking the death penalty. A natural response to such heinous crimes is a thirst for vengeance. ... Retribution is the most common basis of support for the death penalty. A recent study found that 37% of death penalty supporters cited "an eye for an eye/they took a life/fits the crime" as their reason for supporting capital punishment. Another 13% cited "They deserve it." The next most common reasons—"saving taxpayers money/cost associated with prison" and deterrence—were each cited by 11% of supporters.

In 2008, the California Commission on the Fair Administration of Justice noted that the additional cost of confining an inmate to death row, as compared with the maximum security prisons where those sentenced to life without possibility of parole ordinarily serve their sentences, is $90,000 per year per inmate. With California's current death row population of 670, that accounts for $63.3 million annually. Using conservative rough projections, the commission estimates the annual costs of the present (death penalty) system to be $137 million per year. The cost of a system that imposes a maximum penalty of lifetime incarceration instead of the death penalty would be $11.5 million per year (California Commission on the Fair Administration of Justice, 2008).

A study released by the Urban Institute forecast that the lifetime expenses of capitally prosecuted cases since 1978 will cost the state of Maryland taxpayers $186 million. That equals at least $37.2 million for each of the state's five executions since the state reenacted the death penalty. The study estimates that the average cost to Maryland taxpayers for reaching a single death sentence is $3 million—$1.9 million more than the cost of a case without the death penalty. The study examined 162 capital cases that were prosecuted between 1978 and 1999 and found that those cases will cost $186 million more than what those cases would have cost had the death penalty not existed as a punishment. At every phase of a case, according to the study, capital murder cases cost more than noncapital murder cases. The 106 cases in which a death sentence was sought but not handed down in Maryland cost the state an additional $71 million. Those costs were incurred simply to seek the death penalty when the ultimate outcome was a life or long-term prison sentence (McMenamin, 2008).

In its review of death penalty expenses in 2008, the state of Kansas concluded that capital cases are 70 percent more expensive than comparable noncapital cases. The study counted costs of death penalty cases through to execution and found that the median death penalty case costs $1.26 million. Cases without the death penalty were counted through to the end of incarceration and were found to have a median cost of $740,000. For death penalty cases, the pretrial and trial-level expenses were the most expensive part, 49 percent of the total cost. The costs of appeals were 29% of the total expense, and the incarceration and execution costs accounted for the remaining 22%. In comparison with cases without the death penalty, the following findings were revealed (State of Kansas, 2008):

- The investigation costs for death sentence cases were about three times greater than for cases without the death penalty.
- The trial costs for death penalty cases were about 16 times greater than for cases without the death penalty ($508,000 and $32,000, respectively).
- The appeal costs for death penalty cases were 21 times greater.
- The costs of carrying out (i.e., incarceration and/or execution) a death sentence were about half the costs of carrying out a nondeath sentence in a comparable case.
- Trials involving a death sentence averaged 34 days, including jury selection; trials without a death penalty averaged about 9 days.

The average cost of a trial in a federal death case is $620,932, about eight times that of a federal murder case in which the death penalty is not sought. A study found that those defendants whose representation was the least expensive, and thus who received the least amount of attorney and expert time, had an increased probability of receiving a death sentence. Defendants with less than $320,000 in terms of representation costs (the bottom one-third of federal capital trials) had a 44% chance of receiving a death sentence at trial. On the other hand, those defendants whose representation costs were higher than $320,000 (the remaining two-thirds of federal capital trials) had only a 19% chance of being sentenced to death. Thus, the study concluded that defendants with low representation costs were more than twice as likely to receive a death sentence (Gould & Greenman, 2008). This last study also brings up the issue that the less that is spent on a defendant's counsel, the more likely the defendant will receive a death penalty.

## Is It Ethical to Medicate Someone so that He or She Will Be Sane Enough to Execute?

In *Ford v. Wainwright* (1986), the U.S. Supreme Court held that the Eighth Amendment prohibits the execution of the insane. In line with its prior decisions, the Court explained that the Eighth Amendment prohibits punishments that were considered cruel and unusual at the time the Bill of Rights was adopted, as well as punishments that are contrary to "evolving standards of decency." The Court found that execution of the insane was prohibited at common law and remains prohibited in every state in the union. The Court noted that it is as true today as in Lord Edward Coke's time that most men and women value the opportunity to prepare, mentally and spiritually, for their death. Moreover, today, as at common law, one of the death penalty's critical justifications, its retributive force, depends on the defendant's awareness of the penalty's existence and purpose. Accordingly, the Court concluded, "The Eighth Amendment prohibits a State from carrying out a sentence of death upon a prisoner who is insane."

## Michael Owen Perry

Michael Owen Perry is on death row in the state of Louisiana. He will probably never be executed. Perry was convicted of killing five members of his family on July 17, 1983. Apparently Perry went to his grandmother's house and calmly blew the heads off his two sleeping cousins. He then walked across the back yard to his parents' house, where he killed his mother and two other people. He was found guilty of capital murder and sentenced to death. At his trial, the issue of his sanity was never raised.

The U.S. Supreme Court ruled that the state could not execute him until he regained his sanity and could therefore understand the nature and gravity of his punishment. In addition, the Louisiana Supreme Court ruled that the state could not forcibly medicate him to assist him in regaining his sanity for the purposes of executing him.

*State's argument that he should be medicated to execute:* The state argued that neither the Eighth Amendment nor the Fourteenth Amendment requires application of a broader standard of incompetency. While on death row, Perry was determined to be insane. The state court found that when Perry was treated with antipsychotic medication, he was competent to be executed. The evidence presented at the competency hearings demonstrated that as long as Perry is medicated, he understands that he was convicted of the murders of five members of his family and that, as a result, he was sentenced to die. Thus, when Perry is maintained on medication, his understanding of his sentence of death satisfies the Eighth Amendment competency standard articulated by Justice Lewis Powell in *Ford v. Wainwright* (1986).

*Perry's attorneys' argument:* Perry's attorneys argued that the medication that the trial court ordered for Perry is not treatment; it is a step toward his execution and part of his punishment. The doctors at Louisiana State Penitentiary have been treating Perry for years. This order to forcibly medicate Perry goes beyond the treatment that has been administered in the past and permits no exercise of professional medical judgment.

Perry has a history of developing side effects as a reaction to psychotropic medication. This order does not consider potential side effects or permit termination of the medication if side effects develop. Perry has received psychotropic medication in the past. This medication has not been successful in achieving sustained or predictable competency. Yet the order does not permit termination of the medication even if it does not work. The Eighth Amendment and contemporary standards of human decency prohibit the use of forced medication solely to create competency to be executed.

Louisiana has no statute, case law, or policy permitting the use of forced medication to create competency to be executed. Neither the legislature nor the Supreme Court of Louisiana has authorized the type of order that the trial court has entered for Perry. No state executes the insane. The majority of states commit an insane inmate for treatment. The majority of states place limits on the use of forcible medication and medication for nontreatment purpose. This consensus shows that the trial court's order to forcibly medicate to create competency for execution violates the Eighth Amendment. Louisiana law prohibits the execution of the insane and requires that insane inmates be treated. Louisiana law also defines the conditions under which an inmate can be forcibly medicated.

These laws create expectations that are protected by the due process clause of the Fourteenth Amendment. By ordering Perry to be medicated for nontreatment purposes, the trial court has violated Perry's rights under the due process clause. The trial court's order to forcibly medicate Perry considered only the state's interest in carrying out its sentence. It did not balance this interest against Perry's interest in avoiding the nonconsensual administration of psychotropic drugs. This order, therefore, fails to accord Perry the minimal protections guaranteed by the Fourteenth Amendment.

Is it cruel and unusual and thus a constitutional violation to execute a person who does not understand the nature and gravity of the punishment?

- Does it make sense to wait until an individual is sane before we kill him or her?
- What difference does it make if the individual understands the nature and gravity of the punishment if he or she is going to die immediately?

In *Singleton v. Norris* (2003), the state of Arkansas attempted to force Singleton, who had been convicted of capital murder and aggravated robbery, to take medication to regain his mental capacity so that he could be executed. A U.S. Court of Appeals held that the state's interest in carrying out the sentence outweighed Singleton's interest in avoiding medication and that his due process interests in life and liberty were foreclosed by the lawfully imposed death sentence and the procedures for imposing the medication. The appellate court found that the Eighth Amendment did not prohibit executing a prisoner who had become incompetent while on death row but did prohibit executing one who regained competency through appropriate medical care. The U.S. Supreme Court denied Singleton's petition for review by the Supreme Court.

## Methods of Execution: Is It Ethical to Inflict More Pain Than Necessary in Carrying Out the Death Penalty?

In preindustrial societies, the death penalty was carried out by banishing the criminal to the wilderness, where death was relatively certain. The effectiveness of banishment diminished as human skills and culture advanced and the chances of an individual surviving banishment greatly increased. Some of the ancient methods of execution include being burned, hanged, stoned, boiled in oil, beheaded, disemboweled, buried alive, thrown to wild beasts, crucified, drowned, crushed, impaled, shot, flayed alive, and torn apart. The list, although long, is not exhaustive of the creative methods used to carry out death sentences. As noted previously, Socrates was forced to drink poison as his method of execution. Table 12.1 contains a list of significant U.S. Supreme Court decisions on the death penalty.

By the middle of the 19th century, "hanging was the 'nearly universal form of execution' in the United States" (*Campbell v. Wood*, 1994). In 1888, following the recommendation of a commission impaneled by the governor to find "the most humane and practical method known to modern science of carrying into effect the sentence of death," New York became the

### Table 12.1.  Significant U.S. Supreme Court Decisions and the Death Penalty

| | | |
|---|---|---|
| *Furman v. Georgia* | 1972 | Overturned death penalty in Georgia |
| *Gregg v. Georgia* | 1976 | Death penalty declared constitutional in Georgia |
| *Ford v. Wainwright* | 1986 | State prohibited from executing the insane |
| *McCleskey v. Kemp* | 1987 | Rejected racial injustice of the death penalty |
| *Thompson v. Oklahoma* | 1988 | Prohibits execution of juveniles under the age of 16 |
| *Perry v. Lynch* | 1989 | Mental retardation is no bar to capital punishment |
| *Stanford v. Kentucky* | 1989 | 17-year-olds can be executed |
| *Wilkins v. Missouri* | 1989 | 16-year-olds can be executed |
| *Atkins v. Virginia* | 2002 | It is unconstitutional to execute the mentally retarded |
| *Roper v. Simmons* | 2005 | May not execute defendants who were juveniles when the crime was committed |
| *Baze v. Rees* | 2008 | Lethal injection approved a method of administering the death penalty |

first state to authorize electrocution as a form of capital punishment (*Glass v. Louisiana*, 1985). By 1915, 11 other states had followed suit, motivated by the "well-grounded belief that electrocution is less painful and more humane than hanging" (*Malloy v. South Carolina*, 1915, p. 185).

Electrocution remained the predominant mode of execution for nearly a century, although several methods, including hanging, firing squad, and lethal gas, were in use at one time. In 1977, legislators in Oklahoma, after consulting with the head of the anesthesiology department at the University of Oklahoma College of Medicine, introduced the first bill proposing lethal injection as the state's method of execution. A total of 36 states have now adopted lethal injection as the exclusive or primary means of implementing the death penalty, making it by far the most prevalent method of execution in the United States (*Baze v. Rees*, 2008).

In colonial America and in early England, hanging was the most common form of execution. The use of a firing squad was the second-most common. The preferred form in France and other European countries was the use of the guillotine, a device consisting of a heavy blade that falls freely between two perpendicular grooved posts. The use of the electric chair began in New York in 1890. The electric chair has been called "America's most innovative contribution to the method of execution." On August 6, 1890, William Kemmler, a convicted murderer from Buffalo, was the first person executed in an electric chair, at the Auburn Penitentiary in New York. The electric chair was hailed as a more humanitarian way to execute people. Many, however, claimed it was merely a promotional device for the developer of a New York electrical company (*Baze v. Rees*, 2008).

Kemmler was strapped in a chair with leather straps. A headpiece connected with electric wires was placed on his head. When the voltage was transmitted through the headpiece, Kemmler's shoulders shot up. It appeared as though every muscle in his body went rigid. His face turned an intense red, then an ashen pallor. His eyes were glazed, pupils dilated. His right hand was clenched so tightly that a nail had dug into the flesh. Spots appeared on his face. The electricity was shut off. His body sagged like a limp rag. They began to unstrap him from the chair. Suddenly, foam bubbled out of his mouth, and a gurgling sound came from his throat. Quickly they replaced the headpiece and turned on the current again. He then sat up in the chair taut and then slumped. A wisp of smoke came from the top of his head (*Baze v. Rees*, 2008).

In an unusual case, a convicted murderer (Willie Francis) was sentenced to die in the electric chair. He was strapped in the chair, and the execution began. The electrical system malfunctioned, however, and he was not killed when the current passed through his body. He then contended that to subject him to the process a second time was cruel and unusual punishment and thus a violation of the Eighth Amendment to the U.S. Constitution. By a five-to-four decision, the Supreme Court ruled against him, and he was finally executed (*Baze v. Rees*, 2008).

## Is the Death Penalty Biased?

Private and public groups have been increasingly scrutinizing the death penalty. Many speculate that the death penalty is unequal justice in light of minorities' being disproportionately sentenced to death. In February 1994, two months before his retirement from the Supreme Court, Justice Harry A. Blackmun articulated his personal conviction that capital punishment in the United States is not applied fairly and consistently and is therefore unconstitutional.

Justice Blackmun stated in *Callins v. Collins* (1994, p. 1146),

> From this day forward, I no longer shall tinker with the machinery of death. For more than 20 years I have endeavored—indeed, I have struggled—along with a majority of this Court, to develop procedural and substantive rules that would lend more than the mere appearance of fairness to the death penalty endeavor. Rather than continue to coddle the Court's delusion that the desired level of fairness has been achieved and the need for regulation eviscerated, I feel morally and intellectually obligated simply to concede that the death penalty experiment has failed. It is virtually self-evident to me now that no combination of procedural rules or substantive regulations ever can save the death penalty from its inherent constitutional deficiencies. The basic question—does the system accurately and consistently determine which defendants "deserve" to die?—cannot be answered in the affirmative. It is not simply that this Court has allowed vague aggravating circumstances to be employed. ... The problem is that the inevitability of factual, legal, and moral error gives us a system that we know must wrongly kill some defendants, a system that fails to deliver the fair, consistent, and reliable sentences of death required by the Constitution.

Justice Blackmun noted that most of the research centering on racial disparities in death penalty sentences, concluded, among all other things being equal, defendants who kill white victims are much more likely to receive the death penalty than those who kill black victims. According to Justice Blackmun, black defendants charged with killing white victims received a death sentence 22% of the time, while white defendants charged with killing black defendants received the death penalty in only 3% of the cases.

## Should the Death Penalty Be Used Only in Aggravated Murder Cases?

Patrick Kennedy, in *Kennedy v. Louisiana* (2008), sought to set aside his death sentence under the Eighth Amendment. He was convicted by the state of Louisiana of aggravated rape of his then-8-year-old stepdaughter. After a jury trial, Kennedy was convicted and sentenced to death under a state statute authorizing capital punishment for the rape of a child younger than 12 years of age. The question before the Supreme Court in the *Kennedy* case was whether the Constitution bars a state from imposing the death penalty for the rape of a child when the crime did not result, and was not intended to result, in the death of the victim. The Court held that the Eighth Amendment prohibits the death penalty for this offense and that the Louisiana statute was unconstitutional.

Associate Justice Anthony Kennedy, writing for the majority, noted that the Eighth Amendment, applicable to the states through the Fourteenth Amendment, provides that "excessive bail shall not be required, nor excessive fines imposed, nor cruel and unusual punishments inflicted." The Court held that the amendment proscribes all excessive punishments, as well as cruel and unusual punishments, that may or may not be excessive and that the Eighth Amendment's protection against excessive or cruel and unusual punishments flows from the basic precept of justice that punishment for a crime should be graduated and proportioned to the offense. Justice Kennedy stated that whether this requirement has been fulfilled is determined not by the standards that prevailed when the Eighth Amendment was adopted in 1791 but by the norms that currently prevail. He concluded that the amendment draws its meaning from the evolving standards of decency that mark the progress of a maturing society. This is because the standard of extreme cruelty not merely is descriptive but necessarily embodies a moral judgment. The standard itself remains the same, but its applicability must change as the basic mores of society change.

The Court contended that the evolving standards of decency must embrace and express respect for the dignity of the person, the punishment of criminals must conform to that rule, and the punishment be justified under one or more of three principal rationales: rehabilitation, deterrence, and retribution. Justice Kennedy noted that it was the last of these, retribution, that most often can contradict the law's own ends. This is of particular concern when the Court interprets the meaning of the Eighth Amendment in capital cases. When the law punishes by death, it risks its own sudden descent into brutality, transgressing the constitutional commitment to decency and restraint. The Court stated,

> For these reasons we have explained that capital punishment must "be limited to those offenders who commit 'a narrow category of the most serious crimes' and whose extreme culpability makes them the most deserving of execution." Though the death penalty is not invariably unconstitutional, the Court insists upon confining the instances in which the punishment can be imposed. (*Kennedy v. Louisiana*, 2008, p. 2642)

# Illicit Behavior by Correctional Employees

John Moriarty, inspector general for the Texas Department of Corrections (TDC), stated that smuggled contraband constitutes the biggest security problem in the Texas prison system. If this is a significant problem, logic seems to imply that employees caught smuggling contraband into the prisons would be severely punished. Studies, however, reflect otherwise.

In a 2009 study by the TDC, it was noted that correctional employees seldom lose their jobs when caught smuggling goods to inmates. Detected smuggled items include knives, drugs, cell phones, smokeless tobacco, and even McDonald's hamburgers. Of the 263 employees disciplined during the period of 2003 to 2008 by the TDC for smuggling, about three-fourths received probation, 26 received no punishment, and only 35 were fired. Only one of the 263 was criminally prosecuted, and he served no prison time. Contraband trafficking in the Texas prisons gained national attention in 2008 when a death row inmate used a smuggled cell phone to threaten a state legislator. It was discovered that other death row inmates had used the cell phone to place more than 3,000 calls. Most of the employees discovered were correctional employees (84%). There were 32 employees who were considered managers or supervisors. The most popular contraband smuggled into the Texas prisons appears to be smokeless tobacco (Sandberg & Stiles, 2009, p. A1).

## Does a Correctional Officer Have a Right to Cohabit with an Ex-inmate?

In *Poirier v. Mass. Dep't of Corrections* (2009), this question was before an appellate court on an appeal. Melissa Poirier was employed for 15 years as a correction officer with the Massachusetts Department of Correction (DOC). She received positive performance evaluations over the course of her career. She was dismissed for violating the following departmental regulation:

> Rule 8(c) of the "Rules and Regulations Governing All Employees of the Massachusetts Department of Corrections" states that: You must not associate with, accompany, correspond, or consort with any inmate or former inmate except for a chance meeting without specific approval of your Superintendent, DOC Department Head, or Commission of Correction. Your relations with inmates, their relatives, or friends shall be such that you would willingly have them known to employees authorized to make inquiries. Conversations with inmates' visitors shall be limited only to that which is necessary to fulfill your official duties.

In 2000 and 2001, the DOC investigated allegations that Poirier (1) maintained an inappropriate relationship with a current inmate, (2) delivered contraband to an inmate, and (3) communicated with a relative of an inmate. After conducting an investigation and hearing, the DOC found no evidence to support the first two charges, but it sustained the third.

The former prison guard brought a civil action under 42 U.S.C.S. § 1983 against the state corrections department and its commissioner. She claimed that her constitutional right to intimate association was violated when she was fired for conducting a romantic relationship with a former inmate in violation of department rules. The U.S. District Court for the District of Massachusetts dismissed for failure to state a claim. The federal district court concluded that the corrections department's actions survived rational basis review. The federal court of appeals affirmed. The guard failed to present a sufficiently precise definition of the type of relationship at stake. Even if the right she sought to vindicate was that of cohabitation between unmarried adults, her claim nonetheless failed. Such right did not fall under any of the Supreme Court's bright-line categories for fundamental rights, and the court of appeals declined to expand on the list. The court afforded significant deference to prison administrators in regard to prison security measures, and the prospect of a guard–prisoner or guard–former prisoner relationship posed a clear and obvious threat to the maintenance of prison order and security.

## Questions in Review

1. Why should criminals be punished?
2. Should the death penalty be an authorized punishment? Justify your answer.
3. Explain the subculture of corrections.
4. What safeguards can be imposed to prevent the death penalty from being discriminatorily applied?
5. Is the death penalty effective in crime prevention? Explain.
6. Should executions be televised? Justify your answer.

# Ethical Issues Involving Victims' Services* 13

## Abstract

The test of a true leader is his/her capacity to adhere to a strong foundation of ethics, articulate them as standards for colleagues and staff, and "practice what s/he preaches" by example on a daily basis. Personal leadership values form this ethical foundation, and are based upon past life experiences and current work processes that seek to improve rights and services for victims of crime. Ethical behavior reflects a sense of self-respect that translates into respect for others in all encounters. The process of living one's personal values in a leadership role requires being in touch with one's inner world of purpose, dreams, principles, aspirations, and ethics, which in the end gives meaning to one's life. The application of a leadership lifestyle is challenging and requires total commitment to the concept of integrity.

## Learning Objectives

Upon completion of this chapter, students will understand the following concepts:

- The various themes of ethics in leadership roles.
- Ethical behavior as an organizational theme and how to measure one's own ethical principals and behaviors.
- Personal leadership values that promote ethics and integrity and how to apply them in a leadership role.
- Challenges to ethical leadership and strategies for facing such challenges.
- The essential role of ethics and integrity in conveying a "unity of purpose" for an organization.

* The material in this chapter was reprinted with permission from *Leadership in Victim Services*, Chapter 2. Integrity and Ethics in Leadership. Authors/Editors: Anita Drummond, Carroll Ellis, Melissa Hook, Morna Murray, and Anne Seymour, Office for Victims of Crime, U.S. Department of Justice, April 2008. Not only does the material discuss victim issues, but it also provides for an excellent summary of ethical leadership practices.

## Introduction

The greatest leaders of history, regardless of their age, gender, race, or platform, all share one quality in common—absolute commitment to the principles they serve. Integrity in leadership is a quality that cannot be contrived and, in turn, is unmistakably apparent when a leader is truly committed to the cause s/he serves. Consider the words of Nelson Mandela, arguably one of today's most revered and honored world leaders, a man who emerged from twenty-six years as a political prisoner to be hailed as the triumphant leader and hero of a new South African democracy by allies and former enemies alike. In 1963, as he faced, before a British court in the strict apartheid regime of South Africa, charges of government sabotage which carried a possible death sentence by hanging, he made what many consider to be the most effective political speech of his career, detailing his efforts on behalf of democracy and freedom. In his authorized biography on Mandela, Anthony Sampson quotes a powerful portion of Mandela's speech in the following descriptive narrative:

"During my lifetime I have dedicated myself to this struggle of the African people. I have fought against white domination, and I have fought against black domination. I have cherished the ideal of a democratic and free society in which all persons live together in harmony with equal opportunities." He paused and looked at the judge: "It is an ideal which I hope to live for and achieve." Then, dropping his voice, he concluded: "But, if needs be, it is an ideal for which I am prepared to die." (Sampson, 1999, p. 192)

Mandela had dedicated his entire adult life to the struggle for freedom and democracy for black Africans. His long ordeal as a political prisoner of the South African regime had barely begun. His lawyers, in every attempt to spare him the death penalty, initially begged him to leave out the statement "it is an ideal for which I am prepared to die." Mandela refused to leave out these words, finally agreeing only to insert the phrase, "if needs be." (Ibid., p. 191).

While leaders are rarely called upon to risk their own lives for the integrity of the causes they serve, it is this kind of unwavering and heartfelt commitment that can propel men and women into positions of great leadership. Often magnificent displays of integrity are recognized only with hindsight, after the drama and tension surrounding a situation have subsided and the atmosphere has cleared sufficiently so that the nature and intent of the act and the opposition to it are manifest. It requires great courage in periods of adversity and dramatic change for leaders to conduct themselves ethically. They are often alone, misunderstood, and under fire for taking on powerful opponents or for struggling to change the status quo. Subtle acts of integrity go unnoticed and thus unappreciated. Yet without a leader's constant adherence to the precious core values that underwrite the entity that s/he represents, an organization's well-being can rapidly deteriorate. Ethical conduct in leadership and trusting relationships among the participants—be they a company, a victim services agency, a political constituency, or a family—are prerequisites for healthy environments.

George Norris, whom John F. Kennedy memorialized in Profiles in Courage, was the freshman Senator from Nebraska who took on the Senate and President Wilson in 1917 to resist the United States' entry into the Great War in Europe. He led a small but committed opposition to the Armed Ship Bill that would have authorized the arming of American merchant ships in the war zone. Norris believed that Wilson was pandering to the munitions business that was seeking military protection for their commercial shipments to Europe, and that it would encourage German attacks and push the country into the war unnecessarily. Importantly, passage of the Bill would also have set a precedent for transferring the authority to declare war that resides with the Congress to the President, which is in violation of the laws of our nation (Kennedy, 2000, pp. 174–178).

Although a three-day filibuster prevented the passage of the Bill, President Wilson managed to arm the ships and "let lose a scathing indictment of the little group of willful men who had rendered the great government of the United States helpless and contemptible." Norris came under brutal attack from his peers and constituency; his unpopularity soared; and he expected to be recalled to his state at any moment. He kept his office by explaining the simple truths of his argument while making personal appearances throughout the country. Even though the nation soon entered the war, in hindsight Norris was honored for his integrity and deemed a hero for his opposition to the Bill (Kennedy 2000, pp. 178–191). Norris' commitment to the principles upon which he staked his political career is memorialized in the following quote:

> I would rather go down to my political grave with a clear conscience than ride the chariot of victory as a Congressional stool pigeon, the slave, the servant, or the vassal of any man, whether he be the owner or manager of a legislative menagerie or the ruler of a great nation . . . I would rather lie in the silent grave remembered by both friends and enemies as one who remained true to his faith and who never faltered in what he believed to be his duty. (Kennedy, 2000)

As a service-based field, integrity in leadership is crucial in the victims' rights discipline. The efforts of victim advocates in the last thirty years to get the nation to focus on the plight of crime victims in the criminal and juvenile justice systems has been a battle in which the exercise of integrity has been essential. Securing the passage of laws that mandate victims' rights has required that the principles of justice to victims become established components of criminal and constitutional law. It is an ongoing process. Caring for victims and seeing that their rights are honored and justice is served is, by definition, "ethical behavior."

Victim services is a dynamic, exacting, and developing profession that both compels and consumes those who have made it their profession. It spans local, state, and federal criminal justice systems and allied professionals, and sweeps across every aspect of daily life. Victim service professionals deal daily with traumatized people who but for giant strides made by the victims' rights discipline would be unattended or poorly served. What crime victims need, want, and are entitled to receive has been learned out of necessity and in a relatively short period. The knowledge has come as a result of increasing collaboration between policy-driven systems and individual crusaders for crime victims. Ethical and uncompromising leadership across the wide spectrum of victim concerns and issues has been a powerful catalyst in the development of comprehensive services currently available to victims, and such leadership is essential for further progress. Integrity, that unwavering commitment to purpose, has been responsible for the many gains made in the effort to gain recognition and rights for victims. Integrity in leadership, then, is nonnegotiable. To be effective, a leader must understand and embrace a strong set of ethics, communicate them as a valued standard to co-workers, and live by them. Integrity is the cornerstone on which trusting relationships are built and from which all honest consensus is created. This chapter defines elements of integrity and discusses how these elements are essential to effective and authentic leadership in any field and specifically in victim services. In what ways does a profession that deals largely with human emotions affect the nature of leadership? The chapter will look at ownership and the different kinds of boundaries that are relevant to leadership in victim services. Finally, it will discuss integrity, both practically and philosophically, in human relationships and in leadership roles.

## Applying Ethics in Leadership Roles

> Ethics is a way of teaching you how to live as though you were one with the other. —Joseph Campbell

Ethical behavior often has a great deal to do with reconciling interests: the moral principles behind the choices one must make are often in conflict; choosing one option over the other requires critical analysis and deliberation. Recognizing an ethical problem within a complex set of circumstances is a test of one's ability to reason moral issues. Often, making moral choices in a family situation is clearer and more straightforward than making moral choices in professional life where the positive and negative repercussions of an ethical choice may occur at a greater distance from the decision maker and have little direct impact on him/her. In the corporate world, leaders frequently find themselves caught between their professional duties and general morality. Do their actions serve the good of the staff? Do their actions serve the good of the community-at-large?

Those whose task it is to watch over the general well-being often see their mission as a career; at the center of which their own person occupies pride of place. Under such conditions, it's difficult for them to disregard the immediate term—especially their own popularity—and consider what would be best for everyone's good in the long term (Ricard and Revel, 1998, p. 195).

Making ethical choices requires a clear idea of one's moral mandate and the ability to critically analyze choices to determine how they stand up to principle. Although there are many approaches to making ethical choices, all basically reflect on good and evil and whether or not an action taken will be harmful to someone or something. The long-term positive results of a decision emphasizes its validity. Some of the different (and sometimes contradictory) choices are:

- The categorical imperative: Always act so as to treat others as an end and never only as a means.
- Be courageous but not rash, liberal but not stingy, righteously indignant but not malicious. Have pride but not vanity.
- Take account of the preferences and interests of all those affected to bring about the greatest net satisfaction of preferences.
- Resist what appears to be good in the short run for what appears to be really good in the long run.

## Classical Ethical Principles

Arriving at moral decisions (or in some cases, the most moral decision possible in a circumstance) is about asking the right questions. Socially responsible business ethics attempt to apply classical ethical principles to modern business practices by proposing the questions below. The ten principles illustrated are tests to determine whether a decision can be considered ethical. It is recommended that seven out of ten be satisfied before a decision is made and the consideration should be for the long-term good:

1. Is the action contemplated in the long-term self interest of yourself and/or of the organization to which you belong?

2. Is the action contemplated honest, open, and truthful? Is it one that you would not mind being widely reported to the media?
3. Is the action contemplated kind and does it build a sense of community, a sense of all working together toward a commonly accepted goal?
4. Is the action contemplated in violation of any laws (as the law represents the minimum moral standard in society)?
5. Does the action contemplated result in the lesser harm for society of which you are a part?
6. Is the action contemplated something you would like to see others take when faced with a similar dilemma?
7. Does the action contemplated abridge any agreed upon and accepted rights of others?
8. Does the action contemplated seek to maximize profits subject to legal and market restraints?
9. Is the action contemplated one that harms the least among us in any way?
10. Does the action contemplated interfere with the right of all of us for self-development and self-fulfillment? (Eighinger, 1998)

Further, the elements to consider when faced with an ethical decision are:

- What are the ethical issues in this case?
- Whose rights are involved?
- What are the social justice issues?
- What solution strategies are available?
- How does the strategy measure:
  - reduction of harm?
  - maximization of benefit?
  - respect of rights?
  - fair treatment of all parties involved?
- What are the potential consequences of solution strategies? Who will be most affected by the choices? Are there unintentional consequences that have not been considered? Will the positive outcome outweigh the negative ones? (Ibid.)

It is clear that leaders must consider a multiplicity of issues and concerns in making consistently ethical decisions and in developing a code of ethical behavior for their organizations. It is the leader's role to set a clear and uniform example of ethical behavior and to articulate specific expectations and goals so that ethical behavior becomes an integral theme of the organization.

## Leadership and Trust

True leaders gain the trust of those they lead. While it is difficult to define exactly what trust is and what it means to those who follow a particular leader, we certainly know when it is present and when it is not. We know that it involves predictability, consistency, clarity of communication and purpose, and that it is essential to the maintenance of good leaders. The establishment and maintenance of trust allows leaders to guide and shape an organization through good as well as difficult times. A strong foundation of trust sustains an organization or any group through challenging obstacles so that the proper care and time can be taken to find the right solutions.

Warren Bennis and Joan Goldsmith, in their book, Learning to Lead (1997), describe four qualities of leadership that, when practiced, create and engender trust. They are vision, empathy, consistency, and integrity. The authors, through their extensive research on leaders, argue that a leader who is trusted demonstrates these four characteristics:

- The leaders have a vision for the organization that is clear, attractive, and attainable. We tend to trust leaders who create inspiring visions. The leader's vision functions as a context that provides shared beliefs and a common organizational purpose with which we can identify and feel that we belong. The leader involves us in the visions, empowers us to create it, and communicates the shared vision so that we integrate it into our lives.
- The leader has unconditional empathy for those who live in the organization. We tend to trust leaders who can walk in our shoes and are able to let us know that although they may have a different point of view, they are able to see the world as we see it and understand the sense we make of it.
- The leader's positions are consistent. We tend to trust leaders when we know where they stand in relation to the organization and how they position the organization relative to the environment. We understand how our leaders' positions evolved and know that they are willing to reconsider them in the face of new evidence.
- The leader's integrity is unquestionable. We tend to trust leaders who stand for a higher moral order and who demonstrate their ethical commitments through actions that we can observe. Leaders uphold a standard of ethics and call themselves and others to account for deviations from this moral code.

It is helpful to consider these four qualities as we consider the importance of trust and integrity in leadership. Oftentimes, as we reflect on leaders in our past and present that have influenced us and/or continue to play an important role in our lives, we see these qualities in action.

# Ethical Behavior as a Theme in the Organization

> We should therefore examine whether we should act in this way or not as not only now but at all times. —Plato

When the ethical behavior within an organization is suspect or there is an atmosphere of apathy and a need for a strong ethical code to serve as a positive motivating factor for all employees, the effort to establish the ethical code begins with the leader of the organization. The motivation starts at the top.

The National Institute of Ethics reports that leaders who encourage staff to maintain a high level of ethical behavior and to maximize their potential inherently do the following:

- Convey a sincere interest in others.
- Satisfy the needs of subordinates.
- Develop an organizational commitment.
- Are honest and open in dealings with fellow employees.
- Allow co-workers to play an active role in decision making.
- Provide challenges and responsibilities for staff.
- Convey trust and understanding.
- Assist in personal development (Trautman, 1998, p. 41).

## Ethics in the Workplace Assessment

The National Institute of Ethics has developed for law enforcement a series of training tools and manuals to determine what policies, procedures, or practices within an organization need to be added or revised to ensure integrity and ethics in the workplace. Two different surveys are conducted—one with staff and one with management. To encourage staff to speak openly, the surveys are sealed upon completion. Staff are requested to frankly disclose their criticisms about the level of ethics in the workplace, from the top down, and to give suggestions for improvements.

General survey questions that apply to criminal justice (and that also apply to victim service providers) are meant to provoke a discussion about the level of ethics in the organization and what would enhance them: What are the greatest needs in relation to ethics? Do unethical acts occur in the organization? What are the strengths in relation to ethics? How can they address the weak areas? (Ibid., p. 53).

Completion of the surveys allows the staff and leadership to examine and express their ideas, expectations, and shortcomings without risking job security. Once ethics become a central theme of the organization, the group as a whole can decide if they would benefit from ethics training.

## Ethics Assurance Council and Ethics Teams

The National Institute of Ethics also proposes the creation of Ethics Assurance Councils for all kinds of organizations to bring staff together to share ideas, suggestions, and critical information while organizing and directing the effort to make ethics a focal point of the workplace. Councils can identify and resolve any unavoidable ethics-related problems that arise in the workplace as a result of company protocol or policy (Ibid.).

In a similar vein, co-workers who form Ethics Teams can work together to improve each other's ethical decision-making skills. They can coach each other and staff on solving problems, providing resources, and offering objective feedback.

The following are questions used in the National Institute of Ethics Self-Evaluation:

- How do I decide ethical dilemmas?
- Do I have set ethical beliefs or standards?
- If so, do I live by these beliefs or standards?
- How often have I done things that I am ashamed of?
- How often have I done things that I am proud of?
- Do I admit my mistakes?
- What do I do to correct mistakes that I make?
- Do I often put the well-being of others ahead of mine?
- Do I follow the golden rule?
- Am I honest?
- Do people respect my integrity?
- List the three best things that have ever happened to me.
- What is the most dishonest thing I have ever done?
- Did I ever rectify the situation?
- What is the most honest thing that I have ever done? (Trautman, 1998, p. 87)

## Personal Leadership Values

Victim service professionals hold the public trust as surely as do other public servants such as prosecutors, law enforcement, and the judiciary. Victims of crime trust and rely that professionals will adhere to a code of conduct based upon established principles and values. That code of conduct must also require service delivery to be appropriate and of the highest quality in technique and nature. The leader establishes a code of conduct and decision making that s/he adheres to with complete integrity. Integrity is individuals conducting themselves by a code or standard of moral virtue, which prevents untoward behavior in thought, word, or deed. The key to integrity is consistent and unwavering commitment to a standard of principles or virtues.

One of the challenges facing victim services is a lack of clearly agreed upon standards and credentials by which the quality and ethics of services offered by both individuals and programs can be objectively measured. This is not a reflection of dissension within the field, but rather an indication of the maturation and growth that has led to an increasing need for the articulation and creation of a common set of values. The diversity of service professionals within the field makes this a complex and complicated process that requires deep consideration and skilled consensus-building. The process has already begun—several states have developed certification processes and the Office for Victims of Crime has funded a national project that will culminate in recommendations (gathered from a diverse, national advisory board, as well as from grassroots populations throughout the country) regarding individual, program, and ethics standards.

The lack of uniformity in credentialing is a challenge to public recognition of the standards upon which victim service practitioners and programs operate. Therefore, it is incumbent upon leaders to clearly articulate the values and principles that form the cornerstone of their provision of victim services. The individual articulation of these principles and values will guide and shape the overall articulation of standards.

What are some of the virtues by which integrity in victim services leadership should be measured?

> The instructor said, Go home and write a page tonight. And let that page come out of you—Then, it will be true. —Langston Hughes in Theme for English B

> The greatest rewards come only from the greatest commitment. —Arlen Blum, mountain climber, leader American women's Himalayan expedition

*Commitment.* The first virtue of integrity is commitment to a purpose. It is absolute dedication to accomplishing a worthy goal. Commitment is unwavering and uncompromising. It endures doubt, blame, and rejection. Emotional attachment or passion, which is often ignored, begins with commitment and is a function of commitment. Leaders believe—through their own vision of lofty ideals—that they can make a difference. They embrace a goal, and expect and hope that others will devote their lives to the achievement of that goal. Leaders must be willing (in their passion for the purpose) to ensure that others also have a stake in creating and owning the possibility of the purpose.

*Trust.* Without trust, effective leadership is impossible. As a virtue, trust refers to loyalty and truthfulness. When leaders demonstrate that they are consistent in their actions, they create a relationship of safety and engender trust from others—trust that situations and events will be handled in accordance with principled standards. The often cited example of "going to the well with someone in the dark of night" captures the core of trust. Trust means knowing that one is in safe hands even under perilous conditions. Integrity in leadership engenders that kind of assurance. Leaders in victim services must not only establish trusting relationships with staff; they must also serve as teachers to the staff who may not yet be adept at forming trusting relationships with the victims they serve.

*Wisdom.* Daniel Payne said, "Wisdom is the gift, the endowments to know how to use power. Knowledge is only an instrument in the hand of wisdom." (Johnson, 1995) Integrity in leadership requires the ability to use the power of wisdom in positive ways to strengthen people, systems, and institutions. Wisdom allows a leader to predict, distinguish, and discern conflicts, actions, and situations. It clears the vision to see beyond the immediate—to take into account the past, present, and future. Wisdom is the virtue that drives integrity.

*Responsibility.* A sense of responsibility which comes with power is the rarest of things. This virtue allows that leaders will step up to the line, take on the mantle, and demonstrate reliability. Responsibility means modeling a standard of excellence to which others can aspire. Responsibility must be embodied and actual. Victim service professionals are faced daily with the overwhelming responsibility of caring for people during critical periods in their lives. The "responsibility" aspect of their work includes treating every client as a unique individual, whose pain and suffering deserves a consistent, quality response.

*Courage.* One isn't necessarily born with courage, but one is born with potential. Without courage, we cannot practice any other virtue with consistency. We cannot be kind, true, merciful, generous or honest. Victim service professionals need courage to confront the overwhelming issues in a field that hinges on life and death. They are also sometimes called upon to confront allied justice professionals about issues that affect the fair and respectful treatment of victims.

*Competency.* Knowledge is not power, it is potential power that becomes real through use. People with integrity are honest enough to acknowledge when they do not know something. At the same time, they bring a level of proficiency to their work which includes expertise in leadership skills. Leaders will challenge, inspire, and enable others through competent measures, as a function of their integrity. They will always lead by example.

*Sensitivity.* Sensitivity is a powerful source for helping others to feel strong. The victim services field is founded on the principle of empowerment. Integrity is based upon the ability to sense, consider, and regard the feelings and needs of others. Respect for others gives rise to the ability to be sensitive to others. Respect for the human condition should permeate one's standard of conduct. What seems to be most natural for professionals in victim services can sometimes become a "lost art" when one surrenders to isolation, loses touch with others, and focuses only on him/herself. Leadership is not an independent activity, but one that relies on relationships between people.

*Justice.* Injustice anywhere is a threat to justice everywhere. We are caught in an escapable network of mutuality, tied in a single garment of destiny. Whatever affects one directly affects all indirectly. We associate justice with entitlement—giving an individual what s/he is due. Justice is that and more. It is also a virtue of integrity, which permits a range of acknowledgment, consideration, attention, and redress to the needs of individuals that may not fit the definition of what is "strictly owed." This virtue takes patience, foresight, flexibility, and an understanding heart.

*Servitude.* "Real leaders are humble servants and not power-hungry tyrants. This concept proposes that greatness is achieved only through humility. Leaders with integrity refute the idea of superiority through position. Rather, they engage in helping and enabling others to have the leeway and the tools that they need for success—recognizing that the success of others is a positive reflection on them. Servitude means refusing to act with pretense, arrogance, or self-importance; it also means making the welfare of people and organizations—rather than power and prestige for one's own gain—a priority.

*Self-respect.* Joan Didion, in her essay "On Self-Respect," says that to have the sense of one's own intrinsic worth is potentially to have everything: the ability to discriminate, to love, and to remain indifferent. To lack it is to be locked within oneself, paradoxically incapable of either love or indifference (Didion 1968).

These nine virtues comprise minimum requirements for integrity. They require diligent pursuit, which in turn requires strength, time, and the will to persevere.

Can integrity be taught or measured? Integrity develops out of repeated confirmation of self- worth and determination. Integrity is measured by one's actions. In essence, people with integrity are able to successfully integrate these virtues and others into their daily transactions. They live the precepts of honesty, reliability, resourcefulness, and concern and consideration for others. They inspire and challenge others to greater levels. They refuse to demand loyalty, yet are grateful for loyalty when inevitably, it comes. Finally, integrity accepts individual differences—both the frailties and strengths—which are by-products of the human condition.

## Applying Personal Values in a Leadership Role

As the field of victim services matures, so does the need for leadership training and education. Having been integrated into police departments, prosecutor and court offices, probation and parole agencies, and hospitals, direct service professionals are being catapulted into positions of power in these bureaucratic institutions where established supervisors have had the benefit of years of leadership training and practical experience. Many victim service providers have been ground-level employees who were never exposed to leadership training. Now occupying positions of authority, but without the support or funding to acquire training, they may have a tremendous need for training in basic leadership qualities and strategies.

Preliminary advice to victim service professionals who find themselves overwhelmed with the leadership position they have assumed includes the following:

- Learn not only about things to be done, but also about how to do them.
- Learn to accept the new role and function as an equal with other leaders in the hierarchy of agencies and institutions. Embrace the total organization — not just the segment that provides victim services. Relate every conceivable aspect of the organization to the activities of victim services.
- Seek to understand the policies and politics that drive the operation of the organization, and find constructive ways to contribute to both.
- Learn from the experiences — both negative and positive — of colleagues in all divisions of the organization.
- Understand the importance of continuing education and training.
- And finally — believe in yourself.

It is also important to recognize that personal values among victim-serving professionals vary significantly. While the diversity of beliefs should be viewed as an asset, it can also present challenges to professionals who are "set in their ways."

A strong leader encourages and even thrives on diversity in values and beliefs of professional colleagues and staff. The varying perspectives often bring new, innovative approaches to victim services. They help victim service organizations to more appropriately "mirror" the diversity of the clients they serve. Perhaps most significantly, diversity in values and beliefs ultimately improves the quality and scope of victim and justice-related services.

## Maintaining Consistency in Integrity and Ethics

We are all faced with many instances in which we are challenged to put our most dearly held beliefs and values into action. Sometimes there is a gap between what a leader believes is right and the action that s/he takes. This has been referred to as the "integrity gap." Having the courage and commitment to stand up for what we believe in when the time comes to do so is a common and recurring challenge for all human beings (Bennis and Goldsmith, 1997, p. 139). Bennis and Goldsmith (1997) cite a study by authors Everett, Mack, and Ore sick that analyzes the pressures upon corporate executives in maintaining ethical values while working to increase profitability of their corporations. One finding was that the executives fell generally into two types of categories: (1) "principled risk takers," and (2) "conventional decision makers" (Ibid., 139). The executives in the study fell generally into one of these two categories, and the differences were seen in the following three areas:

1. *Self-Consistency: Wholeness or Compartmentalization.* Did individuals see life as an integrated whole in which their beliefs applied to work as well as to church groups, volunteer organizations, and values at home?
2. *Personal Efficacy: High or Limited Sense of Agency.* Did individuals have a sense of power and control in their work life so that they believed they could take action to express their values?
3. *Scope of Awareness: Global or Circumscribed.* Did individuals see themselves as global citizens with responsibilities that are larger than their own corner of the world? (Ibid.)

It is a rare person who is solely a "principled risk taker" or "conventional decision maker." Most of us are combinations of both. Analyzing and reflecting upon the issues raised by the above three qualities is extremely helpful in determining our own capacities for leadership and for withstanding the pressures that oftentimes come with positions of leadership, e.g., pressures to conform, to take the easy way out, to keep everyone happy, to do things the same way they've always been done, or to not "make waves." Maintaining one's personal values and morals consistently and congruently throughout one's personal and professional lives is no easy task like everything discussed in this manual, it is a long and highly personal journey.

## Challenges to Ethical Leadership

The beginning of this chapter addressed the high price of integrity in leadership: learning it and constantly reinforcing its practice. Sometimes the best lessons are learned through failure and mistakes. As the old saying goes, that which does not destroy me, makes me stronger.

Success can be measured by the ability to overcome obstacles. Put another way, success can be measured by one's ability to avoid the mistakes that others have made along the way.

In order to gain some insight into problems that are common to victim service professionals, the following scenarios present examples of possible ethical quandaries.

## Adapting to Change and Remaining Resilient:
## The Age/Experience Factor

Lauren has been involved in the victim's movement for over twenty years. She remembers a time when the word "struggle" applied to the recognition of victims and their rights, the acquisition of resources for victims, funding for programs, and even respect and salaries for professionals in the field. Lauren cherishes her journey in all of these instances, which in some way defines her purpose in life. Her motivation has always been her passion to reach out and help victims; her commitment has often driven her to live her job 24/7. The organization for which she has been the director for twenty years has grown from a staff of three to a staff of eighteen. One of the major contributing factors to the dynamics of the workplace environment is the age and level of experience of the victim advocates, and how each generation's motivations and core values shift dramatically from one age group to another.

Lauren lives by a traditional work ethic. Her primary motivation is to give back and to serve—to do good for others. She works hard at her job to serve victims to the greatest degree possible, and if that involves overtime and home phone calls, so be it. When her staff jumped from three to eighteen people, the first difference she noted between her motivation and that of her new staff (who were generally age thirty and younger) was an apparent lack of shared commitment. They wanted to work a nine-to-five job, and they wanted independence and responsibility assigned to them immediately without regard for learning and earning the work experience. They were fearless but seemed to demonstrate less passion for serving victims than their more senior counterparts. Lauren was frustrated because she did not view them as serious in their quest to serve victims and witnesses of crime in the same passionate sense that she applied to her life's work. An added dynamic of the extremes in age/experience within Lauren's office was a generation disparity. Older, more traditional staff, who entered the field of victim services with considerable experience in related fields, sometimes expressed feeling insecure and inadequate among the younger, more aggressive staff who have not had the years of experience but nevertheless are charged with more responsibility in the work environment. The older individuals, new to victim services, were often trained by first-line supervisors who in some instances could be as much as twenty-five years younger than the trainee, and the dynamics of the training were hampered because of such an age/experience differential.

Specifically, Lauren was concerned about the discomfort of a newcomer, a therapist who joined her staff. She brought with her years of training and experience with clients in crisis. After learning from the young trainer about the speed and efficiency required in dealing with the great number of victims who require speedy referrals and case processing, the therapist (who is fifty-six years old) felt that she was being asked to ignore her victim counseling skills to help streamline office protocols. Not only did this newcomer resent the lack of recognition of her experience in helping those in need, she also felt that the younger staff members did not respect her as an individual.

Issues to consider:

- In a discipline where people often deal with high intensity emotional experiences, how does this example demonstrate a common theme in the workplace? Why is this situation an ethical quandary for Lauren?
- What type of serious long-term damage can result from allowing a situation of this nature to go unchecked? Tolerance, as a virtue of integrity, might allow Lauren to connect/communicate/understand her younger, less experienced staff. In what ways can she expand her own perspective by broadening her lens?
- While part of the problem with the new therapist may be related to the therapist's dislike of her subordinate position to a young trainer, Lauren must deal with the essential issue of her employee's self-respect as well as the fundamental well-being of the organization. Lauren may need to reassure the therapist that she was hired precisely because of her experience as a therapist. How can Lauren help the therapist to frame the responsibilities of her new job in such a way that she will employ those skills, improve and expand them, and pass them on to others?

Lauren's challenge as a leader is to recognize that she cannot impose her work ethic on others, a critical factor in the leader/follower relationship. How much is too much in that relationship? Lauren as a leader must be capable of supporting all of her staff to do very good work on their own terms. The ultimate challenge, however, is to make the trials of others easier to bear.

Current leadership theorists have examined with great interest how sensitivity to generational differences is becoming a factor in motivating staff to improve their performance. Essex and Kusy (1999) write that:

> For generation X (born from 1964 through 1975), growing up with computers and MTV and being the first generation of latchkey kids, it's no surprise that they are not used to being closely supervised. While loyal to a profession or a cause, they are not necessarily loyal to an organization, having witnessed the downsizing of many baby boomers. They may want rewards based on performance, not longevity or degrees, and don't understand why they should be

required to work their way up if they have the necessary skills now. As Xers enter the workforce, leaders of all generations will need to understand how best to lead and retain them because this is the thinnest labor pool in recent times.

According to Essex and Kusy (1999), baby boomers (those born from 1946 to 1963) typically demonstrate stronger work ethics and company loyalty. They are more open to talking through issues at length with supervisors, brainstorming with colleagues, and working in team efforts. They have a clear sense of the importance of career building and establishing an income base.

The oldest work pool for organizations is made up of people born between 1925 and 1945 who share traditional work ethics, value loyalty and stability, and demonstrate respect for authority. "They bring a strong work ethic, a wealth of life and work experience, as well as commitment to the organizations fortunate enough to have captured their wisdom." (Ibid., 20)

Drawing upon three generations of workers who have powerfully different motivations requires that leaders cease to even consider that what they want—and how they want to achieve it—is transferable. For example, the current rule for dealing with generation Xers is to stop "squeezing them for motivation and commitment." They can be excellent at their job if one remembers that "play and work go hand in hand." To GenXers, "there is life after work" (Ibid.).

Baby boomers have other needs. They are more organizationally loyal and relate profoundly to their work even if they don't like their job. A key motivation to a baby boomer is having adequate opportunities for advancement and participation in key organizational decisions. Essex and Kusy (1999) suggest that boomers need help in stretching their talent, but they also tend to work excessively. "To avoid mid-career burn-out, provide boomers with the self-actualizing experiences for which they hunger." Allow them opportunities to be creative. Give them mobility and offer them sabbaticals.

Essex and Kusy (1999) point out that it is common among older workers with traditional work ethics to feel that what they have accomplished in their careers is not being held in as high esteem as it should be. It is important that their abilities be recognized. Under skillful leadership, they oftentimes become the office "sages" to whom younger staff turn for a wide range of advice about challenges in victim services, as well as general life situations.

## Ownership: The Importance of Clear and Healthy Boundaries

People drawn to the field of victim services are often passionate about crime victims and their issues. Victim service providers, as pioneers and crusaders for victim justice, work tirelessly to ensure that crime victims are afforded

rights and services. Crime victims and providers enter into a close relationship characterized by the victim's dependency on the service provider. When
service providers become so involved with their clients that they become reliant upon their relationship with their clients to address their own needs, this
behavior represents a compromise of ethical standards of professionalism. It
is necessary to recognize the importance of

- Understanding that the "need to be needed" is potentially harmful
  to clients as well as staff.
- Separating from one's work and finding a balance between work and
  other aspects of one's life. Just as there are addictions to drugs, alcohol, and sex, there are addictions to "being needed by others."
- Finding resources to support one's mental health—a mentor, therapist,
  friend, hobby, family, exercise, spiritual leader, or a combination.
- Understanding the tremendous impact that a leader's behavior may
  have upon clients and their families.

Kathy is a victim service provider in a law enforcement agency.
Throughout her years of working victim cases, she has developed close relationships with many homicide survivors, and is deeply aware of the importance of not cultivating a dependence that some survivors may develop
during their interactions with key players within the criminal justice process. Those interactions may be with victim service providers, prosecutors,
police detectives, or other agents.

Kathy observed a phenomenon among some female homicide family survivors that she realized could create a serious problem for them. They have a
tendency to become completely reliant and dependent on the male detectives
investigating the homicide. It is difficult to assess how much of the dependency
is the result of the need for victims to be in touch with every bit of information specific to their cases, the all-consuming aspects of homicide, or possible
issues associated with the investigators' needs beyond professional accom-
plishment. Whatever the reason and extent of these sometimes involved and
intense associations, the end of the investigation often results in the end of the
relationship and can have devastating effects on the grieving survivor.

Kathy believed her duty was to take a stand on helping investigators to
recognize the important influence they have on victims. The climate of her
agency would not permit an open discussion of the situation without jeop-
ardizing her job and the working relationships she had spent so many years
developing.

Issues to consider:

- Kathy may need to establish a policy of meeting with all female
  homicide family survivors early in the investigation. This process

could help educate victims further regarding their right to information, not as a component of their relationship with the investigator, but as a full-scale right required by law.

- Kathy may consult with local mental health professionals familiar with this type of dependent response in victims to develop the most effective means of communicating with the victims whom she considered vulnerable. One option may be to develop training for law enforcement that will assist them in explaining the sort of unusual emotional responses that victims might have in dealing with their loss, i.e., excess alcohol or other drug use; excess medication; and falling in love with an inappropriate person who may be helping them deal with the crime. Kathy communicated this message throughout the staff, and it has been assimilated without causing any harm or creating animosity among co-workers, investigators, or detectives.

## Searching for Approval in All the Wrong Places: Failure to Strive for Wholesome Relationships with Self and Others

In his "Rules" adapted from his autobiography, My American Journey, Colin Powell (1995) indicates that one should never let ego get so close to one's position that when the position goes, one's ego goes with it. It is a mistake to be guided by one's own need for ego fulfillment in leadership situations.

Leaders sometimes find that they are driven by a need to have employees like them, include them in their lives, and identify with them beyond the dictates of the job. These struggling leaders fail to recognize their inner world. They cannot draw a distinction between their own personal needs and the professionalism required for the work environment. Ethical behavior allows that distinction.

Relationships must start with the leader's concept of self and move on to relationships with others. These relationships must be meaningful, empowering, and reciprocal in nature, and must reflect a broader view of respect than one's inherent due. The broad view is the infusion of respect throughout every encountered situation. Rather than look for adoration from followers, real leaders search instead for respect through mutual relationships. Leaders must create a valuing culture in the workplace where relationships are built on appreciation—rather than on tolerance—and all are made to feel an equal part of the whole.

Beth and her co-worker Vickie had worked together in establishing a unique program response to victims of sexual assault. The two colleagues considered themselves crusaders in providing quality service for specific types of crimes. They spent long grueling hours planning and implementing their program. The hours together created a bond that carried over into their personal lives. The two received public acclaim for their contributions to the field and as a consequence, a grant provided the opportunity to hire more staff and Beth was promoted into the position of director of the program. Vickie did not resent the promotion. However, their close friendship proved to be a problem for the newly hired staff, to the extent that Beth experienced major difficulties in retaining staff, based on accusations of favoritism, failure to include total staff in various projects, and a distorted assumption of project ownership.

Issues to consider:

- Prior to the expansion of the program and her promotion, Beth's relationship with Vickie was typical of those shared by colleagues in the workplace environment. When the promotion and staff adjustments changed this, Beth failed to make the appropriate corresponding adjustment.
- What did Beth need to know and understand about her role as a leader? What ethical issues were apparent in her behavior? Could Vickie have helped Beth in modifying their relationship?
- Could Beth also have been struggling with some ego-related issues surrounding her special work with sexual assault victims? Could she have been possessive of the program and her relationship with Vickie and unwilling to bring others into the process? What are her ethical obligations in this situation?

Sometimes individuals placed in leadership roles assume that because they have special responsibilities, particularly those associated with managing people, they are entitled to special privileges and so can take the best of everything … the best office, equipment and materials, holiday time, and other benefits. Being in charge and setting the pace and standard for others is exciting and exhilarating. When leaders become obsessed with their sense of importance they fail ethically. Any amount of this conduct, even seemingly insignificant behavior, ultimately manifests itself in a destructive way. The manager who demands loyalty, extracts favors, and abuses employees cannot hope to become a leader. Employees are quick to discover inequities in a system fueled by exploitation. Integrity demands that leaders let go of petty self-interest.

## Failure to Bring Everyone into the Inner Circle

Valuing diversity means dealing with cultural differences and expanding one's awareness and acceptance of these differences. It means having the integrity to confront and dispel one's own personal negative feelings and attitudes about individual differences among people. Whether the differences relate to sexual orientation, physical or mental disabilities, race, age, ethnicity, socioeconomic or religious affiliation, leaders make a point of including and caring for about everyone. They ensure that appreciation is truly about quality treatment for all. Leaders believe in their followers and promote an environment of respect and support.

## Leadership, Relationship, and Unity of Purpose

A successful organization must be founded on a strong set of core values that are embraced by all of its members. In a group of people with many backgrounds, interests, and motivations, how can one be sure that they will all commit to the same set of values? It is the responsibility of the leader to establish those values within the organization by stating them, restating them, and openly living them in words and deeds. It is the leader's job to inspire co-workers, to take them beyond their everyday selves to a higher level of awareness, motivation, and commitment. The leader must also provide ongoing opportunities for staff to understand and "buy in" to the organization's values, as well as to review and revise them, as needed.

Lincoln shared, emphasized, and continually restated two fundamental values throughout his presidency: the pursuit of liberty and equality. He described the Civil War as the "people's contest," writing that "on the side of the Union it was a struggle for maintaining in the world that form and substance of government whose leading object is to elevate the condition of men [and women] ... to afford all an unfettered start, and a fair chance, in the race of life." (Phillips, 1992, p. 53).

Leadership historian J. M. Burns writes that Lincoln in his role as leader felt the duty to reach down to the person behind him or below him and help to elevate that person to his or her better self. Lincoln was one of those leaders who "perceive their roles in shaping the future to the advantage of groups with which they identify, an advantage they define in terms of the broadest possible goals and the highest possible levels of morality" (Burns, 1978).

In many religions and philosophical teachings it is advised that we share: "[s]haring in all reactions, of all attitudes, of all types of wisdom, of all problems and difficulties and limitations, so that they become constructive in the group sense and cease to be destructive" (Haasnoot, 2000, p. 44) In discussing the leader's role in creating a sharing environment among co-workers, Haasnoot emphasizes the importance of sharing information—both positive and negative—about the health and direction of the company and their individual status within it with staff. Citing Deepak Chopra's second spiritual law of success, he also asserts that

> sharing is a form of giving. Companies and leaders must give and receive in order to keep wealth and affluence. (Ibid., p. 45)

A program that has been frequently cited for its approach to sharing within a traditional corporate environment is the "Work-out" program at General Electric. The tremendous growth of the company in the last decade, as it became an increasingly global entity, created barriers as a result of distance between geographic locations, diversity of functions, and varying corporate structures. The GE leadership concluded that the best way to address the "no-man's land" that was developing between the divisions was to put people together from different units in a noncompetitive environment on a regular basis. A discussion of financial goals and achievements was consciously excluded from the meetings to place emphasis on creativity, discovery of new motivations, open exchange, and generation of open feedback.

In the "Workout" model, managers meet two full days a month with the leadership in "candid, face-to-face exchanges to resolve issues, share new ideas and projects, and identify new opportunities." At the end of their meetings, they go back to their divisions and share information with their co-workers. Within divisions, employees also meet regularly over a period of two days without the presence of supervisors or managers to resolve issues, share information, and learn from each other. On the third day of meetings they invite the managers to be present at their exchanges. The result of the regular open dialogues, according to Danzig, Haasnoot, and other leadership writers, has been the evolution of a unified global attitude in every corner of the corporation. Trust building, employee empowerment and engagement, elimination of unnecessary repetitive work, and the culture of an open, boundaryless workplace have all contributed to the organization's continued success and well-being (Danzig, 2000, p. 36–37).

This chapter has discussed many methods of relationship building with co-workers that leaders can employ to promote ethical behavior and attitudes in the workplace. Perhaps the most important ingredient necessary to maintain trust is deep confidence in the leadership, confidence that they will do the right thing for the staff and for the health of the organization. When times are tough and unpopular decisions are necessary, what maintains the trust, therefore continuing to affirm the shared values of the organization?

## Emotional Bank Accounts

An emotional bank account is a term coined by Steven Covey that describes the amount of trust that has been accumulated in a relationship. Like a financial bank account, the size of the account increases and decreases according to how much is deposited and how much is spent. Deposits are made through acts of courtesy, kindness, honesty, and promise keeping. Withdrawals occur when we show discourtesy and disrespect, ignoring, and betraying trust. Implicit in the description is the suggestion that we should consciously seek to keep a large reserve on account so that when we make mistakes and behave badly, there is good will still available to take us through the negative phase without inflicting further damage (Covey, 1989, pp. 188–189). Leaders make mistakes. They are also forced by necessity to make choices that are detrimental to people within their organization. To sustain a high level of trust in an organization, a leader requires many emotional bank accounts: with the managers, with the staff, with the clients, and with the organization as a total entity.

Covey describes six efforts that we can make in our relationships to build healthy emotional bank accounts:

1. *Understanding.* We can seek to understand individuals and groups so that we better understand what constitutes a deposit in their accounts. "One person's mission is another person's minutia." Deposits should be based on what is important to the individual or the group with whom we are dealing.
2. *Paying attention to the small things.* Little kindnesses and courtesies are important.
3. *Keeping promises.* Breaking promises and ignoring commitments constitute a major withdrawal from the emotional bank account. People build their hopes around promises and when they are broken, the level of trust is weakened.
4. *Taking the time to clarify expectations.* When individuals do not understand what is expected of them, they are uncomfortable in the relationship. When they misunderstand the role that they are meant to play, they may feel inconsequential, ignorant, or distrustful. In any new situation, it is important to spell out expectations and, in particular, to allow time for the differences in interpretation to be voiced and addressed before they create conflict.
5. *Personal integrity.* Integrity creates trust; lack of it will destroy the fabric of almost any relationship.
6. *Apologize when you are in error.* Sincerely apologize and express your regret when you make a withdrawal from the emotional bank account. A sincere apology can be a deposit in the account, although repeated apologies are eventually seen as insincere and are interpreted as withdrawals (Ibid., pp. 190–199).

The leadership qualities that have been addressed—commitment, trust, ethics, integrity, and emotional bank accounts—are all what many consider moral qualities. What is the role of a leader in a spiritual or moral context? The concept of the "servant leader," is at the heart of any discussion of leadership values and integrity.

## Servant Leadership

An examination of the effectiveness of the servant leader focuses upon the impact of the leader's actions upon the well-being of those served:

- Are those served growing as individuals?
- Are they healthier, wiser, freer, more autonomous, and more likely themselves to become servants?
- What is the effect on the least privileged of society? Will they benefit or at least not be further deprived? (Spears, 2001)

When a leader pays attention to values—makes values the "boss in the organization"—the organization and its people can flourish. It requires "implementing a "values-platform" by clarifying values, then communicating them and working diligently to align organizational actions and practices with them. Furthermore, it requires a rethinking of how we use power: we must learn the distinction between power over staff and power with staff. So much unethical behavior in the workplace results from poor use and abuse of power. Ideally, the servant leader creates the means by which there can be a reconciliation between what is good for the soul, good for the customer, good for the employee, and good for the health of the larger institution and yet still has viability in the marketplace (Ibid.).

In practice, the servant leadership concept is being applied in several areas: as a working philosophy for profit and not-for-profit organizations; as a model in management and leadership courses; and by independent consultants who work directly with companies to develop new organizational models. In its purest form, servant leadership advocates the power of persuasion and the seeking of consensus so that the mind of the servant leader and the needs of the employees, customers, constituents, and community, become the most important reason for the organization's existence.

## Conclusion

The heartfelt desire to lead with fairness, justice, and integrity requires a strong commitment to knowing oneself and to living in accordance with a clearly established set of core values and principles. Stated simply, respect for one's self transcends to respect to and for others. While a leader must be flexible and open in numerous contexts so that the needs of his/her organization can be met most effectively, integrity is not a negotiable issue but must be adopted as a way of life. Becoming a leader with true integrity is never easy and the journey is filled with challenges, mistakes, and lessons along the way. But the rewards of ethical leadership with integrity cannot be measured, and the effects will live on long after the leader is gone.

Combining a solid foundation of ethics and integrity with flexibility in the face of challenges and problems is key for leaders in facing the everyday problems of organizational life. There are a multitude of solutions to every problem, and knowing how to choose the right one is a skill that can be developed and refined. In the next chapter, we will discuss an essential skill of leadership: creative problem solving.

# References

## Court Cases

*Allen v. Scribner*, 812 F.2d 426, 432 (9th Cir. 1987).
*Anderson v. Central Point School Dist.*, 746 F.2d 505, 506 (9th Cir. 1984).
*Andrews v. City of Philadelphia*, 895 F.2d 1469 (3d Cir. 1990).
*Atkins v. Virginia*, 536 U.S. 304 (2002)
*Bates v. United States*, 766 A.2d 500 (D.C. 2000).
*Baze v. Rees*, 128 S. Ct. 1520 (2008).
*Berger v. United States*, 295 U.S. 78, 84–85 (1935).
*Bigby v. State*, 2008 Tex. Crim. App. LEXIS 716 (Tex. Crim. App. 2008).
*Bracy v. Gramley*, 520 U.S. 899, 904 (1997).
*Brady v. Maryland*, 373 U.S. 83 (U.S. 1963).
*Briscoe v. Lahue*, 460 U.S. 325, 346 (U.S. 1983).
*Bundy v. Jackson*, 205 U.S. App. D.C. 444 (D.C. Cir. 1981).
*Callins v. Collins*, 510 U.S. 1141, 1145–1146 (U.S. 1994).
*Campbell v. Wood*, 511 U.S. 1119 (1994).
*Civil Service Charges and Specifications v. Hunt*, 1993 Ohio App. LEXIS 103 (Ohio Ct. App., 1993).
*Cleveland Metro. Bar Ass'n v. McFaul*, 120 Ohio St. 3d 293 (Ohio 2008).
*Cochran v. City of Los Angeles*, 222 F.3d 1195 (2000, 9th cir.)
*Collazo v. Estelle*, 940 F.2d 411, 414, 417–418 (9th Cir. 1991).
*Colombrito v. Kelly*, 764 F.2d 122 (2d Cir. N.Y. 1985).
*Connick v. Myers*, 461 U.S. 138 (1983)
*Daniels v. City of Arlington*, 246 F.3d 500, 506 (5th Cir. 2001).
*Durmer v. Rogers*, 2006 U.S. Dist. LEXIS 74612 (D.N.J. Oct. 13, 2006).
*Ellison v. Brady*, 924 F.2d 872 (9th Cir. Cal. 1991).
*Eubanks v. Gerwen*, 40 F.3d 1157 (11th Cir. Fla. 1994).
*Fontain v. Ravenel*, 58 U.S. 369 392–393 (1854).
*Ford v. Wainwright*, 477 U.S. 399 (1986).
*Fraternal Order of Police Newark Lodge No. 12 v. City of Newark*, 170 F.3d 359 (3d Cir. 1999).
*Frazier v. Cupp*, 394 U.S. 731 (1969).
*Furman v. Georgia*, 408 U.S. 238 (1972)
*Garcetti v. Ceballos*, 547 U.S. 410, 126 S. Ct. 1951, 164 L. Ed. 2d 689 (2006).
*Glass v. Louisiana*, 471 U.S. 1080 (1985).
*Gomez-Perez v. Potter*, 128 S. Ct. 1931 (2008).
*Government of Virgin Islands v. Bryan*, 731 F. Supp. 720, 720–721 (D.V.I. 1990).
*Gregg v. Georgia*, 428 U.S. 153 (1976)

*Griego v. Hogan*, 377 P.2d 953, 955–956 (N.M. 1963).

*Griggs v. Duke Power Co.*, 401 U.S. 424 (U.S. 1971).

*Hall v. State*, 113 Ga. App. 587 (Ga. Ct. App. 1966).

*Hugh M. Caperton, Harman Dev. Corp. v. A.T. Massey Coal Co.*, 2009 U.S. S. Ct. Briefs LEXIS 111.

*In Interest of Von Rossum*, 515 So.2d 1100 (La. 1998).

*In re Gault*, 387 U.S. 1 (1967).

*Jackson v. Litscher*, 194 F. Supp. 2d 849, 857 (E.D. Wis. 2002).

*Johnson v. Jones*, 515 U.S. 304 (1995)

*Kannisto v. San Francisco*, 541 F.2d 841, 843–44 (9th Cir. 1976).

*Kennedy v. Louisiana*, 2008 U.S. LEXIS 5262 (2008).

*Kent v. United States*, 383 U.S. 541 (1965).

*Kyles v. Whitley*, 514 U.S. 419 (U.S. 1995).

*Lopez v. United States*, 373 U.S. 427 (1963).

*Malloy v. South Carolina*, 237 U.S. 180 (1915).

*Manning v. Chevron Chemical Co., LLC*, 332 F.3d 874 (5th Cir. 2003).

*Matter of LaBombard*, 2008 NY Slip Op 7990, 1–2 (N.Y. 2008).

*McCleskey v. Kemp*, 482 U.S. 920 (1987)

*McDonnell Douglas Corp. v. Green*, 411 U.S. 792 (1973).

*Miller v. Fenton*, 796 F.2d 598 (3d Cir. 1986).

*Nixon v. City of Houston*, 511 F.3d 494 (5th Cir. Tex. 2007).

*N.J. v. T. L. O.*, 469 U.S. 325 (U.S. 1985).

*People v. Carter*, 77 N.Y. 2d 95 (1990).

*People v. Harrell*, 2002 Cal. App. Unpub. LEXIS 8647 (Cal. App. 2d Dist. 2002).

*People v. Lawery*, 43 Misc. 2d 1084, 1085–1086 (N.Y. City Crim. Ct. 1964).

*People v. Marin*, 686 P.2d 1351 (Colo. App. 1983).

*People v. Nunn*, 46 Cal. 2d 460 (1964).

*People v. Woods*, 146 Cal. App. 4th 106 (Cal. App. 2d Dist. 2006).

*Perry v. Lynch*, 493 U.S. 1068 (1989)

*Picha v. Wielgos*, 410 F.Supp. 1214 (ND Ill. 1976).

*Poirier v. Mass. Dep't of Corr.*, 2009 U.S. App. LEXIS 3940, 2–3 (1st Cir. Mass. Feb. 27, 2009).

*Powell v. Alabama*, 287 U.S. 45 (1932).

*Robinson v. County of Los Angles*, 2009 U.S. App. LEXIS 458 (2009, CA 9th Cir.).

*Roper v. Simmons*, 543 U.S. 551 (2005)

*Roth v. Veteran's Admin.*, 856 F.2d 1401 (1988, 9th cir.)

*Sanchez v. City of Santa Ana*, 936 F.2d 1027, 1039 (9th Cir. 1990).

*Shedelbower v. Estelle*, 885 F.2d 570 (9th Cir. 1989).

*Singleton v. Norris*, 319 F.3d. 1018 (2003, 8th Cir. Ark.).

*Smithson v. State*, 275 Ga. App. 591, 594 (Ga. Ct. App. 2005).

*Stanford v. Kentucky*, 492 U.S. 361 (1989)

*State v. Goode*, 278 N.J. Super. 85, 92 (App. Div. 1994).

*State v. Noriega*, 142 Ariz. 474, 484 (Ariz. 1984).

*State v. Udell*, 34 Kan. App. 2d 163 (Kan. Ct. App. 2005).

*Stewart v. City of St. Louis*, 2007 U.S. Dist. LEXIS 38473, 1–2 (E.D. Mo. 2007).

*Thompson v. Oklahoma*, 487 U.S. 815 (1988)

*Trujillo v. Bd. of Educ.*, 2006 U.S. Dist. LEXIS 95377 (D.N.M. 2006).

*United States v. Al Jibori*, 90 F.3d 22, 25 (2d Cir. N.Y. 1996).

*United States v. Anderson*, 929 F.2d 96 (2d Cir. 1991).
*United States v. Correa-Gomez*, 160 F. Supp. 2d 748 (E.D. Ky. 2001).
*United States v. Gist*, 2008 U.S. Dist. LEXIS 48010, 11–13 (M.D. Pa. June 20, 2008).
*United States v. Heath*, 58 F.3d 1271, 1276 (8th Cir. Minn. 1995).
*United States v. Keogh*, 391 F2d 138, 34 ALR3d 1 (CA2 NY1968).
*United States v. Mariani*, 121 F. Supp. 2d 803, 809 (M.D. Pa. 2000).
*United States v. Orso*, 275 F.3d 1190, 1194 (9th Cir. 2001).
*United States v. Theodore F. Stevens*, 593 F. Supp. 2d 177, 182–183 (D.D.C. 2009).
*United States v. Velasquez*, 885 F.2d 1076 (3d Cir. 1989).
*United States v. Young*, 470 U.S. 1 (1985).
*Vernonia School District 47J v. Action*, 515 U.S. 646 (1995).
*Webb v. City of Philadelphia*, 2009 U.S. App. LEXIS 7169 (CA 3rd, 2009).
*Wilkins v. Missouri*, 492 U.S. 937 (1989)
*Williams v. State*, 103 Nev. 106, 109–110 (Nev. 1987).
*Wisconsin v. Yoder*, 406 U.S. 205 (1972).

## Literature

Ackerman, B. A. (1980). *Social justice in the liberal state*. New Haven, CT: Yale University Press.
Alan Dershowitz interview. (1982, May 26). *Los Angeles Herald-Examiner*, p. 7.
Albanese, J. (2008). *Professional ethics in criminal justice* (2nd ed.). Boston: Allyn & Bacon.
Ali, Mohamed. (1907). Thoughts on the Present Discontent Bombay, India: Kessinger Publications.
American Bar Association. (2003). The function of defense counsel. In *ABA standards for criminal justice: Prosecution and defense function*. Chicago: Author.
Aquino, K., & Reed, Americus, II. (2002). The self-importance of moral identity. *Journal of Personality and Social Psychology*, 83(6), 1423–1440.
Arrigo, B. (1999). *Social justice/criminal justice: The maturation of critical theory in law, crime, and deviance*. Belmont, CA: Wadsworth.
Arrington, R. (1983). A defence of ethical relativism. *Metaphilosophy, 14*, 225–239.
Banks, C. (2004). *Criminal justice ethics*. Thousand Oaks, CA: Sage.
Barnes, J. (2001). Roman Aristotle. In G. Nagy (Ed.), *Greek literature* (Vol. 8, pp. 176–182). New York: Routledge.
Bazelon, L. (2009, March 15). A crack in jurist discipline. *Houston Chronicle*, p. E1.
Beccaria, Cesare. (1774). *Essay on Crimes and Punishment*, translated by Henry Paolucci. New York: Bobbs-Merrill, 1963.
Bennis, W., & Goldsmith, J. (1997). *Learning to lead*. Reading, MA: Perseus Books.
Bentham, J. (1970). *An introduction to the principles of morals and legislation* (J. Burns & H. L. A. Hart, Eds.). London: Athlone Press. (Original work published 1789.)
Blasi, A., Lapsley, D. K., & Narváez, D. (2004). *Moral development, self, and identity*. Mahwah, NJ: Lawrence Erlbaum.
Boetig, B. (2007). Leadership spotlight: Above reproach. *FBI Law Enforcement Bulletin, 76*(4), 12–13.
Bok, S. (1999). *Lying: Moral choice in public and private life* (2nd ed.). New York: Vintage Books.

Brennan, T. (2005). *The stoic life*. Oxford: Oxford University Press.

Brinkley, David. (2005, October 21). "The Talk of the Town, "What It Takes," *The New Yorker*. page 78.

Brun, Jean. (1978). *Socrate*. Paris: Presses universitaires de France.

Burke, E. *Thoughts on the cause of the present discontent*.

Burns, J. M. (1978). *Leadership*. New York: Harper & Row.

California Commission on the Fair Administration of Justice. (2008, June 30). *Report of the California Commission on the Fair Administration of Justice*. Sacramento: State of California.

Campbell, J. (1988). *The power of myth with Bill Moyers*. New York: Doubleday.

Capaldi, N. (2004). *John Stuart Mill: A biography*. Cambridge: Cambridge University Press.

Carpenter, S. (2009, February–March). Speaking of race. *Scientific American Mind*, 12.

Carroll, L. (1865). *Alice's adventures in wonderland*. London: Macmillan & Co.

Carter, D. L., & Radelet, L. A. (1999). *The police and the community* (6th ed.). Upper Saddle River, NJ: Prentice Hall.

Chase, C. A. (2001, January). *Loyola of Los Angeles Law Review*, 34, 767–792.

Cherniss, J. (2008). *Ethical pluralism*. Retrieved August 17, 2008, from http://www.bookrags.com/research/ethical-pluralism-este-0001_0002_0/

Clement, J., & Lochhead, J. (1980). *Cognitive process instruction*. Proceedings of the third annual meeting of the Cognitive Science Society, Berkeley, CA.

Cloud, M. (1994, Fall). The dirty little secret. *Emory Law Journal*, 43, 1311–1346.

CNN.com. (2009). *Ted Stevens*. Retrieved April 21, 2009, from http://topics.cnn.com/topics/ted_stevens

Coleman, Stephen. (2003, June). "When Police Should Say 'NO!' to Gratuities," Centre for Applied Philosophy and Public Ethics, Charles Sturt University, Australia, working paper.

Commentary on Plato's *Republic*. (2008). *Encyclopædia Britannica*. Retrieved November 25, 2008, from Encyclopædia Britannica Online, http://www.britannica.com/EBchecked/topic/127843/Commentary-on-Platos-Republic

Confidentiality and the case of Robert Garrow's lawyers. (1975). *Buffalo Law Review*, 25, 211, 213–214.

Covey, S. (1989). *The 7 habits of highly effective people*. New York: Simon & Schuster.

Covey, S. (1999). *Living the 7 habits: The courage to change*. New York: Simon & Schuster.

Crisp, R. (1997). *Mill on utilitarianism*. London: Routledge.

Danzig, R. (2000). *The leader within you*. Hollywood, FL: Frederick Fell.

Delattre, E. J. (1990, September 5). Teaching integrity: The boundaries of moral education. *Education Week*.

Delattre, E. J. (1994). *The new police officer: Integrity and temptation*. Retrieved May 19, 2009, from www.neiassociates.org/integrty.htm

Delattre, E. J. (2002). *Character and cops: Ethics in policing* (4th ed.). Washington, DC: AEI Press.

DePree, M. (1992). *Leadership jazz*. New York: Dell.

Didion, J. (1968). On self-respect. In *Slouching towards Bethlehem*. New York: Farrar, Straus & Giroux.

Dimock, S. (2001). The natural law theory of St. Thomas Aquinas. In *Classic readings and Canadian cases in the philosophy of law*. Toronto: Pearson Education Canada.

Dolhenty, J. (n.d.). *An overview of natural law theory*. Retrieved December 29, 2009, from http://www.radicalacademy.com/philnaturallaw.htm

Donaldson, D. M. (1953). *Studies in Muslim ethics*. London: SPCK.

Eighinger, L. (1998). *Condensed version of the study of ethics*. Retrieved from Interpreter's Network Web site, http://www.terpsnet.com/resources/99r003.htm

Essex, L., & Kusy, M. (1999). *Fast forward leadership*. London: Prentice Hall.

Ethics. (2008). *Encyclopædia Britannica*. Retrieved August 17, 2008, from Encyclopædia Britannica Online, http://www.britannica.com/EBchecked/topic/194023/ethics

Etzioni, A. (1998). *The new Golden Rule: Community and morality in a democratic society*. New York: Basic Books.

Fakhry, M. (1970). *A history of Islamic philosophy*. New York: Columbia University Press.

Ferm, V. (1956). *Encyclopedia of morals*. New York: Vintage.

Foot, P. (1985). Utilitarianism and the virtues. *Mind, 94*, 107–123.

Gamer, M. (2009, February/March). Telling the truth. *Scientific American Mind*, 52–56.

Gardner, S. (1999). *Kant and the critique of pure reason*. New York: Routledge.

Garner, R. T., & Rosen, B. (1967). *Moral philosophy: A systematic introduction to normative ethics and meta-ethics*. New York: Macmillan.

Gates, H. L., Jr., & West, C. (2000). *The African-American century*. New York: Free Press.

Geach, P. (1969). *God and the soul*. New York: Shocken Books.

Gert, B. (1970). *The moral rules: A new rational foundation for morality*. New York: Harper & Row.

Goldberg, Jay. (1969, March 24). New York Times, col. 2 p. 14)

Goleman, D. (1995). *Emotional intelligence*. New York: Bantam Books.

Gould, J., & Greenman, L. (2008, June). *Update on cost, quality, and availability of defense representation in federal death penalty cases*. Washington, DC: Office of Defender Services of the Administrative Office of the U.S. Courts.

Haasnoot, R. (2000). *The new wisdom of business*. Chicago: Dearborn.

Hadot, Pierre. (1998). *The Inner Citadel: The Meditations of Marcus Aurelius*. Translated by Michael Chase. Cambridge, MA: Harvard University Press.

Hall, R. A. S. (2000). *The ethical foundations of criminal justice*. Boca Raton, FL: CRC Press.

Hardy, S. A., & Carlo, G. (2005). Identity as a source of moral motivation. *Human Development, 48*, 232–256.

Harvey, P. (2000). *An introduction to Buddhist ethics*. Cambridge, MA: Cambridge University Press.

Heffernan, W. C. (2001). Two approaches to police ethics. In W. Bruce (Ed.), *Classics of administrative ethics* (Rev. ed., pp. 313–329). Bellevue, TN: Westview.

Hertzler, J. O. (1975). *The social thought of the ancient civilizations*. New York: McGraw-Hill. (Original work published 1936.)

Hirsch, Jeffrey L. (2003). Labor and Employment in Connecticut: A Guide to Employment Laws, Regulations & Practices, 2nd ed. Conklin, NY: Michie

Hobbes, T. (1985). *Leviathan* (C. B. Macpherson, Ed.). London: Penguin Books. (Original work published 1691.)

Houtsma, M. T., et al. (Eds.). (1938). *The encyclopædia of Islam: A dictionary of the geography, ethnography, and biography of the Muhammadan peoples*. London: Luzac.

Hyslop, J. (1903). *Ethics of the Greek philosophers: Socrates, Plato, and Aristotle*. New York: Brooklyn Ethical Association.

Irwin, T. (1977). *Plato's moral theory: The early and middle dialogues*. Oxford: Clarendon.

Jackman, T. (2006, February 14). Detective allowed to receive sexual services at parlor. *Houston Chronicle*, p. A8.

Johnson, E. H. (1974). *Crime, correction, and society*. Homewood, IL: Dorsey Press.

Johnson, V. (1995). *Heart full of grace: A thousand years of black wisdom*. New York: Simon & Schuster.

Jones, J. R., & Carlson, D. P. (2004). *Reputable conduct* (2nd ed.). Upper Saddle River, NJ: Pearson/Prentice Hall.

Josephson Institute for Ethics. (n.d.). Retrieved September 1, 2008, from josephson-institute.org/sixpillars.html.

Kant, I. (1898). *The critique of practical reason*. New York: Longsman and Green. (Original work published 1788.)

Kant, I. (1967). *Groundwork of the metaphysics of morals*. New York: Barnes & Noble. (Original work published 1797.)

Kauffman, K. (1988). *Prison officers and their world*. Cambridge, MA: Harvard University Press.

Keefe, T. (1998). *Simone de Beauvoir*. New York: St. Martin's Press.

Kennedy, J. F. (2000). *Profiles in courage* (perennial ed.). New York: HarperCollins.

Keown, D. (1992). *The nature of Buddhist ethics*. New York: Macmillan.

Kidston, R. R. (1958). The office of crown prosecutor. *American Law Journal, 32*, 148.

Kouzes, J. (1995). *The leadership challenge*. San Francisco: Jossey-Bass.

Kovach, G. (2009, February 19). A Texas judge accused of misconduct draws mixed opinions on her fairness. *New York Times*, p. A26.

Kupfer, J. (1982). The moral presumption against lying. *Review of Metaphysics, 36*, 103–126.

Lane, N., & Piercy, N. (2003). The ethics of discrimination: Organizational mindsets and female employment disadvantage. *Journal of Business Ethics, 44*, 313–325.

Lavery, J. (2007). Plato's *Protagoras* and the frontier of genre research: A reconnaissance report. *Poetics Today, 28*, 191–246.

Lavine, T. Z. (1984). *From Socrates to Sartre: The philosophic quest*. Toronto: Bantam Books.

Lightfoot, S. L. (2000). *Respect*. Cambridge, MA: Perseus Books.

Liptak, A. (2008, May 4). When law prevents righting a wrong. *New York Times*, p. 2.

Locking justice's door: Texas Court of Criminal Appeals chief justice's unethical, outrageous blocking of a death row appeal merits the most severe legal sanctions. (2007, October 16). *Houston Chronicle*, p. B8.

Los Angeles Police Department's Board of Inquiry. (2000, March 1). *Rampart area corruption incident*. Los Angeles: City of Los Angeles.

*Los Angeles Times*. (2009, February 13). p. A13.

Lynch, J. E. (1997). Natural law. *Microsoft® Encarta® Online Encyclopedia*. Retrieved December 31, 2008, from encarta.msn.com

Manz, C. C. (1998). *The leadership wisdom of Jesus: Practical lessons for today.* San Francisco: Berrett-Koehler.

Marx, G. T. (2001). In M. Amir & S. Einstein (Eds.), *Policing, security, and democracy: Theory and practice.* Huntsville, TX: Office of International Criminal Justice. Journal of Contemporary Criminal Justice, *Vol. 18 No.2*, pp.147–166

Masters, R., & Roberson, C. (1990). *Inside criminology.* Englewood Cliffs, NJ: Prentice Hall.

McManus, K. (2008). Morality bites. *Responsibility.* Retrieved July 27, 2008, from http://www.responsibilityproject.com/blog/post/morality-bites

McMenamin, J. (2008, March 6). Death penalty costs Md. more than life term. *Baltimore Sun.*

Milhizer, E. R. (2006, Fall). Rethinking police interrogation: Encouraging reliable confessions while respecting suspects' dignity. *Valparaiso University Law Review, 41,* 1–18.

Miller, D. (1987). *The Blackwell encyclopedia of political thought.* London: Blackwell.

Miller, H.A., Mire, S.M., & Kim, B. (2009). Predictiors of job satisfaction among police officers: Does personality matter? Journal of Criminal Justice. In press. Accessed 09/09/2009. Available on line at http://www.elsevier.com/wps/find/journaldescription.cws_home/366/description#description

Mollen, M. (1994). *Commission to investigate allegations of police corruption and the anti-corruption procedures of the police department.* City of New York Commission Report 36.

Moshman, D. (2004). False moral identity: Self-serving denial in the maintenance of moral self-conceptions. In D. K. Lapsley & D. Narvaez (Eds.), *Moral development, self, and identity* (pp. 83–109).

Murphy, M. (2002). The natural law tradition in ethics. *Stanford Encyclopedia of Philosophy.* Retrieved December 31, 2008, from plato.stanford.edu/entries/natural-law-ethics

Natural Law (Ethics). (2008). *Microsoft® Encarta® Online Encyclopedia.* Retrieved December 31, 2008, from http://encarta.msn.com

Navia, L. E. (1989). *Socrates: The man and his philosophy.* New York: Garland.

O'Toole, J. (1995). *Leading change: Overcoming the ideology of comfort and the tyranny of custom.* San Francisco: Jossey-Bass.

O'Toole, J. (1999). *Leadership A to Z: A guide for the appropriately ambitious.* San Francisco: Jossey-Bass.

Packer, H. L. (1968). *The limits of criminal sanction.* Stanford, CA: Stanford University Press.

Pasnau, R. (1995). Henry of Ghent and the twilight of divine illumination. *Review of Metaphysics, 49,* 49–75.

Perkins, D. (with Holtman, M. P., Kessler, P. R., & McCarthy, C.). (2000). *Leading at the edge.* New York: Amacom.

Phillips, D. (1992). *Lincoln on leadership: Executive strategies for tough times.* New York: Warner Books.

Plato. (1981). *Five dialogues: Euthyphro, Apology, Crito, Meno, Phaedo* (G. M. A. Grube, Trans. & J. M. Cooper, Ed.). Indianapolis: Hackett.

Pogge, T. (2007). *John Rawls: His life and theory of justice.* Oxford: Oxford University Press.

Pollock, J. M. (2006). *Ethics in crime and justice: Ethical dilemmas and decisions in criminal justice* (5th ed.). Belmont, CA: Wadsworth.

Pollock, J. M., & Becker, R. F. (1996, November). Ethics training: Using officers' dilemmas. *FBI Law Enforcement Journal*, 17–23.

Portalié, E. (1907). Life of St. Augustine of Hippo. In *The Catholic encyclopedia*. New York: Robert Appleton. Retrieved January 1, 2009, from New Advent, http://www.newadvent.org/cathen/02084a.htm

Porter, B. F. (1980). *The good life: Alternative in ethics*. New York: Macmillan.

Postow, B. (2007). Toward honest ethical pluralism. *Philosophical Studies*, 132(2), 191–210.

Powell, C. (with Persico, J. E.). (1995). Rules. In *My American journey*. New York: Random House.

Ramstad, Jim. (2008, September 17). "Amendment to ADA" in U.S. House of Representatives Congressional Record, page H8286.

Rand, A. (2006). *Normative ethics: The virtuous egoist*. New York: Cambridge University Press.

Rawls, J. (1971). *A theory of justice*. Cambridge, MA: Harvard University Press.

Reynolds, S., & Ceranic, T. (2007). The efforts of moral judgment and moral identity on moral behavior: An empirical examination of the moral individual. *Journal of Applied Psychology*, 92(6), 1610–1624.

Ricard, M., & Revel, J. F. (1998). *The monk and the philosopher*. London: HarperCollins.

Robbins, S. (2005). *Organizational behavior* (5th ed.). Upper Saddle River, NJ: Prentice Hall.

Roberson, C. (1997). *Introduction to corrections*. Incline Village, NV: Copperhouse.

Roberson, Cliff, and Harvey Wallace. (1998). *Introduction to Criminology*, Incline Village, NV: Copperhouse.

Roosevelt, Theodore. (1913). An Autobiography: XV. The Peace of Righteousness, Appendix B, New York: Macmillan.

Rotelle, J. (Ed.). (1997). *The complete works of St. Augustine: A translation for the 21st century*. New York: New City Press.

Ruiz, J., & Bono, C. (2004, Winter–Spring). At what price a "freebie"? The real cost of police gratuities. *Criminal Justice Ethics*.

Sampson, A. (1999). *Mandela: The authorized biography*. New York: Vintage Books.

Sandberg, L., & Stiles, M. (2009, March 15). Texas prisons: An illicit bazaar. *Houston Chronicle*, pp. A1, A3.

Schafer, S. (1969). *Theories in criminology*. New York: Random House.

Schafersman, S. D. (1991, January). *An introduction to critical thinking*. Retrieved April 20, 2009, from http://www.freeinquiry.com/critical-thinking.html

Schmalleger, F. (2008). *Criminal justice: A brief introduction*. Upper Saddle River, NJ: Pearson/Prentice Hall.

Shamoo, A., & Resnik, D. (2003). *Responsible conduct of research*. New York: Oxford University Press.

Shaw, W. H. (1999). *Contemporary ethics: Taking account of utilitarianism*. Oxford: Blackwell.

Singer, M. (1995). *Cults in our midst*. San Francisco: Jossey-Bass.

Singer, P. (1995). *How are we to live? Ethics in an age of self-interest*. Amherst, NY: Prometheus Books.

Skolnick, J. H. (1982, Summer–Fall). Deception by police. *Criminal Justice Ethics, 1,* 40–48.

Slobogin, C. (1996, Fall). Testilying: Police perjury and what to do about it. *University of Colorado Law Review, 67,* 1037–1061.

Smith, R. L. (1974). *The tarnished badge.* New York: Arno Press.

Solomon, R. C. (1987). *From Hegel to existentialism.* Oxford: Oxford University Press.

Souryal, S. (2007). *Ethics in criminal justice: In search of the truth.* Newark, NJ: LexisNexis.

Spears, L. C. (2001). *Servant leadership: Quest for caring leadership.* Retrieved January 21, 2001, from the Robert Greenleaf Web site, http://www.greenleaf.org

*Stanford encyclopedia of philosophy.* (2008). Retrieved January 16, 2009, from plato. stanford.edu/

Stark, D. (2005). *Christ-based leadership.* Minneapolis, MN: Bethany House.

State Commission on Judicial Conduct. (2009, February 18). *Notice of formal proceedings.* Austin, TX: Author.

State of Kansas. (2008). *Performance audit report: Costs incurred for death penalty cases; A K-GOAL audit of the department of corrections.* Topeka: Author.

Stockdale, J. (1993). *Courage under fire: Testing Epictetus's doctrines in a laboratory of human behavior.* Stanford, CA: Hoover Institution.

Stroh, L. K., Brett, J. M., & Reilly, A. H. (1992). All the right stuff: A comparison of female and male managers' career progression. *Journal of Applied Psychology, 77,* 251–260.

Taylor, C. (1991). *The ethics of authenticity.* Cambridge, MA: Harvard University Press.

Trautman, N. (1998). *Integrity leadership.* Longwood, FL: National Institute of Ethics.

Travis, J. (1998, June). *Policing in transition.* Plenary address at the fourth biennial conference on International Perspectives on Crime, Justice, and Public Order, Budapest, Hungary. Retrieved August 31, 2008, from http://www.ojp.usdoj.gov/ nij/speeches/budapest.htm

Velasquez, M., Andre, C., Shanks, T., & Meyer, M. J. (1987). What is ethics. *Issues in Ethics, 1*(1).

Velasquez, M., Andre, C., Shanks, T., & Meyer, M. J. (1988). A framework for thinking ethically. *Issues in Ethics, 1*(2).

Von Hirsch, A. (1976). *Doing justice.* New York: Hill and Wang.

Waldroop, J., & Butler, T. (2000). *Maximum success.* New York: Doubleday.

Walker, R. C. S. (1999). *Kant.* London: Routledge.

Wallace, J. (2000, May). Lying. *The ethical spectacle.* Retrieved January 14, 2009, from www.spectacle.org

Weisburd, D., Greenspan, R., Hamilton, E. E., Bryant, K. A., & Williams, H. (2001). *Abuse of police authority: A national study of police officers' attitudes* (NCJ 189242). Washington, DC: Police Foundation.

Wheelock, John Hall. (1920). *A Bibliography of Theodore Roosevelt.* New York: Charles Scribner's Sons.

Williams, R. W., & Arrigo, B. A. (2008). *Ethics, crime, and criminal justice.* Upper Saddle River, NJ: Pearson/Prentice Hall.

Wuthnow, R. (1989). *Meaning and moral order: Explorations in cultural analysis.* Berkeley: University of California Press.

Wylen, S. M. (2001). *Settings of silver: An introduction to Judaism.* Mahwah, NJ: Paulist.

# Index